GUERCINO MIND TO PAPER

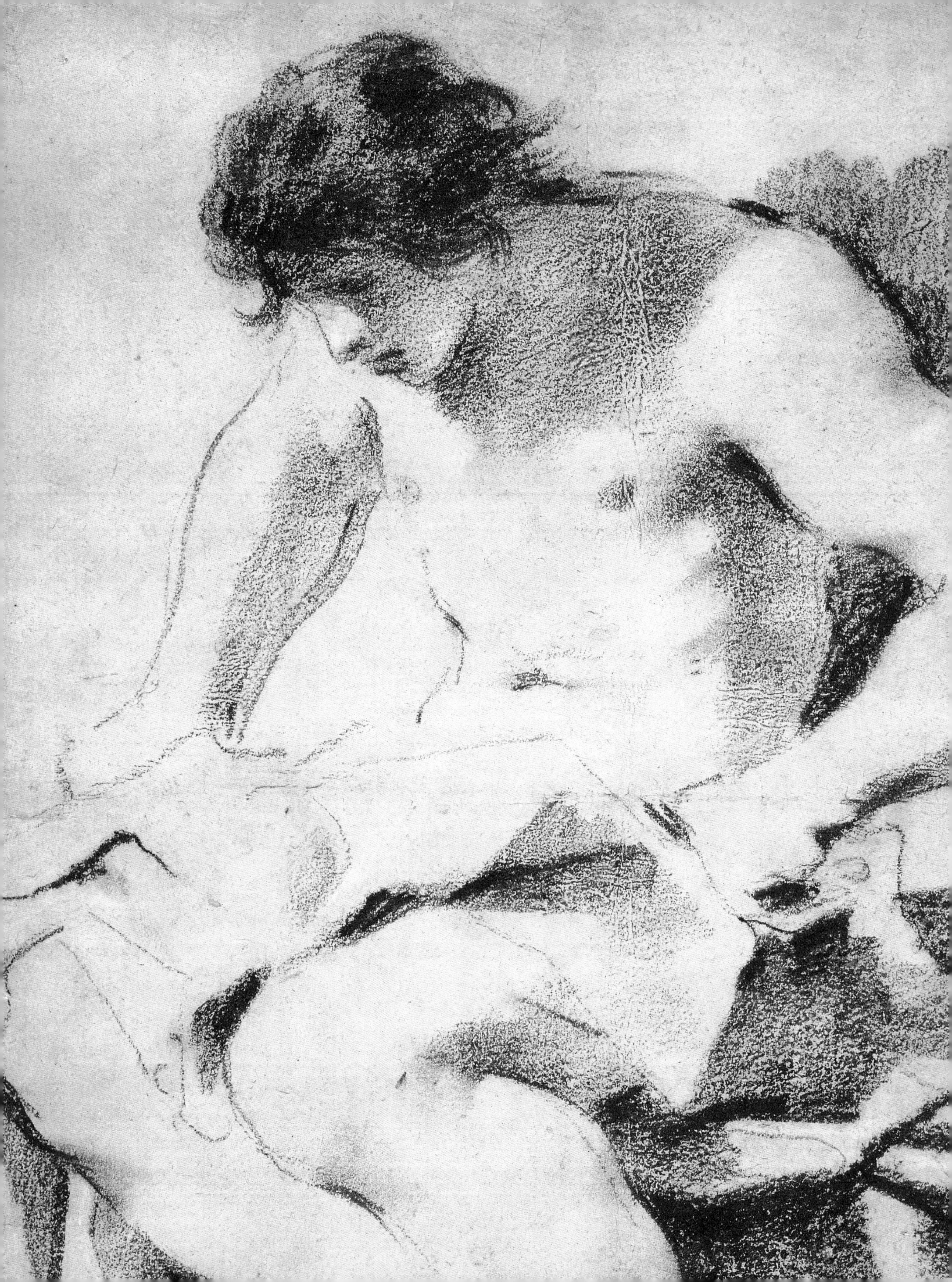

GUERCINO MIND TO PAPER

Julian Brooks

with the assistance of Nathaniel E. Silver

The J. Paul Getty Museum, Los Angeles

Front and back covers: Guercino. Details from *The Assassination of Amnon* (cat. no. 14), 1628. London, Courtauld Institute of Art Gallery

Frontispiece: Guercino. Detail from *Study of a Seated Young Man* (cat. no. 2), ca. 1619. Los Angeles, J. Paul Getty Museum

Pages 18–19: Guercino. Detail from *Landscape with a View of a Fortified Port* (cat. no. 22), ca. 1635. Los Angeles, J. Paul Getty Museum

This catalogue was published to accompany the exhibition *Guercino: Mind to Paper,* held at the J. Paul Getty Museum, Los Angeles, October 17, 2006, to January 21, 2007, and at the Courtauld Institute of Art Gallery, London, February 22 to May 13, 2007.

Getty Publications
1200 Getty Center Drive, Suite 500
Los Angeles, California 90049-1682
www.getty.edu

Mark Greenberg, *Editor in Chief*

Patrick E. Pardo, *Project Editor*
Tobi Levenberg Kaplan, *Copy Editor*
Catherine Lorenz, *Designer*
Suzanne Watson, *Production Coordinator*

Typesetting by Diane Franco
Printed by The Studley Press, Dalton, Massachusetts

Library of Congress Cataloging-in-Publication Data

Brooks, Julian, 1969–
Guercino : mind to paper / Julian Brooks with the assistance of Nathaniel E. Silver.
p. cm.
"This catalogue was published to accompany the exhibition 'Guercino: mind to paper' held at the J. Paul Getty Museum, Los Angeles, October 17, 2006, to January 21, 2007."
Includes bibliographical references and index.
ISBN-13: 978-0-89236-862-4 (pbk.)
ISBN-10: 0-89236-862-4 (pbk.)
1. Guercino, 1591–1666—Criticism and interpretation. 2. Guercino, 1591–1666—Exhibitions. I. Silver, Nathaniel E. II. Title.
NC257.B27B76 2006
795.5—dc22
2006014159

CONTENTS

FOREWORD

OVER THE LAST FOUR YEARS the close partnership between the J. Paul Getty Trust and the Courtauld Institute of Art has flourished. It has brought to the Los Angeles public outstanding works of art from the Courtauld and yielded a superb exhibition of oil sketches by Giambattista Tiepolo, which was shown at the Getty Museum and, in a modified format, at the Courtauld in London. In extending this collaboration, the present project aims to illuminate the draftsmanship of the painter Giovanni Francesco Barbieri, il Guercino, called "the Rembrandt of the South," and probably the greatest Italian draftsman of the seventeenth century.

The appeal of Guercino's draftsmanship is apparent from even the briefest look through this catalogue. One sees drawings so spontaneous that one senses the artist's pen scratching the paper and an extraordinary aptitude with effects of light and shade. The Courtauld possesses an important group of drawings by Guercino, thanks to Sir Robert Witt's 1952 bequest, and twenty-six are presented here. The four Guercino drawings from the Getty collection in the exhibition—though few in number—also make a significant contribution, since they show aspects of Guercino's work not otherwise represented. The Getty has an early "academy" study, a stunning landscape, a large, highly finished compositional drawing, and a caricature, none of which categories feature in the Courtauld collection.

The neat dovetailing of the Courtauld and Getty Guercino drawings has been supplemented by a few choice loans—for which we are immensely grateful—from the Los Angeles County Museum of Art and from two West Coast collectors. These include a superb red-chalk "close-up" study of Saints John the Baptist and John the Evangelist; a profile view of Dante, which makes a wonderful parallel with the Getty profile caricature; and a drawing of Bathsheba that shows better than almost any other sheet both Guercino's grasp of texture and his use of the blank page. Using this selection of drawings, the exhibition and catalogue seek both to provide an introduction to the defining characteristics of Guercino's draftsmanship and to investigate why his work is so highly esteemed. The drawings span the range of Guercino's lengthy and successful career and illustrate the many facets of his work.

For putting the exhibition and catalogue together, our thanks are due to Julian Brooks, assistant curator of drawings, working under the direction of curator Lee Hendrix. We would also like to thank William M. Griswold, former acting director of the Getty Museum, for his support of the project from the outset. The result is a testament to the ongoing warm and productive collaboration between our two institutions.

MICHAEL BRAND
Director
The J. Paul Getty Museum

DEBORAH SWALLOW
Märit Rausing Director
The Courtauld Institute of Art

ACKNOWLEDGMENTS

GUERCINO WAS SUCH a talented draftsman that it has been a great pleasure to study his work in such depth. At every turn, one encounters the footprints of Sir Denis Mahon, who rediscovered our neglected cross-eyed artist and on whose writings any subsequent consideration of Guercino must depend. Nicholas Turner and Carol Plazzotta's 1991 British Museum exhibition catalogue *Drawings by Guercino from British Collections* has likewise been a vital precedent.

I am extremely pleased that one of the results of the collaboration between the J. Paul Getty Museum and Courtauld Institute of Art Gallery is *Guercino: Mind to Paper.* Deborah Swallow, Courtauld director, kindly supported the project from the outset. Ernst Vegelin van Claerbergen and Caroline Campbell provided encouragement at every stage, while Joanna Selborne and Alexandra Gerstein were particularly helpful in giving access to the drawings and files. William Clarke, Julia Blanks, and Emma Hayes all played vital roles.

At the Getty I would like to thank Michael Brand, director, and Mikka Gee Conway, assistant director for museum advancement, for their warm support of the project. Former Getty Museum acting director William Griswold suggested Guercino as a fruitful subject of possible collaboration even as the idea was germinating in my own mind. Lee Hendrix, curator of drawings, has been a constant source of advice and encouragement to me, and Stephanie Schrader, Christine Giviskos, and David McCormick, my colleagues in the Drawings Department, have been generously supportive at every stage. I am extremely grateful for the help of Nathaniel Silver, the 2005–6 Drawings Department Graduate Intern, who conscientiously compiled the catalogue apparatus, and wrote part of the essay and some labels; he also kindly assumed—with unwarranted cheer—any number of dull tasks associated with the project. Associate conservator Nancy Yocco was the source of much useful advice. Quincy Houghton, assistant director, and Susan McGinty, exhibitions coordinator, guided the project with supreme efficiency and sense. Sally Hibbard, chief registrar, and Amy Linker, associate registrar, brought the exhibition together, and designers Robert Checchi and Levi Lewis, working under exhibition design manager Merritt Price, conceived a fitting design, well installed by Bruce Metro's department. I would also like to thank Stephanie Ford, Catherine Comeau, Maite Alvarez, Rael Lewis, and Miranda Carroll for their contributions.

The team at Getty Publications has been a pleasure to work with. Mark Greenberg oversaw the project with aplomb, and Ann Lucke, Karen Schmidt, Suzanne Watson, and Cecily Gardner all played important roles. I am especially grateful to the designer Catherine Lorenz, working with design manager Deenie Yudell, for such an appealing and clear volume. Tobi Kaplan was an engaged editor, and Patrick Pardo has been an attentive project editor.

In addition, I would like to thank the following for not-so-random acts of kindness: Carmen Bambach, Rhea Sylvia Blok, Hugo Chapman, David Ekserdjian, Kate Heard, Catherine Jenkins, George Knox, Henrietta Ryan, Sabrina Shim, and Catherine Whistler (a constant inspiration).

It is a hope that—fifteen years after the rash of quatercentenary Guercino exhibitions in 1991—the present exhibition and catalogue might enable many other people to make his acquaintance, and I am profoundly grateful to all those who have helped.

JULIAN BROOKS
Assistant Curator of Drawings
The J. Paul Getty Museum

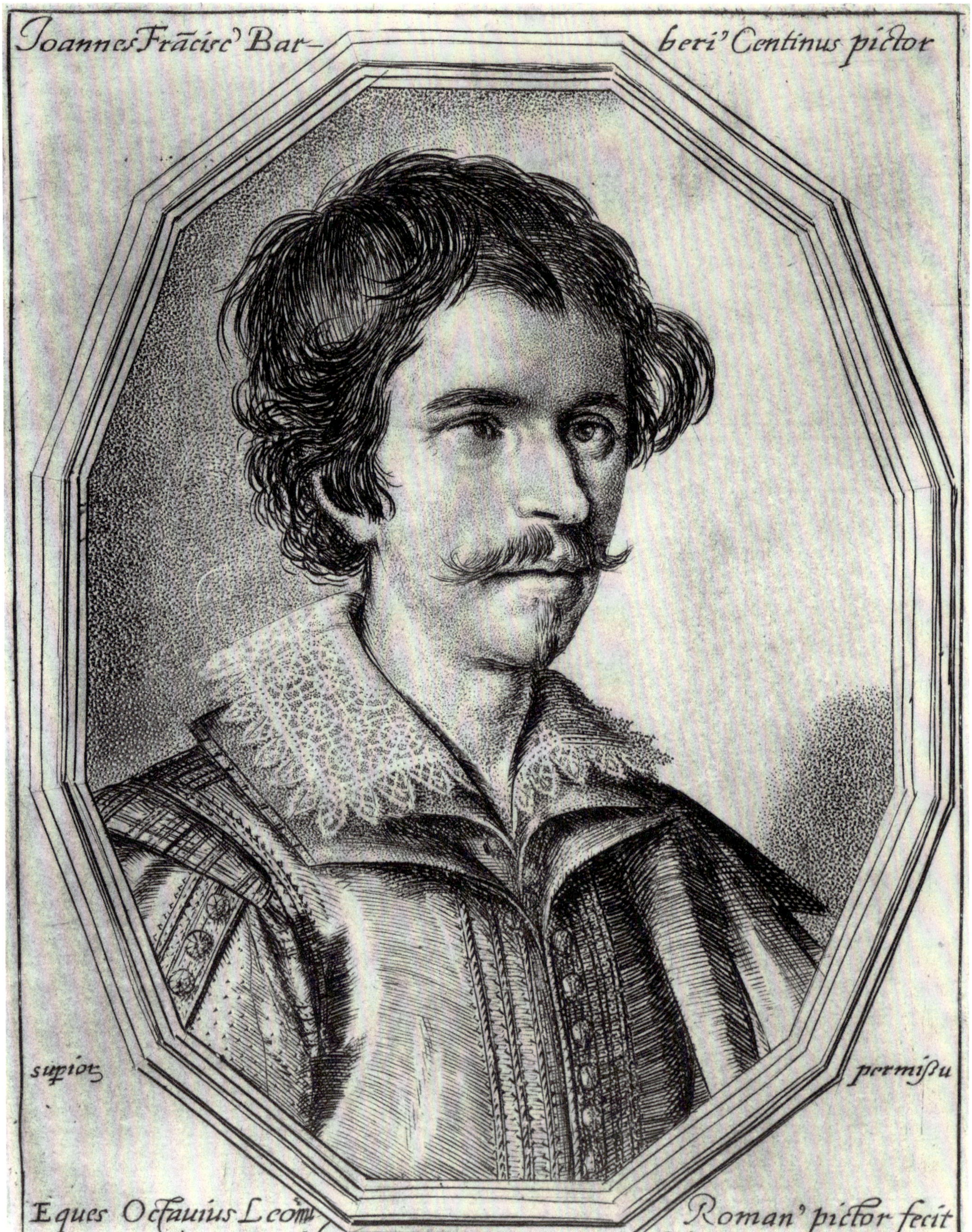
Joannes Fracisc' Bar-
beri' Centinus pictor
supior
permissu
Eques Octauius Leoni
Roman' pictor fecit
16
23

INTRODUCTION

WHY IS A CROSS-EYED MAN from the small town of Cento (between Bologna and Ferrara) in north Italy now regarded as one of the greatest Italian draftsmen of the seventeenth century? What makes his drawings so special? Why are they among the most distinctive and sought-after creations of graphic art? To explore the answers to these questions, this book examines the draftsmanship of Giovanni Francesco Barbieri (1591–1666), nicknamed *Guercino* ("squinter").

In studying Guercino and the nature of his drawings, we are fortunate for two reasons. First, Guercino's life is exceptionally well documented. In addition to two biographies by contemporaries who were close to the artist—Count Carlo Cesare Malvasia (1616–1693) and Francesco Scannelli (1613–1663)—there survives a well-maintained account book that details Guercino's commissions from 1629 until his death in 1666. These sources make it possible to reconstruct the chronology of Guercino's paintings with unusual precision, to learn details about his patrons, and to glean biographical notes about the artist and his lifestyle.[1]

Second, an extraordinarily large proportion of Guercino's drawings survive, allowing us to assess and appreciate his draftsmanship fully. Despite repeated requests from patrons, the artist was reluctant to part with his drawings and kept the majority in his studio (see pp. 5–7 for their history). We can estimate that about 40 percent of them still survive today, a remarkably high percentage that is perhaps unparalleled among other sixteenth- or seventeenth-century artists.[2] For example, Paul Joannides calculates that only around 1 percent of Michelangelo's graphic production survives, an extreme figure reflecting the fact that the artist deliberately burned a large number of his drawings.[3] Many of Guercino's surviving drawings were created as studies for painted works, and these offer an insight into his creative process; they help us understand how and why he drew. Any artist's drawings provide, to some extent, a glimpse into their maker's mind, and we can see ideas evolving on the page. Given the large number of his surviving sheets, we feel this process even more keenly with Guercino and consequently can develop a great sympathy for him. □

FIGURE A
Ottavio Leoni (Italian, 1578–1630). *Portrait of Giovanni Francesco Barbieri, called Guercino*, 1623. Engraving, 14.6 × 11.6 cm ($5\frac{3}{4} \times 4\frac{9}{16}$ in.). Los Angeles County Museum of Art, AC1994.138.2. Gift of Bruce Davis

GUERCINO'S LIFE

ALTHOUGH HE WAS GIVEN the name Giovanni Francesco (Barbieri) when he was born in early February 1591, the artist became better known by the nickname *Guercino* ("squinter"). His distinctive squint came about in early childhood: while in the care of a nurse, he was suddenly awakened by a loud noise, which left one of his eyes permanently fixed at an angle in its socket.[4] Despite being cross-eyed, the boy showed a talent for drawing even at the age of six; by age nine, he was apprenticed to a local painter. Other apprenticeships followed, including to a *quadraturista* based in Bologna and, most profitably, in 1607 to the Centese artist Benedetto Gennari the Elder (1563–1658); Guercino remained close to the Gennari family throughout his life.

Despite his apprenticeships and training, Guercino felt that he was largely self-taught. Early on, he studied the work of Lodovico Carracci (1555–1619), who had painted an altarpiece in 1591 for the church of the Cappuccini in Cento, the town where Guercino lived. Guercino also traveled to Bologna to look at works by Lodovico and his cousins Annibale (1560–1609) and Agostino Carracci (1557–1602), and it was no doubt at that time that he learned about the Carraccis' working methods, saw the way they used preparatory drawings, and perhaps visited their academy.[5] Guercino's early work also shows the stylistic influences of the Ferrarese artists Ippolito Scarsella, called il Scarsellino (ca. 1550–1620), and Carlo Bonone (1569–1632).

Like many artists at the time, the youthful Guercino honed his skills by drawing from posed nude figures. His biographer Malvasia reported that he was in such high demand as a teacher that he set up an *Accademia del nudo* in two rooms lent by a Centese patron, Bartolomeo Fabri. There, Guercino taught drawing from the live nude model, especially using black chalk (see cat. no. 2 for an example).[6] In setting up his academy, the artist was no doubt inspired by the Carracci academy in Bologna, which included a rigorous program of drawing from life and ran parallel to such activities in the studios of Florence.[7] By 1617, Guercino's *Accademia del nudo* had grown to twenty-three students, but it fell victim to the artist's growing popularity as a painter, and soon Guercino was too busy with commissions to run it.

Guercino's early success as a painter was due largely to the influence of one of his first supporters and patrons, Padre Antonio Mirandola, canon of San Salvatore in Bologna, who arranged a number of local commissions at this time, and continued to do so. These commissions attracted the attention of Cardinal Alessandro Ludovisi, archbishop of Bologna, and Cardinal Jacopo Serra, the papal legate in Ferrara, each of whom commissioned groups of paintings. A commission from the Grand Duke of Tuscany (see cat. no. 1) provides additional evidence of Guercino's growing status outside his native Cento and Bologna.

Guercino traveled little over the course of his life, but in 1618 he went to Venice with Padre Pietro Martire Pederzani. He took with him a series of anatomical drawings,

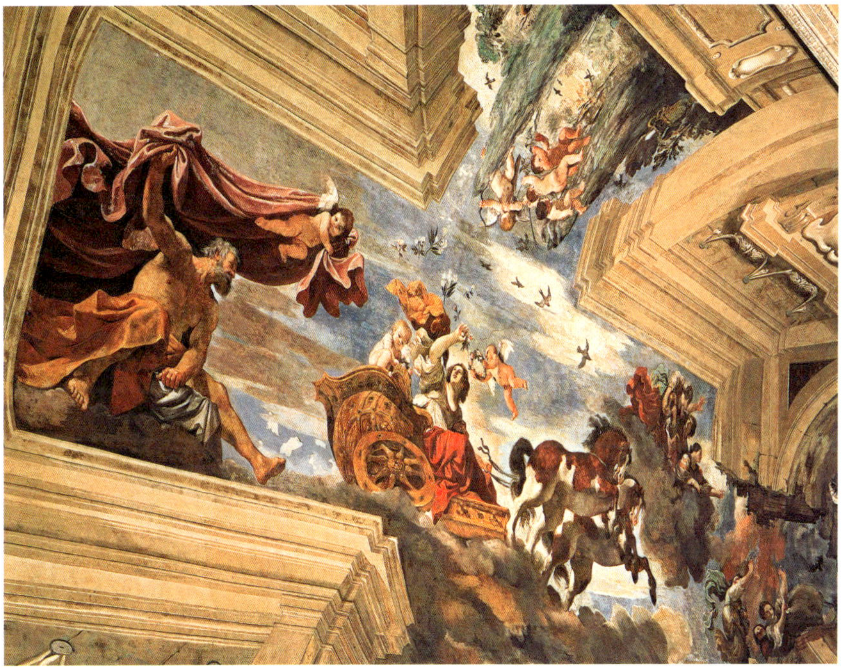

FIGURE B
Guercino. *Aurora*, 1621. Dry fresco. Rome, Casino Ludovisi, ceiling. Photo: Scala/Art Resource, New York

which he intended to publish for the instruction of young artists, and showed them to Jacopo Palma, il Giovane (ca. 1548–1628). The following year, the drawings were engraved by Oliviero Gatti and published with a dedication to Ferdinando Gonzaga, Duke of Mantua.[8] In 1621, Guercino's supporter Alessandro Ludovisi became pope, taking the name Gregory XV. This was an event of pivotal importance for Guercino. He was summoned to Rome to paint the Loggia delle Benedizioni in St. Peter's basilica, and moved to the Eternal City.

In Rome, Guercino's alignment with the pope won him important commissions, including his *Aurora* for the Casino Ludovisi (fig. B) and a large-scale altarpiece for St. Peter's (see cat. nos. 3 and 4). These commissions not only brought him international fame but also pitted him against competing artists such as Guido Reni (1575–1642); indeed, Guercino's style became more classicizing, reflecting that of Reni. Ottavio Leoni drew Guercino's portrait, and the engraving made from that drawing in 1623 (fig. A) shows a finely dressed young artist with a wiry moustache and a distinctive squint.

In broad terms, Guercino's career is characterized by two styles. His *prima maniera*, developed during his youth in Cento and Bologna, yielded bold compositions and employed strong effects of light and shade. From 1623 to 1632, Guercino's style went through a period of transition, culminating in his *seconda maniera*: in the latter part of his career he used a subtler palette to create refined compositions in a more idealized, classical style.

Guercino's runaway success in Rome was abruptly ended by the death of Pope Gregory XV on July 8, 1623. Guercino returned to Cento, where he continued producing church altarpieces, depictions of saints, and half-length pictures of biblical and mythological scenes for private clients. However, his patrons now came not only from local centers such as Reggio and Piacenza but also from international markets. He often shipped paintings abroad (for example, see cat. no. 31), and royal patrons sought him out. In the mid-1620s, King Charles I of England invited Guercino to London to become a court painter there, and in 1639 King Louis XIII invited him to become a painter at the French court. Guercino declined both invitations, preferring instead to stay with home and family in Cento.

In 1628, Guercino's sister Lucia married Ercole Gennari (1597–1658), one of Guercino's assistants, further strengthening the connection between the artist and the Gennari family. Later, Ercole's two children—Guercino's nephews Benedetto (1633–1715) and Cesare (1637–1688)—also joined the workshop.

Throughout his career, Guercino adhered to a strict system of fees for his work. He charged for his paintings by the figure—approximately 100 ducats per full-length figure, 50 ducats for a half-length, and 25 for a head—a practice not uncommon at the time.[9] However, Guercino does not seem to have been as commercially savvy or self-promoting as some artists of his day, for example Domenichino (1581–1641) or Guido Reni. Curiously, for someone who clearly took great care and time to prepare a composition, Guercino apparently set no premium on originality: throughout his career, he asked the same fee for a replica of a composition as for the original work.[10]

In 1642, Guercino moved to Bologna with his entire extended family, perhaps to avoid the Wars of Castro, which were encroaching on nearby territory. The move may also have been prompted by the death of Guido Reni. For years, Reni's workshop had dominated Bolognese artistic commissions; by relocating, Guercino could seize the opportunity to work for some of Reni's patrons. Over the next twenty years, Guercino's business went from strength to strength, and his many international clients reflected his widespread renown. In 1655, Queen Christina of Sweden (1626–1689) visited his studio "to have the pleasure of touching a hand that has worked such miracles."[11] In his last few years, Guercino was beset by illness, and on December 22, 1666, he died. Having never married, he bequeathed his house and studio—the Casa Gennari—to his nephews Benedetto and Cesare Gennari. They carried on the business, preserved Guercino's studio props, and protected the legacy of his drawings.

Guercino's biographer Malvasia, writing shortly after his subject's death, provides a touching account of the artist as humble, well-mannered, honest, respectful, chaste, and agreeable.[12] □

THE CASA GENNARI AND THE PROVENANCE OF SIR ROBERT WITT'S GUERCINO DRAWINGS

MANY OF THE DRAWINGS reproduced in this book are now in the Witt Collection at the Courtauld Institute of Art Gallery, London. Their history can be traced directly back to the Casa Gennari, Guercino's house and studio in Bologna.

As the custodians of Guercino's studio after his death, Benedetto and Cesare Gennari preserved their uncle's drawings in a relatively intact corpus and cherished his memory. A drawing in the Witt Collection shows one of the ways in which Benedetto and Cesare chose to honor their uncle (fig. C). It is a design by Cesare Gennari made as the frontispiece to a series of fourteen etchings of Guercino landscape drawings, published in the 1670s with a dedication to Francesco II d'Este, Duke of Modena.[13] Benedetto, who was in Paris working for the French court between 1672 and 1674, had the series etched there by Jean Pesne (1623–1700). The plates were then sent to Bologna, where Cesare drew a frontispiece (engraved by Gioseffo Roli) that is a testament to "Guercinosity." Cesare's drawing uses the entire range of media at his disposal, resulting in a collage-like effect. Two putti drawn in stumped black chalk hold a medallion portrait in red ink of a youthful Guercino, whose squint is not emphasized (in contrast to Leoni's engraving, fig. A). One putto pulls

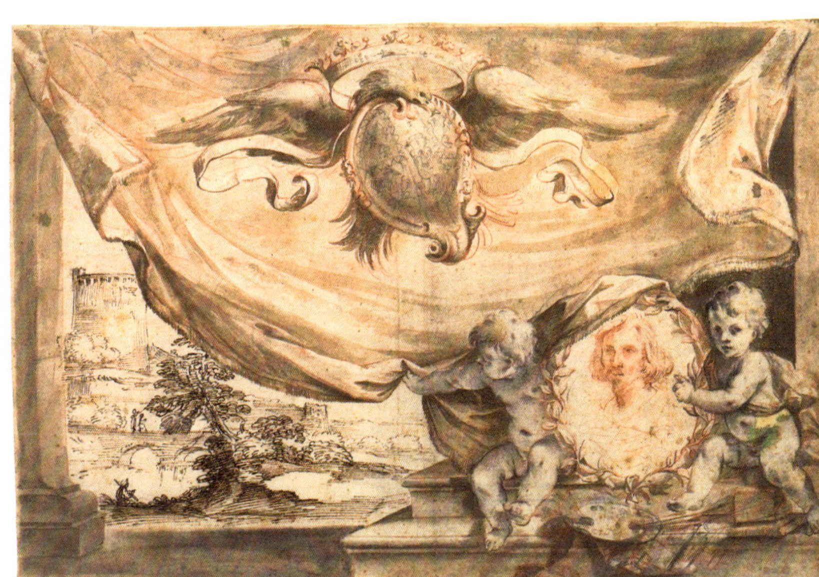

FIGURE C

Cesare Gennari (Italian, 1637–1688). *Design for a Frontispiece: Two Putti Supporting a Medallion Portrait of Guercino*, ca. 1675. Black chalk, red chalk, pen with brown and red inks, brush with brown wash, 28 × 40.7 cm (11 × 16 in.). London, Courtauld Institute of Art Gallery, D.1952.RW.567

back a curtain drawn in brown wash and red chalk, revealing a striking landscape that is clearly also a homage to Guercino's style.[14]

Benedetto Gennari probably sold the fourteen original landscape drawings to one of his patrons, the 4th Earl (later 1st Duke) of Devonshire, and the drawings remained thereafter at Chatsworth. One (fig. D) was acquired by the Ashmolean Museum, Oxford, in

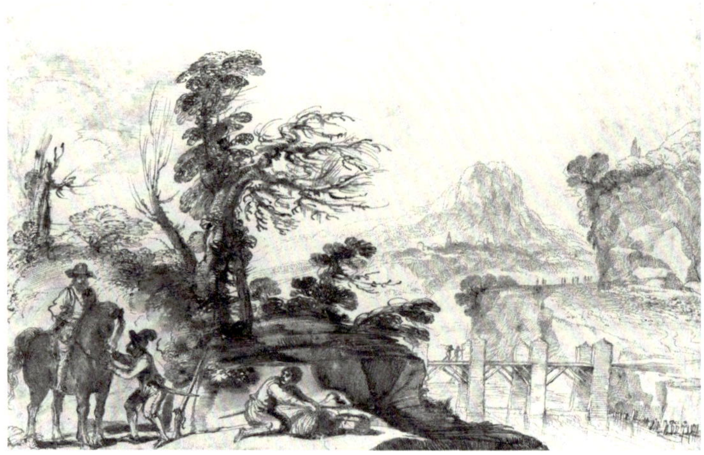

FIGURE D
Guercino. *Landscape with a Man on a Horse and Two Armed Men*, ca. 1630s. Pen and brown ink, brush with brown wash, 25.8 × 42.3 cm (10 1/8 × 16 5/8 in.). Oxford, Ashmolean Museum, 873B

1987, and another by the Fitzwilliam Museum, Cambridge. By the eighteenth century, the prints made in the 1670s and numerous copies of them had helped to generate a taste for Guercino's landscape drawings. To meet demand, forgeries were rife.[15] Unfortunately, the Witt Collection has no original landscape drawings by Guercino.[16]

It is unclear exactly how many of Guercino's drawings Cesare and Benedetto inherited in 1666, but an inventory of the Gennari property taken after Benedetto's death in 1719 records 1,689 drawings in albums, 136 framed, and about 660 loose, an astonishing number.[17] Benedetto had never married, and the 1719 inventory allowed his nephews Filippo Antonio (1677–1751) and Gianfrancesco Gennari (1671–1727) to divide up the studio property. Some of the drawings had, like the Chatsworth landscapes, already begun to filter out of the Gennari family, but Gianfrancesco's son Carlo Gennari (1716–1790), heir to both shares of the collection, probably sold off the first large groups of the drawings, which were sought by an eager market.[18]

John Bouverie (ca. 1723–1750), a young collector who went on to form one of the most important drawings collections of the eighteenth century, wasted no time capitalizing on this opportunity. Although it is impossible to reconstruct fully Bouverie's access to the Gennari collection, he appears to have purchased his Guercino drawings through intermediaries (primarily Francesco Forni in Bologna, son of an established drawings dealer) during his first Grand Tour (1740–42) at age eighteen. Bouverie's purchases formed the core of the first major collection of Guercino drawings to arrive in England, some fifteen years before King George III began acquiring works by the artist.[19] The king added more than 800 drawings by Guercino and school to the Royal Collection through the purchases of his agents, who also recognized the opportunity provided by the Gennari collection.

In 1750, when he was only twenty-seven years old, John Bouverie died. The drawings passed to Bouverie's sister Anne and were later inherited by her [?] son Christopher Hervey (d. 1786). It was while the collection was in Hervey's possession that the drawings connoisseur Henry Reveley described Bouverie's careful selection: "But perhaps the finest collection of Guercino's drawings in England, is in the possession of Mr. Hervey of Welbeck Street. They are contained in about twelve volumes; and were inherited from his uncle Mr. Bouverie."[20] When Hervey died, in 1786, the drawings passed to his aunt, Elizabeth Bouverie, the other of John Bouverie's two sisters.[21] She had never married, and although it has long been unclear why she chose to leave the drawings and part of her estate, Barham Court, to Sir Charles Middleton (1726–1813), it now appears that they had a close connection: his wife was Elizabeth Bouverie's close childhood friend.[22] Upon Middleton's death, the drawings were inherited by Charles Noel (1781–1866)—eldest son of Middleton's only child, Diana (d. 1823), and Sir Gerald Noel Noel (1759–1838)—probably via Sir Gerald.

In 1841, Charles Noel was elevated to the peerage, becoming the 1st Earl of Gainsborough. Eighteen years later, he offered the first major portion of the Bouverie collection for sale at auction, including 116 sheets by Guercino.[23] Over the next sixty-plus years, gifts and purchases scattered small numbers of drawings from the Gainsborough family to other owners.[24] In 1922, the 3rd Earl of Gainsborough provided the next significant opportunity for collectors to purchase drawings from the Bouverie collection when he sold his property at auction.[25]

One collector who seized this chance was Sir Robert Witt (1872–1952). A solicitor by profession, Witt developed a great interest in art while studying at Oxford and later helped to establish the National Art Collections Fund. In addition, he collected photographs of works of art that became the foundation for the indispensable Witt photographic reference library at the Courtauld Institute of Art. When the Bouverie collection came up for sale, Witt probably followed a common practice and commissioned a dealer to bid for him; it appears that the respected firm F. R. Meatyard successfully purchased one lot on his behalf.[26] It contained 60 drawings by Guercino, together considered by many scholars to be the finest surviving group from the Bouverie collection. Witt bequeathed 32 of the drawings to the Courtauld Institute of Art.[27] Of the drawings in the present volume that are from the Witt Collection, all but one carry the Bouverie provenance.[28]

A number of physical clues on the drawings by Guercino from the Witt Collection reflect the sheets' illustrious provenance.[29] For example, the distinctive kinetic lined mounts visible on catalogue numbers 10, 27, and 34, among others, are known as "Casa Gennari" mounts. They were made with some sensitivity (for example, on cat. no. 34, the lines on the mount are red, instead of black, to complement the red-chalk technique of the drawing), and may have been added by the dealer Francesco Forni in the eighteenth century. Some of the drawings (see cat. nos. 4 and 7) have early inscriptions that might be Gennari location references, and many of the sheets have numeration in graphite in the lower left corner that seems to record a Gainsborough collection numbering. □

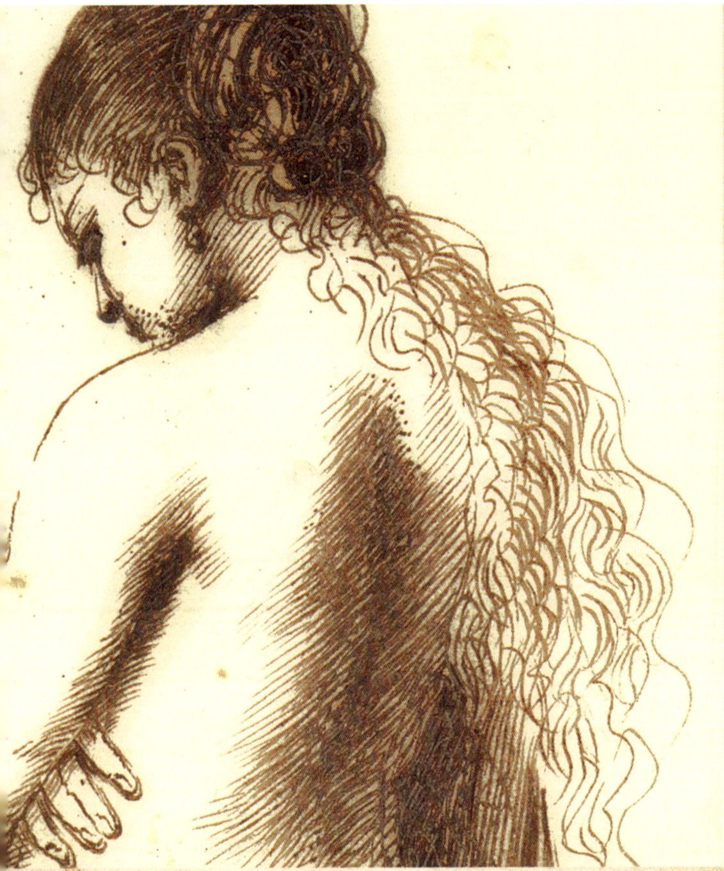
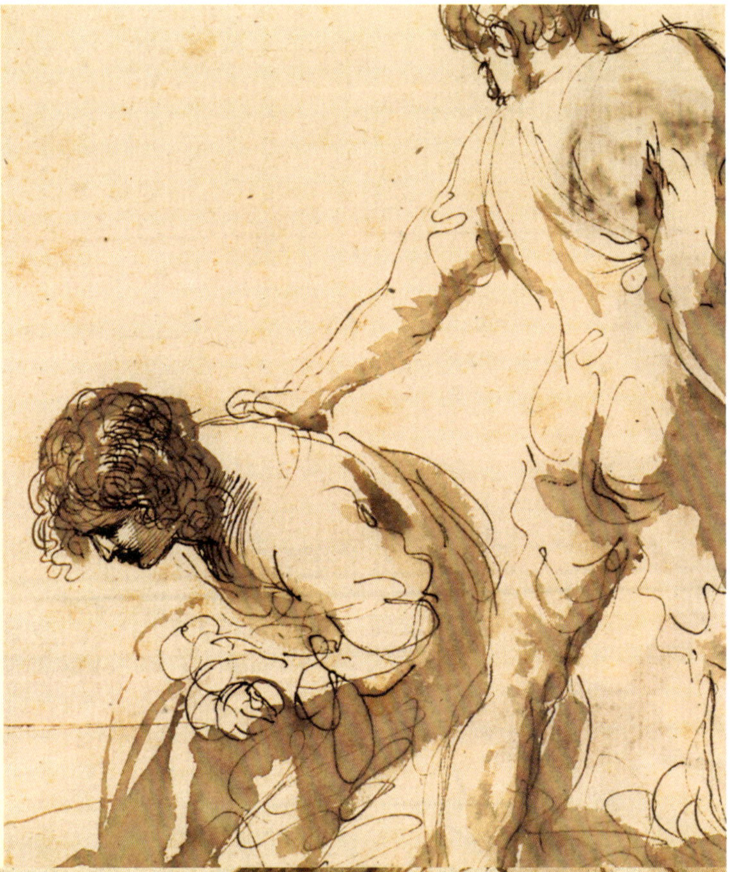
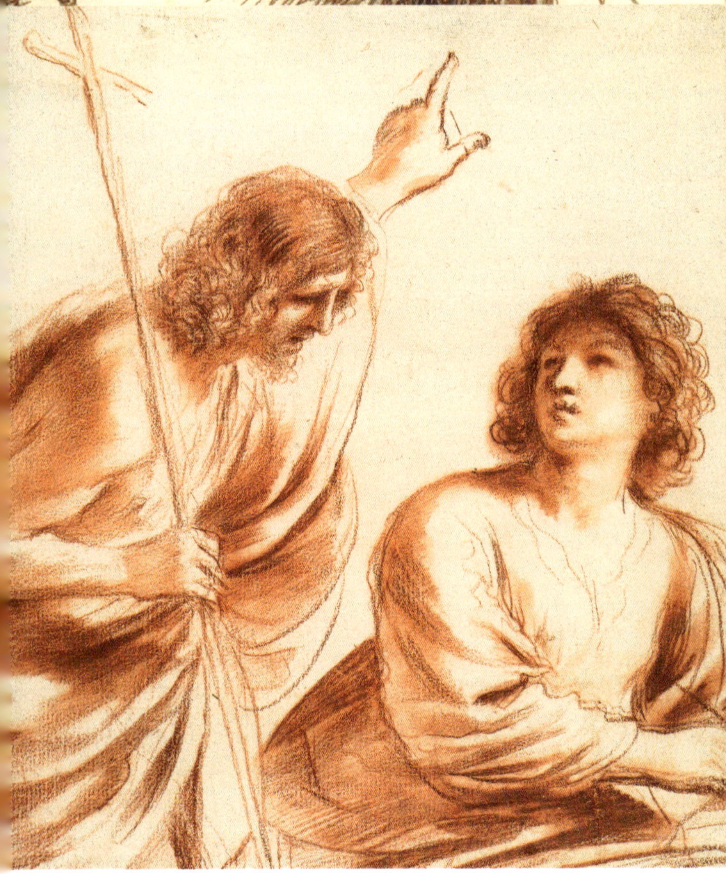
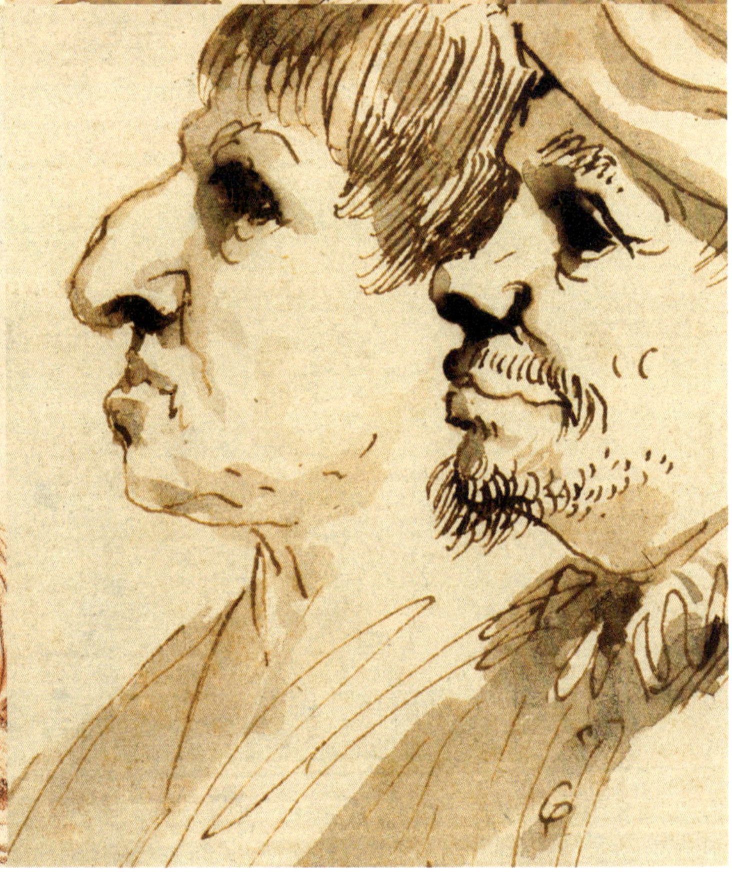

CHARACTERIZING GUERCINO'S DRAFTSMANSHIP

IN 1741, THE COLLECTOR and writer Pierre-Jean Mariette (1694–1774) eloquently summed up Guercino's draftsmanship as follows:

> One cannot say that Guercino was a scrupulous draftsman. Very far from it. One could even accuse him of being strongly mannered. Yet he pleases at least as much as a more severe draftsman. His contours are fluid and robust, his compositions large and noble, and in his distribution of light and shade there is a marvelous intelligence and effect. This painter has a completely seductive pen, and when combined with a few touches of wash, it gives his drawings a beauty that one cannot find in the drawings of any other master.[30]

In reviewing what people have written about Guercino's drawings in the distant and recent past, and considering the drawings themselves as a whole, four groups of attributes emerge to characterize what is special and distinctive about the artist's draftsmanship: (1) inventiveness and process, (2) energy and spontaneity, (3) texture, shadow, light, and space, and (4) humor and humanity. These attributes are not mutually exclusive; in fact, they are often profoundly interlinked, and some drawings are excellent examples of all four. Taken together, they express the essence of Guercino's draftsmanship.

1. INVENTIVENESS AND PROCESS

The majority of drawings created by artists in the late sixteenth and early seventeenth centuries were used in the preparatory stages of making paintings. While individual artists used drawings in different ways, almost all seem to have made drawings in the following formats: finished *modelli*, compositions, individual figures (from imagination or life), groups of figures, heads, and details of drapery or limbs. Guercino used all of these types of drawing (although he did not make many *modelli* [see p. 12]), but he differed from his contemporaries and predecessors in two ways: he created repeated large-scale studies, and he made "close-up" drawings that focused on the emotional relationship between two figures in a scene. These two types of drawing formats are at the root of Guercino's compositional inventiveness.

Clockwise from top left: Details from cat. no. 28, cat. no. 16 (recto), cat. no. 20, and cat. no. 15

Repeated Large-Scale Studies

In their indispensable 1989 survey of drawings by Guercino in the Royal Collection, Sir Denis Mahon and Nicholas Turner note how Guercino "submitted his compositions to a continuous process of change and refinement."[31] This is particularly evident in the sequences of preparatory drawings for commissions such as *The Burial and Reception into Heaven of Saint Petronilla* and *The Martyrdom of Saints John and Paul* (see cat. nos. 4, 14, 16, and 18). Whereas most artists might think through a composition and scatter a selection of their thoughts—on a small scale—across a sheet of paper, fully working up only the most successful ideas, Guercino abandoned this technique early in his career in favor of a much more innovative approach.

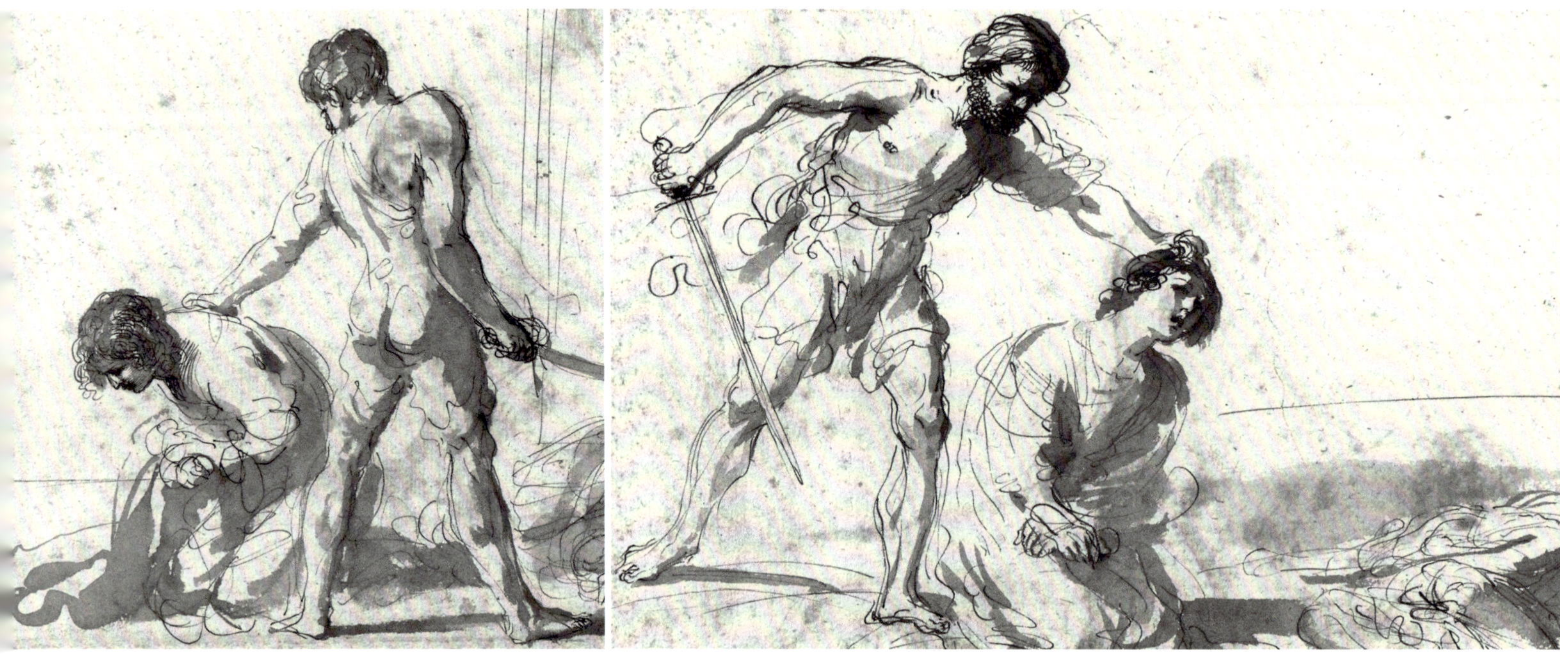

Left to right: Details from cat. no. 16 (recto), cat. no. 16 (verso), and fig. 16.4

For each composition, Guercino would study the principal figures in one arrangement across a whole sheet of paper, take a new sheet and study them in another full-scale arrangement, and then do this again and again, repeating the process numerous times with numerous sheets of paper. As Mahon says, it is as if, on receiving a commission, Guercino felt compelled to consider many ways of representing the scene in pen and ink before proceeding.[32] Guercino's study sheets seem to capture the progress of his thoughts, allowing us to see the contents of his mind on paper. Each drawing occupies a full sheet, a testament to the importance given by the artist to every thought. Likewise, each drawing is worked up—albeit rapidly—to a relatively full degree of finish. Guercino's repeated large-scale studies reflect great inventiveness in approaching a scene; like a skilled choreographer or film director, he orchestrates the actions of his characters.

Beyond Guercino's sheer enjoyment of drawing, there was also a practical aspect to his approach; he no doubt realized that a library of such compositions could be very useful for his own future reference. It is clear that the artist valued his drawings highly, and he probably kept them in albums for safekeeping and ready access. Examples abound of the artist reusing figures, motifs, and compositional solutions from previous projects. For example, some of his ideas for *Sisyphus* (see cat. no. 23) were reused ten years later when he approached the subject of Atlas.[33] Guercino was also not above "borrowing" motifs from other artist's works, a subject of much speculation among scholars.[34]

The ideas that Guercino explores in a suite of drawings for a composition often vary so much that it can be difficult to reconstruct fully the order in which they were made. Occasionally, it is obvious that he is working out a specific problem, such as the visibility of a figure's face, or an awkward pose. Mostly, however, Guercino doesn't seem to concentrate on one particular problem but rather turns the whole composition around in three dimensions, first in his head and then on the paper.

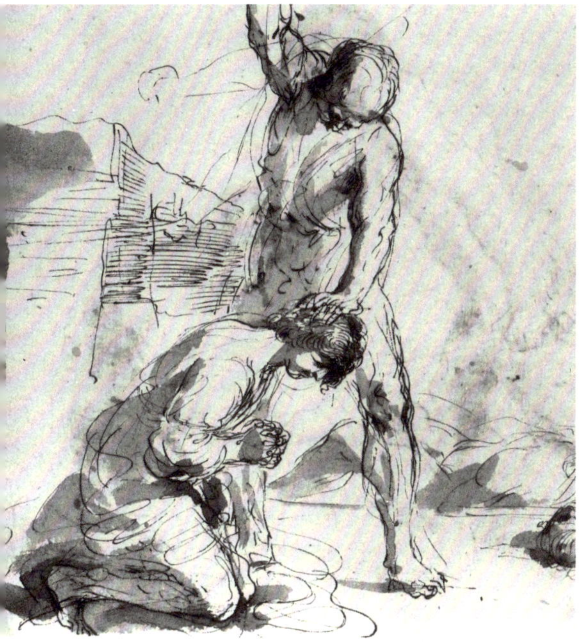

One workshop tool that helped him visualize compositions and figures from different viewpoints, and of which he made great use, was the counterproof, or offset. This was a technique whereby a damp sheet of blank paper was laid on top of a drawing in red or black chalk; when the sheet was removed, chalk particles would stick to it, creating a weaker, reversed version of the image. This enabled the artist to "flip" a composition or figure easily; the technique was common in sixteenth-century Bolognese, Florentine, and Roman drawing practice.[35]

"Close-Ups"

David Stone has identified a particular type of drawing made by Guercino, which he calls a "close-up" because it seems to zoom in on one part of a larger composition.[36] A typical Guercino "close-up" is a fairly finished study of two figures from a larger composition that examines the emotional relationship between the figures (for an example, see cat. no. 15). Generally, Guercino would already have made studies of the relevant figure or group in full length, but would draw them again up close, in half-length. Such drawings occur frequently in Guercino's oeuvre but are unusual for other artists. Guercino often used "close-ups" to characterize the figures studied through details of facial type, hair, or dress. More importantly, however, they examine the facial expressions and gestures of the characters in relation to one another. These studies seem to be Guercino's way of getting inside the emotional dynamics of a scene, analyzing its psychological disposition, and developing a real understanding of the narrative of the story. As Stone has pointed out, Guercino's "close-ups" were often made relatively late in the preparatory process, yet they could, in turn, significantly affect the focus of the entire composition.

These two distinctive types of drawings—repeated large-scale studies and "close-ups"—reflect Guercino's specific way of working. Through them, he sought to develop on paper the ideas that were in his mind. They are evidence of a fertile and inventive imagination looking to tell a story in the most convincing and satisfactory way possible. For Guercino, the process of devising a composition continued right up to—and included—

the moment he was actually making the finished painting.[37] While most artists showed their patrons drawings (often highly finished *modelli*) of a commission to ensure that they would like the result, Guercino refused to do so, on the basis that he would then be bound to a particular solution.[38] In only a single instance do we have a *modello* from his hand, and it is far from what Guercino actually painted (see cat. no. 4).

2. ENERGY AND SPONTANEITY

Going hand in hand with Guercino's inventiveness and creativity was his ability to put ideas on paper at the moment of inspiration. He worked very quickly, placing subjects on a sheet deftly and surely. The speed of his draftsmanship conveys an appealing energy, which Malvasia memorably characterizes using the word *guizzanti*, from *guizzare*, meaning to "dart with a flick of the tail, as fishes."[39] All modern commentators have noted the spontaneity of Guercino's draftsmanship.

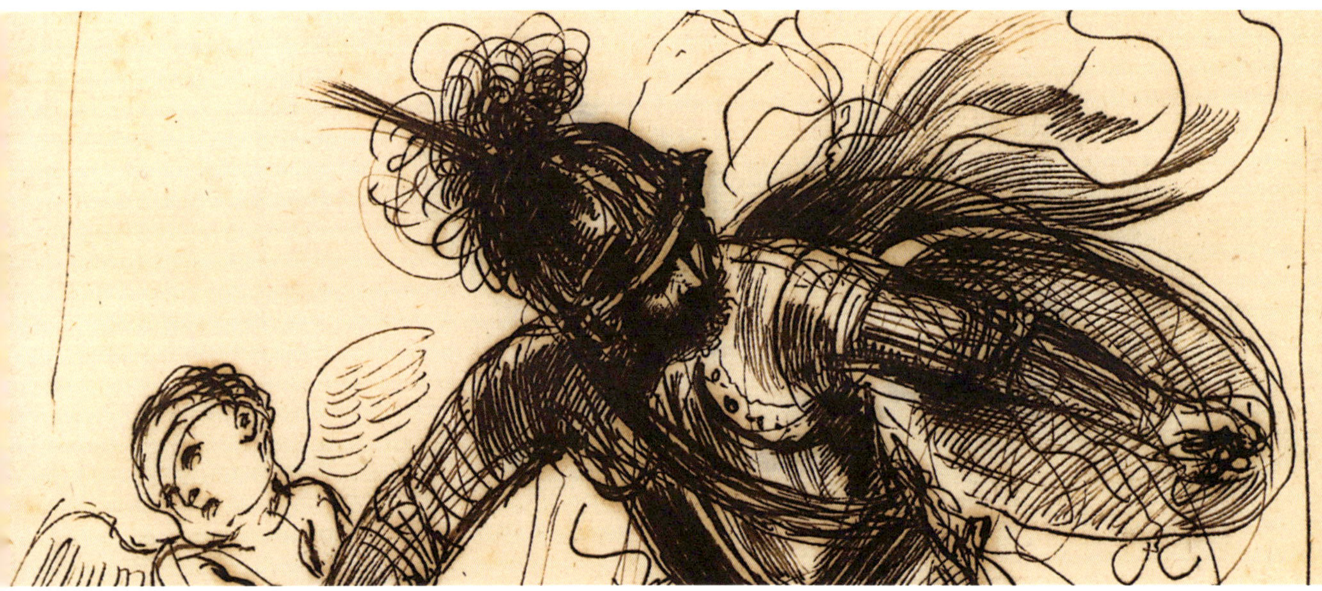

Detail from cat. no. 26

The medium through which Guercino found he could express himself best remained the same for most of his career. He made the majority of his drawings using pen dipped in brown ink, over which he applied brown or gray wash with a brush. These media, in particular, allow great fluidity and speed. In contrast to most of his contemporaries, Guercino did not generally first sketch out his ideas on the page in black chalk, which could be erased; instead—in a testament to his confidence and capability—he reached straight for his pen. Guercino mostly used a quill pen (a type made from a goose feather), which could hold more ink than a reed pen and thus allowed longer, more calligraphic lines. The pen still had to be dipped in ink at regular intervals, and Nicholas Turner and Carol Plazzotta have noted the skillful way Guercino used a fully loaded nib for the passages requiring darker accents.[40] His mastery of line also allowed a conspicuous brevity of draftsmanship; in many cases, he delineates only as much as the human visual brain needs to identify a scene (for example, see cat. nos. 6 and 28). He achieves the same economy — and thus speed — when he adds wash (see cat. nos. 10 and 31).

Very often, Guercino actually conveys movement in a subject by the speed with which he attacks the paper with the pen and the brush, as in his studies of *The Annunciation* and *Cupid Restraining Mars* (cat. nos. 25 and 26). In these drawings, the vigor of the draftsmanship matches that of the subjects. Guercino often also consciously or unconsciously uses pentimenti (minor changes) to blur a line or form and thereby create a kinetic effect. Examples of this include the wheel of Aurora's chariot (cat. no. 3), and Jupiter's arm (cat. no. 32).

Guercino was well aware that diagonal axes could be used in a composition to convey unsteadiness and movement, and he often further exploited this on a small scale with angled lines. In his drawings of Saint Sebastian and Jupiter, for example, Guercino cleverly uses sets of differently angled parallel lines to heighten movement and drama in the scenes (cat. nos. 30 and 32).

3. TEXTURE, SHADOW, LIGHT, AND SPACE

While these four elements might seem unrelated, together they provide a key to the appeal and success of Guercino's draftsmanship. In many drawings, dense texture is contrasted with blank sections of the page that represent either patches of light or space, or both.

From his early years, Guercino trained by drawing the nude body with an emphasis on tonal effects and chiaroscuro (see cat. no. 2). A major strength of Guercino's draftsmanship rests on his understanding of the nature of form defined by shadow, whether that form is a landscape, a body, or an arm (see cat. nos. 10 and 22). Many great draftsmen have such a skill, but Guercino uses it in conjunction with an expression of the texture of the underlying form in a way that is compelling. This is further emphasized by his selection of the most suitable media for each subject. For example, in his study of a warrior (cat. no. 31), he used brown wash to convey both the solid nature of the armor and the fluttering softness of the drapery; these contrast with the soldier's wiry moustache, made of pen lines. In a study of two women drying their hair in front of a fire (cat. no. 21), brush and wash brilliantly evoke long wet hair, while pen-and-ink lines indicate the licking flames.

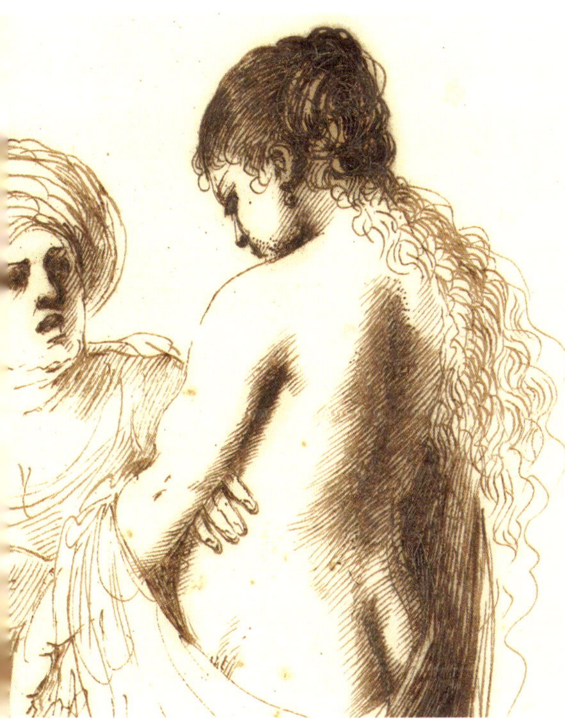

Detail from cat. no. 28

Indeed, the texture of hair seems to have fascinated Guercino, and few draftsmen represented it as adeptly. Whether head-borne or face-worn, hair is used subtly to bring a sense of verisimilitude and realism to Guercino's figures and compositions. The falling lock of hair on the saint about to be martyred in cat. no. 16 (recto), for example, heightens the pathos of the scene. In some cases, Guercino's approach is less subtle: Jupiter's turbulent curls (cat. no. 32) and Bathsheba's seductive ringlets (cat. no. 28) demonstrate just how powerfully the artist could use hair to characterize a figure.[41]

Throughout his career, but particularly during the 1630s, Guercino relished using brown wash, both to create strong effects of light and shadow, as in his Dante (cat. no. 19),

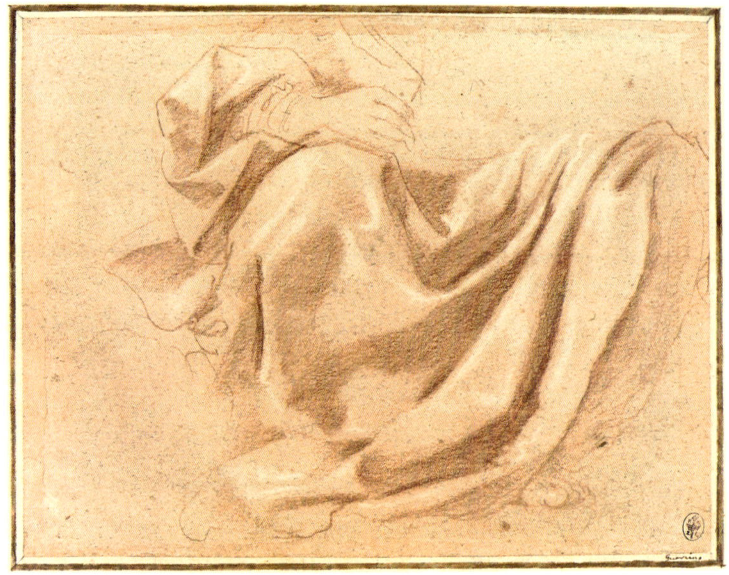

FIGURE E
Guercino. *Study for the Drapery of the Madonna*, ca. 1632. Red chalk, white heightening, 21.2 × 27.7 cm (8 3/8 × 10 7/8 in.). Stuttgart, Staatsgalerie, Graphische Sammlung, Koenig-Fachsenfeld Collection, 11/63

and—in varying subtle shades—to emphasize planes of space, as in *The Annunciation* (cat. no. 25). Artists would not use wash with such freedom again until the eighteenth century, when draftsmen in Venice exploited its effects. Giambattista Tiepolo (1696–1770), in particular, appreciated Guercino's draftsmanship and owned a number of his drawings.[42] Yet Guercino often seems intentionally to contrast the smooth and flowing wash with scratchy penwork, bestowing a conspicuous variety of texture upon the sheet.

Through virtuoso penwork and a multiplicity of lines, many of Guercino's designs for prints exemplify the artist's particular awareness of texture (see the scene of an old seamstress and child in cat. no. 5, for example). Unfortunately, such details were often lost on the engraver.[43] In his drawings for printmakers, Guercino chose pen and ink, intended to be most suitable for translation through the engraver's burin.

Guercino's sensitive choice of media is also clear in his deployment of red chalk. He used the medium throughout his career, especially toward the end of his life, applying it with particularly great effect in his studies of drapery and children, for which its soft modeling was especially suitable. Figure E and catalogue number 9 exemplify the way Guercino used red chalk to manipulate texture, shadow, light, and space, with stunning results.

4. HUMOR AND HUMANITY

Guercino's biographer Malvasia emphasized the artist's concern for those around him. Guercino was, he wrote, "affectionate towards the poor, who flocked around him whenever he left his house, as if he were their father; he enjoyed conversing with them."[44] Certainly, the artist's large corpus of caricatures and genre scenes reveal his great sensitivity to, and sympathy for, a range of human situations. Yet, perhaps more importantly, Guercino had the powers of observation to see the details of this in everyday life, and the capability—and desire—to record them on paper.

Some of the artist's drawings are strict caricatures: figures whose features are exaggerated for the purpose of mockery (see cat. no. 20). But there are also a large number of genre scenes and caricatures that reflect a detached, gentle sense of amusement rather than derision (cat. nos. 6 and 17, for example). These seem to have been observed in the course of daily life. As Sir Denis Mahon and Nicholas Turner aptly put it, "they are remarkable for their informality and lack of staginess, and it is precisely this uncontrived naturalism that makes them seem so true to life."[45] Furthermore, as Carel van Tuyll observed, Guercino's genre drawings do not have the patronizing or moralizing air of those produced by his northern contemporaries, for example the Dutch genre painter Adriaen van Ostade (1610–1685).[46]

Guercino's caricatures and genre drawings seem to have been made with no purpose in mind other than the amusement of the artist and his friends. As the provenance of the Witt sheets demonstrates, Guercino kept the drawings in his studio throughout his lifetime, and he likely enjoyed showing them off to his visitors. They follow a strong Bolognese tradition of caricature and genre drawings, of which Guercino must have been aware. In particular, he probably saw Annibale Carracci's drawings of tradesmen; Carracci made eighty of them

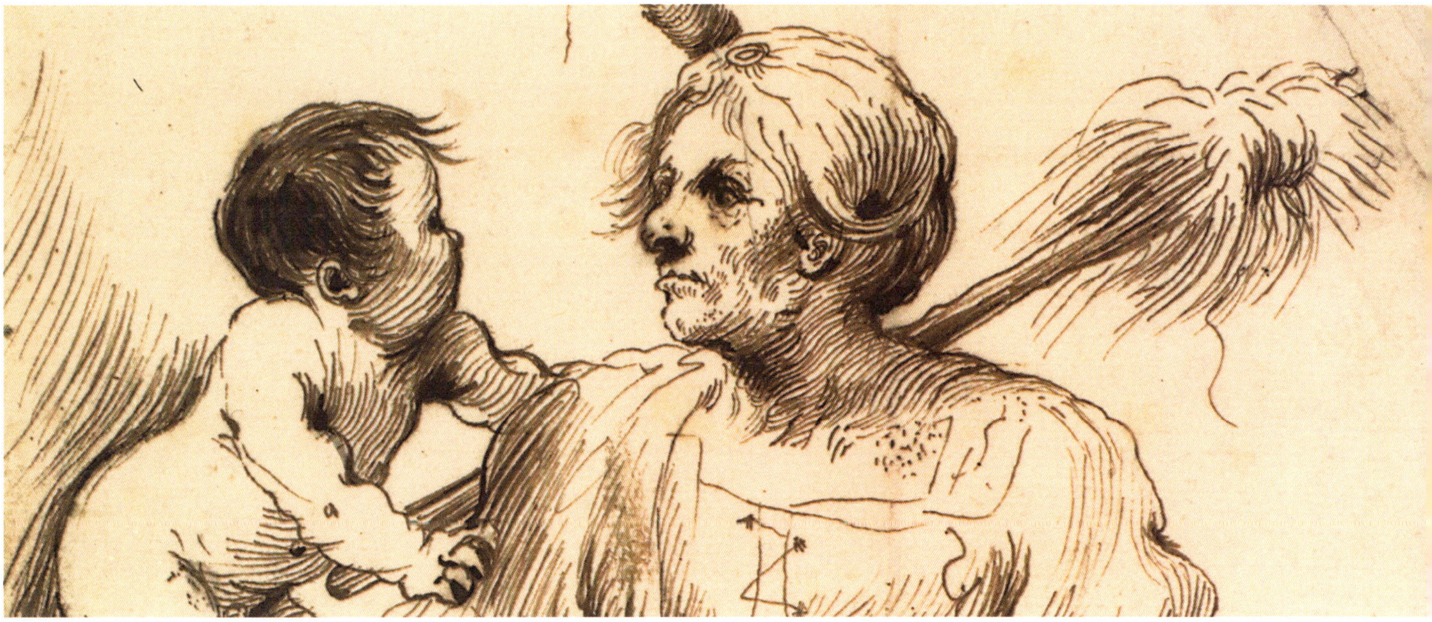

Detail from cat. no. 5

in the 1580s and used them for teaching in his studio; they were later published in a series of prints as *Le arti di Bologna*.[47] Guercino was also familiar with the work of the Lorraine-born caricaturist Jacques Callot (1592–1635) and owned a number of Callot's prints and drawings, including a book of twenty-seven sheets representing beggars.[48]

Given that Guercino traveled little and spent so much of his career in provincial Cento, it is no surprise that his caricatures and genre scenes reflect local life rather than political subjects. A gentle, sensitive humor and humanity characterize his work in this field and indeed pervade his entire graphic output. □

CASA GENNARI / BOUVERIE FAMILY / SIR ROBERT WITT PROVENANCE

Casa Gennari; John Bouverie (ca. 1723–1750); his sister Anne Bouverie (d. 1757); her husband, John Hervey (d. 1764); his son Christopher Hervey (d. 1786); his aunt Miss Elizabeth Bouverie (d. 1798; surviving sister of John Bouverie); by bequest to Sir Charles Middleton, later 1st Baron Barham (1726–1813); his son-in-law Sir Gerard Noel Noel, 2nd Baron Barham (1759–1838); his son Sir Charles Noel, 3rd Baron Barham and later 1st Earl of Gainsborough (1781–1866); thence by descent to the 3rd Earl of Gainsborough (sold, Christie's, London, July 27, 1922, lot 81); purchased by F. R. Meatyard; Sir Robert Witt (1872–1952); by bequest to the Courtauld Institute of Art, 1952.

NOTES

1 Carlo Cesare Malvasia, *Felsina pittrice: Vite de' pittori bolognesi*, 2 vols. (Bologna, 1678); Francesco Scannelli, *Il Microcosmo della pittura* (Cesena, 1657); *Il Libro dei conti del Guercino*, most recent edition by Barbara Ghelfi (see Ghelfi 1997).

2 Letter of February 15, 1650, to Don Antonio Ruffo (Mahon *Disegni* 1969, 7–8). The 1719 inventory records roughly 2,500 drawings by Guercino: 1,689 autograph drawings in albums, 136 framed drawings, and about 660 loose sheets. One could estimate that there are about a thousand genuine sheets by Guercino in collections worldwide today. None of these numbers includes the artist's very numerous counterproofs or works by his studio or followers. Nicholas Turner postulates a number as high as 3,000 surviving drawings, presumably including such sheets (Turner in Adam et al. 2005, 23). The number of drawings Guercino parted with during his lifetime is difficult to estimate.

3 Paul Joannides, in his introduction to the forthcoming catalogue of Michelangelo drawings in the Ashmolean Museum, Oxford (2006–7).

4 Malvasia ed. 1841, 2:257.

5 Malvasia ed. 1841, 2:256.

6 Malvasia ed. 1841, 2:258, 283.

7 Brooks 2003, 26–27.

8 See Mahon and Turner 1989, 6–7.

9 Spear 1994, 594. See also the in-depth analysis by Bonfait 1990, 71–94.

10 Spear 1994, 596.

11 Malvasia ed. 1841, 2:299 (Mahon *Disegni* 1969, 8).

12 Malvasia ed. 1841, 2:272.

13 The famous project is discussed fully by Mahon and Turner 1989, 105–7, and Bagni 1985, 57–165.

14 A copy of this part of the drawing has been published by Mahon and Turner 1989, 169, no. 585, not ill.

15 The drawing in figure D can be seen in the Print Room at the Ashmolean Museum alongside an eighteenth-century forgery derived from it (repr. Mahon and Ekserdjian 1986, 47–48, no. xxv, pl. xxv). The originals and forgeries are all well reproduced by Bagni 1985, 63–165.

16 Two sheets, invs. D.1952.RW.189 and D.1952.RW.513, seem to be the work of followers.

17 The information in this section draws heavily on the research of Nicholas Turner and Carol Plazzotta (Turner and Plazzotta 1991) and Nicholas Turner (Turner 1994; Turner 2005). For details of the inventory, see Mahon and Turner 1989, xviii–xxii; and Turner and Plazzotta 1991, 20. The inventory has yet to be transcribed and published.

18 Bagni has deduced that the drawings belonging to Filippo Antonio also passed to Carlo Gennari, because Filippo had three daughters and no sons (Bagni 1990, 11; Turner and Plazzotta 1991, 20).

19 It is unclear exactly how many drawings Bouverie purchased from each source and how many sources he had. Bouverie's first documented purchase of drawings by Guercino was probably one album with a few drawings from the Abbé Bonducci during his first Italian visit, 1740–42. Bouverie appears to have purchased the majority of his drawings by Guercino from Francesco Forni in Bologna, during a second visit to Italy about 1745. Turner suggests that Forni had early enough access to the Gennari drawings to enable him to choose some of the finest sheets. For a discussion of the Bonducci transaction, see Turner and Plazzotta 1991, 22. For a discussion of the Forni transaction, see Turner 1994, 96–97. For a discussion of the dating of the arrival of Bouverie's drawings by Guercino in England, see Turner in Adam et al. 2005, 13–17.

20 Reveley 1820, 77. As clarified by Nicholas Turner, "Henry Reveley died in 1798 and the book was published posthumously by his son Hugh." (Turner and Plazzotta 1991, 28n49, 31n82).

21 Turner and Plazzotta 1991, 24.

22 Turner 2005, 511n2. Reinforced by Brydges, according to whom, Middleton married "Margaret Gambier, aunt of the present Lord Gambier; a connection which introduced him to the house of her friend, Mrs. Bouverie at Teston (or Barham-Court), near Maidstone, in Kent, where he spent the greater part of his subsequent life; and who, at her death, left him the greater part of her estate" (Brydges 1829, 408).

23 Christie's, London, "Property of a Nobleman" [1st Earl of Gainsborough], July 20, 1859.

24 For a summary of gifts, bequests to family members, and sales, see Turner 1994, appendices 1 and 2.

25 Christie's, London, "Property of the Rt. Hon. The Earl of Gainsborough, of Exton Park, Oakham, Rutlandshire," July 27, 1922, lots 73–86. Other smaller sales followed. For a summary, see Turner 1994, appendix 2.

26 Lot 81 contained 68 drawings: 8 probably by other artists and 60 attributable to Guercino and his workshop, of which 32 were bequeathed by Witt to the Courtauld Institute of Art in 1952. The remaining 28 drawings by Guercino were probably sold to buy other drawings (Mahon 1967, 14n38; Turner and Plazzotta 1991, 27). One, of Saints Roch and Sebastian, formerly Witt Collection inv. 1340, is noted in Mahon and Turner 1989, 44. Another, of a young woman standing reading, apparently passed by descent until it was sold at Sotheby's, New York, January 26, 2005, lot 71. For the suggestion that Meatyard bid on behalf of Witt, see Turner and Plazzotta 1991, 27; Byam Shaw writes, "... from Parsons in Brompton Road and from Meatyard in Museum Street, both much respected establishments and much frequented by connoisseurs" (Byam Shaw 1989, 493n2).

27 Turner and Plazzotta 1991, 27.

28 *The Race of Atalanta* (cat. no. 8) was purchased by the Courtauld Institute of Art after Witt's death in 1952.

29 Turner and Plazzotta 1991, 25–26.

30 "L'on ne dira point que le Guerchin soit un dessinateur correct. Il s'en faut beaucoup. On peut meme le taxer d'etre fort maniéré. Il plait cependant pour le moins autant qu'un dessinateur plus sévere. C'est que ses contours sont coulons et de chair, que ses compositions sont grandes et nobles, et qu'il y a dans la distribution de son clair-obscur, une intelligence et des effets merveilleux. Ce peintre a outre cela una plume tout-à-fait séduisante, et lorsqu'il y joint quelques coups de lavis, il met dans ses desseins une vaghesse qu'on ne trouve dans les desseins d'aucun autre maitre" (Pierre-Jean Mariette, *Description Sommaire des Dessins des Grands Maistres... du Cabinet de Feu M. Crozat* [Paris, 1741], 57–58, as noted by Mahon and Turner 1989, xiv). Mariette had more than 350 drawings attributed to Guercino in his collection.

31 Mahon and Turner 1989, xv.

32 Mahon *Disegni* 1969, 29–30.

33 See Turner and Plazzotta 1991, 134–35, 173–78; Stone 1991, 4–5.

34 See Turner and Plazzotta 1991, 15–17 (where a woodcut by Antonio da Trento after Parmigianino is identified as the source for *The Martyrdom of Saints John and Paul* [cf. cat. no. 16 in the present volume]); Stone 1991, 58, instead postulates a derivation from Correggio.

35 For a full discussion of Guercino's use of counterproofs, see Mahon and Turner 1989, 177–78. For an interesting example, see Mahon and Ekserdjian 1986, 39.

36 Stone 1991, xxv, 64, 68, 82–83.

37 Mahon and Turner 1989, xvi.

38 Mahon *Disegni* 1969, 28 (citing a letter from Guercino to Don Antonio Ruffo, who had requested such drawings on several occasions).

39 Guercino "sfidano coraggiosamente qual siasi mai stat'altra leggiadra penna, non escludane quella del Primaticcio, ò del Parmigianino, essendo anch'essi que' del Sig. Gio. Francesco così spiritosi, guizzanti, bizzarri, e galanti, che ben danno a conoscere quanto più di qual siasi altro fosse nato pittore, e fatto della natura" (Malvasia ed. 1841, 1:398).

40 Turner and Plazzotta 1991, 18.

41 See also the hair of Samson in a drawing at Holkham Hall, Norfolk, England (Turner and Plazzotta 1991, 172, no. 143, fig. 143).

42 Tiepolo is noted as the owner of two of Guercino's drawings etched by Francesco Bartolozzi and published in 1764: *The Holy Family* and *Adoration of the Magi* (Calabi 1928, 530–32).

43 For example, see Turner and Plazzotta 1991, 62, no. 31, fig. 31.

44 Malvasia ed. 1841, 2:272.

45 Mahon and Turner 1989, 110.

46 Van Tuyll 1991, 184.

47 See Alessandro Marchi, *Le Arti che vanno per via*, in Pulini 2001, 98–105.

48 Mahon and Turner 1989, xx. These could possibly be identifiable with the lost drawings for Callot's series of 25 engravings of beggars, *Les Gueux*, dating from the 1620s (drawings: Ternois 1962, 111–12; engravings: Lieure 1989, 40–41). In general, see also Gozzi in Adam et al. 2005, 38–47 (reprinted from his essay in Pulini 2001, 88–97).

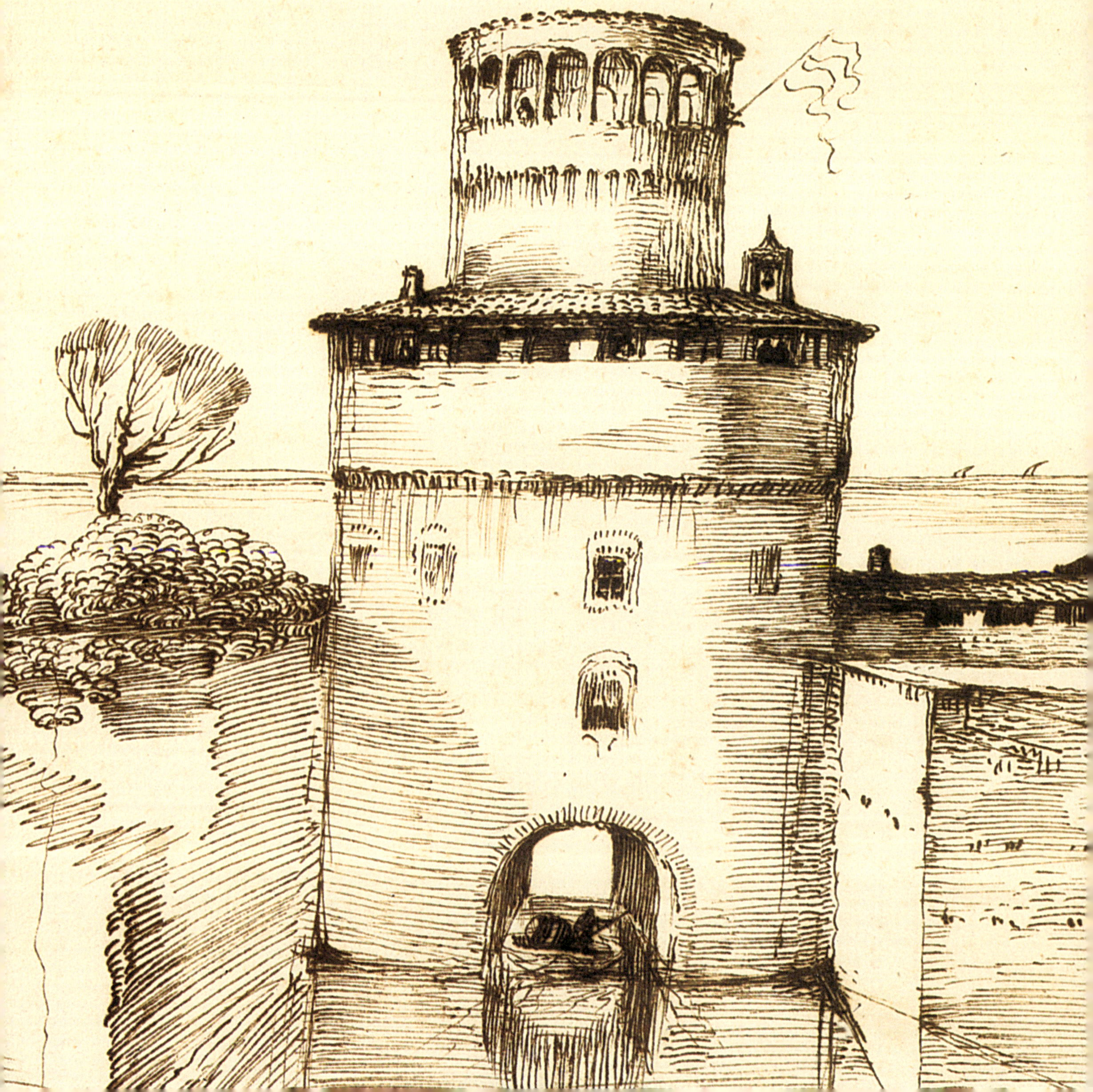

CATALOGUE

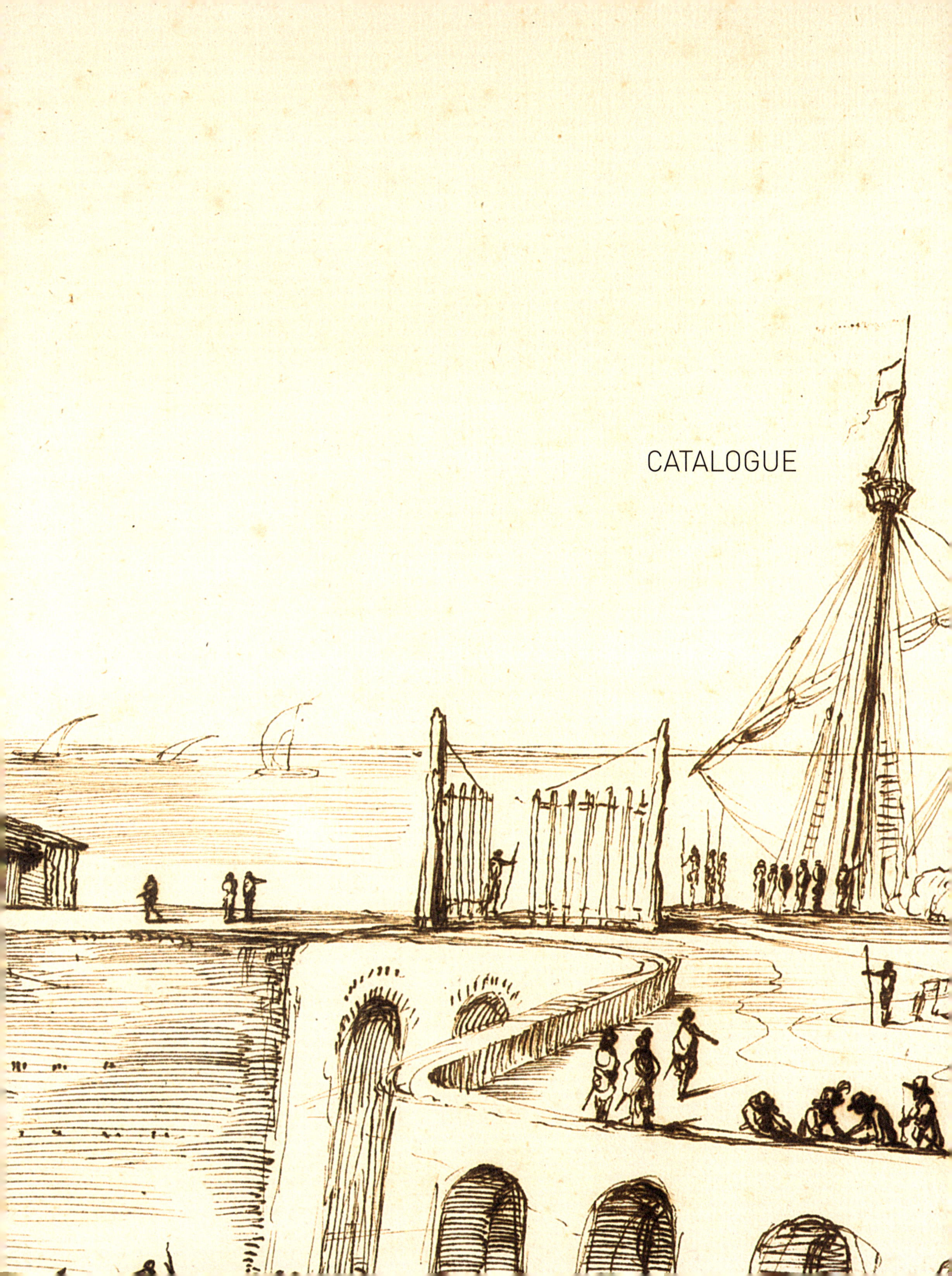

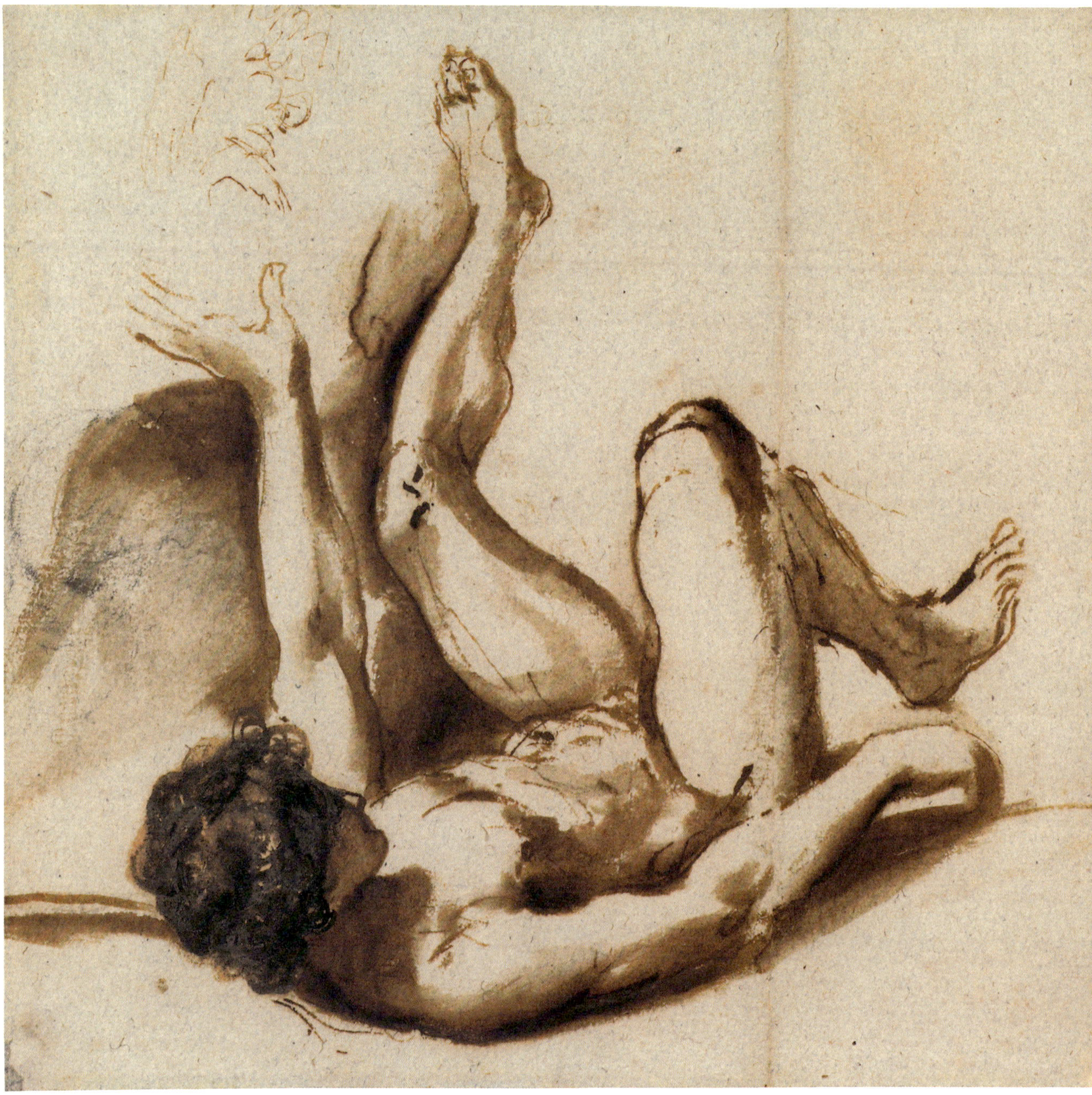

1.

NUDE FIGURE OF A YOUTH LYING ON HIS BACK, WITH HIS LEFT ARM AND LEG RAISED

1618
Pen and brown ink, brush with brown wash, on pale blue-gray paper
22.8 × 23.9 cm (8 15/16 × 9 3/8 in.)
London, Courtauld Institute of Art Gallery, D.1952.RW.1375

PROVENANCE Casa Gennari / Bouverie family / Sir Robert Witt, L.2228B, *verso* (see p. 16).

EXHIBITIONS Windsor 1939, no number; London 1943, no number; Windsor 1950, no number; London 1953a, no. 54; Manchester 1962, no. 82; Bologna 1968, no. 32; London 1971, no. 17; London 1977, no. 34; London 1991, no. 6.

BIBLIOGRAPHY V. and A. 1943, 24; Eton 1950, unpaginated; Arts Council 1953, 21, pl. 5; Blunt 1956, 76; Blunt and Troutman 1962, 38, pl. 82; Mahon *Dipinti* 1968, 69; Mahon *Disegni* 1969, 32, 61, 62, pl. 32; Courtauld 1971, 4; Roli 1972, 20; Hammer et al. 1977, 17; Salerno 1988, 126; Mahon and Turner 1989, 3; Loire 1990, 93; Turner 1991a, 348n7; Turner and Plazzotta 1991, 31n92, 32n108, 38–39, 231, fig. 6; Boccardo 1992, 32, 34, no number.

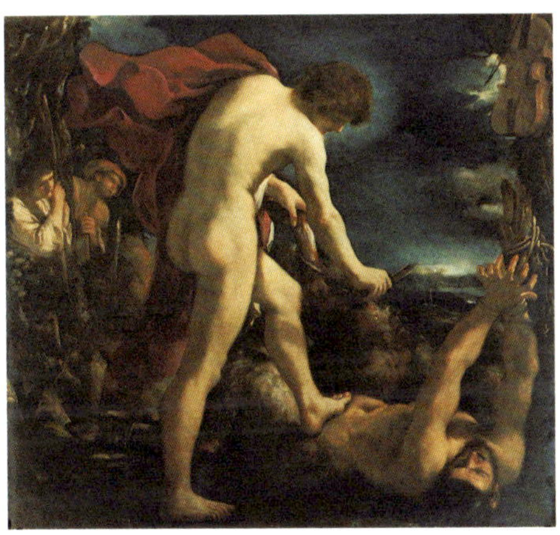

FIGURE 1.1
Guercino. *Apollo Flaying Marsyas*, 1618. Oil on canvas, 185.5 × 200 cm (73 × 78 3/4 in.). Florence, Palazzo Pitti. Photo: Scala/Art Resource, New York

HERE ONE SEES A DRAWING made from a live model, shown in dramatic foreshortening as he almost falls out of the picture space. On this sheet, the artist strictly limited his use of the pen; instead, he created the majority of the form—even the bushy head of hair—with wash applied using the point of a brush. In some parts, such as the left hand, he "starved" the brush of ink to make a less concrete form. Large areas of the paper are left blank as highlights to complement the shadows, and these combine to create a strong sense of chiaroscuro.

This drawing is an early study for the figure of Marsyas, a mythical Greek flute-player; here he is about to be flayed alive by the god Apollo after losing a musical competition.[1] Guercino made the painting for which it is a study (fig. 1.1) in 1618 for Cosimo II, Grand Duke of Tuscany. The commission is a testament to Guercino's growing status, even as a young artist. As can be seen, Guercino "flipped" the composition some time after making catalogue number 1. (For more on Guercino's use of reversal, see p. 11.) A number of preliminary compositional studies exist for the painting, among them a drawing in the Royal Library at Windsor Castle that shows Marsyas on the left, and two other drawings in which the figures are reversed, resulting in a scene closer to the final painting.[2] A charcoal study drawn from a live model shows the figure of Marsyas very close to the final resolution and has a line indicating the bottom edge of the canvas; it must have been made late in the process.[3]

Guercino seems to have used the same model to pose for the figures of both Marsyas and Apollo.[4] Indeed, the head of Apollo in the painting—with light catching the tip of his nose—is similar to Marsyas's head in catalogue number 1.

This drawing was made on blue paper (now faded to a pale blue-gray), an unusual choice for the artist. It might relate to the fact that, in 1618, a few months before he made the drawing, Guercino had been to Venice, where blue paper was widely used. His first biographer, Count Malvasia, records that the artist went to Venice with a certain Padre Pederzani, who introduced him to Palma il Giovane, who in turn showed him works by Titian, among others.[5] The tonal and chromatic effects typical of Venetian art are found in figure 1.1. □

NOTES

1. Ovid, *Metamorphoses*, 6.382–400.
2. Windsor Castle, Royal Library, inv. RL 2469 (M&T 5; Turner and Plazzotta 1991, 39, pl. 7); Vienna, Albertina, inv. 2362 (Mahon *Disegni* 1969, 62, pl. 34); Milan, Biblioteca Ambrosiana, inv. 209, p. 194 bis (Bora 1976, no number, no. 209, p. 194 bis).
3. Paris, École des Beaux-Arts, inv. 156 (Mahon *Disegni* 1969, 62, pl. 35).
4. Hammer et al. 1977, 17; Turner and Plazzotta 1991, 39.
5. Mahon *Dipinti* 1968, 47–48.

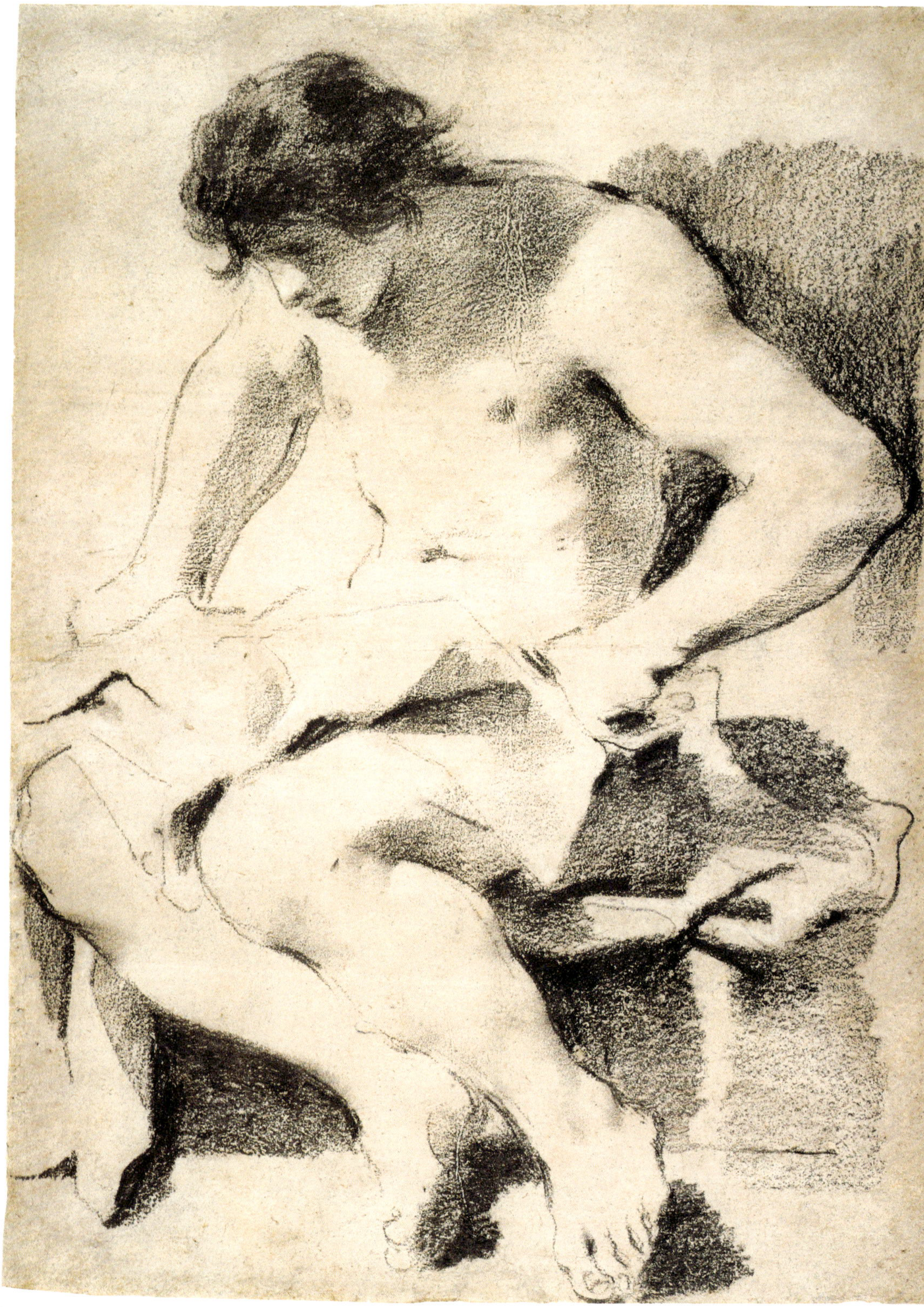

2.
STUDY OF A SEATED YOUNG MAN

ca. 1619
Black chalk dipped in gum, white chalk heightening, on gray-brown paper
52.2 × 42.7 cm (20⁹⁄₁₆ × 16¾ in.)
Los Angeles, J. Paul Getty Museum, 89.GB.52

PROVENANCE Hugh Blaker, London; Sir Colin Anderson, London; Lady Anderson, London (sale, Christie's, London, December 9, 1986, lot 48); art market, London.

EXHIBITIONS London 1948, no. 46; London 1988, no. 26; Cambridge 1991, no. 63; Bologna 1991, no. 207; New York 1993, no. 58; London 1993, no. 20; Los Angeles 1996, no number; Los Angeles 1998, no number; Los Angeles 1999, no number.

BIBLIOGRAPHY Leicester 1948, 10 (as "Bolognese XVII Century: Possibly an early drawing by Piazzetta"); Hazlitt, Gooden, & Fox 1988, unpaginated, under no. 26; Getty 1990, 190, no. 47; Mahon 1991, 51; Stone 1991, xxi, 146–47, 148, 150, 213, pl. 63; Goldner, Hendrix, and Pask 1992, 60, no. 20; Faietti 1993, 47; Goldner 1993, 18; RA 1993, 22; Turner and Hendrix 1997, 38, no. 29; Cricco and Paolo di Teodoro 2004, 992, fig. 22.7; Adam et al. 2005, 212; Bambach 2005, 178–79, fig. a.

THE SCALE AND POWER of this extraordinary drawing are difficult to grasp in reproduction. Guercino used a very large sheet of rough brown paper, fully exploiting it for a dramatic study of a seated youth drawn from life. The model sits at an angle on a low block cushioned by a piece of drapery; the fabric has been pulled up across his lap and hangs down the other side of his knees. With his arms out to the side but bent at the elbow, the sitter focuses on the ground. Guercino no doubt deliberately chose this pose to present complex angles and spatial challenges.

The purpose of the drawing seems to be to study the human body in tonal terms, and the form has been excavated from the paper through the use of varied shadows. Dark foreground lines, such as those marking the edges of the model's left arm, stand in contrast to the well-judged, lighter, more distant delineation of his right arm, the top of which has been left to the viewer's imagination, allowing an unencumbered facial profile. Very light touches of white chalk make up a few highlights on the form, including the tip of the nose, shoulder, and left knee. At a late stage in the drawing, the artist apparently realized that the uppermost line of the drapery (below the youth's navel) was too dark and created spatial ambiguity, so he simply lightened it with white chalk, giving the effect of pushing the fabric deeper into space.

As has been noted, the Getty sheet is one of a number of life studies made on this scale by the artist before his departure for Rome.[1] A sheet at the Metropolitan Museum of Art strongly parallels catalogue number 2: it seems to represent the same model seated on the same block, and in both drawings the composition is strongly lit from the top left.[2] Although the sheets in the group are usually described as having been made in "oiled black chalk or charcoal," the chalk was instead dipped in a gum solution before drawing.[3]

Guercino probably began making "tonal" studies like these after looking at similar drawings by Pietro Faccini (ca. 1562–1602); they may also reflect his trip early in 1618 to Venice, where such effects were widely sought.[4] Guercino seems to have kept the sheets in his studio for reference, and figures in several paintings that he made about this time are clearly derived from them.[5] □

NOTES

1 Mahon *Disegni* 1969, 220–22; Mahon and Turner 1989, 80–81; Turner and Plazzotta 1991, 36–38; Stone 1991, 146–52. The group includes sheets in Florence, Galleria degli Uffizi (inv. 12502 F); Genoa, Palazzo Rosso (invs. 1702, 1703); Melborne, National Gallery of Victoria (inv. 1278/3); Oxford, Ashmolean Museum (inv. 873A); Windsor Castle, Royal Library (invs. RL 2415, RL 01227); and St. Louis, Collection of Evalyne S. Grand.

2 Bambach 2005, 178–79. New York, The Metropolitan Museum of Art, Purchase, Rogers Fund, and Mr. and Mrs. David M. Tobey Gift, 2004 (inv. 2004.250).

3 Bambach 2005, 178–79. Research by Marjorie Shelley.

4 Mahon *Disegni* 1969, 44. It is likely that Guercino actually owned two such studies by Faccini; Mahon and Turner 1989, xx.

5 In particular, the figure of the angel in Guercino's painting *Saint Francis in Ecstasy* (ca. 1620) resembles cat. no. 2—or one made in that session—but is shown in reverse (see Mahon, Pulini, and Sgarbi 2003, 250–51, no. 85 [repr.]).

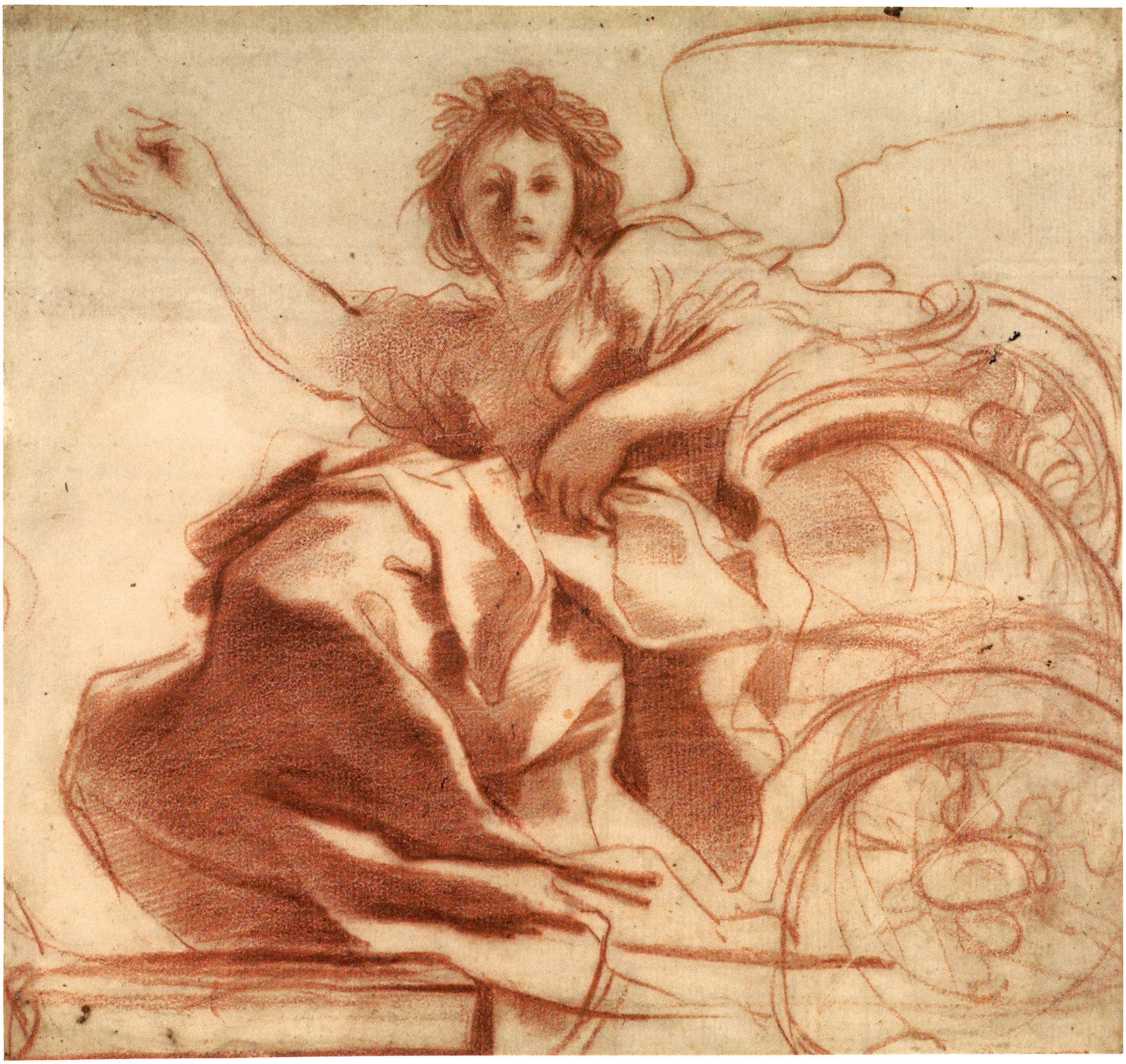

3.
AURORA

ca. 1620
Red chalk, stumping
24.8 × 27.1 cm (9¾ × 10¹¹⁄₁₆ in.)
London, Courtauld Institute of Art Gallery, D.1952.RW.1328

PROVENANCE Casa Gennari / Bouverie family / Sir Robert Witt (see p. 16).

EXHIBITIONS London 1937, no. 32; London 1943, no number; London 1953, no. 128; London 1955, no. 44; London 1958, no. 14; Auckland 1960, no. 24; Bologna 1968, no. 78; London 1971, no. 12; Wellington 1973, no. 31; London 1977, no. 28; London 1991, no. 33.

BIBLIOGRAPHY Ragghianti 1938, XXI, XXII, and fig. 7; V. and A. 1943, 24; RA 1953, 38; Mahon 1955, 54; Blunt 1956, 75; Courtauld 1958, 7; Mahon 1967, 33; Mahon *Disegni* 1969, 19n40, 87, 89–90, pl. 78; Courtauld 1971, 3; Roli 1972, 23, tav. 26; Troutman 1973, 7, 19; Hammer et al. 1977, 16; Salerno 1988, 164, 166; Turner 1991, 50; Ebert-Schifferer 1991, 404; Turner and Plazzotta 1991, 12, 31n92, 32n108, 33, 60, 63–64, 65, 88, 301, 304, pl. 5.

THIS IS THE MOST IMPRESSIVE of a group of drawings that the artist made in preparation for his ceiling decoration in the Casino Ludovisi (fig. B), a dry fresco widely regarded as the masterpiece of his "Roman" period (1621–1623, when he lived and worked in the Eternal City). It studies the winged figure of Aurora (Roman goddess of the dawn) in her chariot moving across the sky. Made in red chalk, the drawing captures frozen movement, suggested by the figure's raised hand, and heightened by the perhaps unintended kinetic effect of several drawn versions of the chariot wheel. Having apparently had some difficulty deciding which angle would look most convincing from below, the artist sketched the wheel in a variety of placements.

The most complete part of the drawing is Aurora's drapery, which includes a number of deep "valleys" rendered using dark chalk hatching with highlights of blank paper. In parts of the face and right shoulder, the artist created subtle tones by rubbing the chalk, either with his finger or with a stump (a stick of tightly rolled paper). The dark eye sockets, raised eyebrows, and smudged mouth combine to form a ghostlike face that looks down and out at the viewer.

Catalogue number 3 was clearly made early in Guercino's creative process for the Casino Ludovisi fresco. It is the only surviving preparatory drawing to depict Aurora flying from right to left.[1] As Sir Denis Mahon and Nicholas Turner have observed, Guercino initially followed Cesare Ripa's iconographical manual (edition of 1618) closely. Among other things, Ripa stipulated that Aurora should have wings and a garland of roses in her hair and that she should scatter flowers with one hand, as she does here. However, in the final painting, Guercino substituted a piece of flying drapery for the wing, and a putto crowns her with the flowers.

Other preparatory studies for the figure of Aurora include two red chalk drawings of seated women holding reins, both apparently made from life, and a simple but beautiful study of her head in a similar position to the painting.[2] Two pen-and-ink studies showing the whole chariot—going from left to right—must have been made after cat. no. 3.[3] □

NOTES

1 Although a drawn copy in Florence, Galleria degli Uffizi (inv. 3671 S), records a lost composition drawing that also shows Aurora, with Pegasus, flying from right to left (Bottari 1966, pl. xxviii).

2 Windsor Castle, Royal Library, invs. RL 2814, RL 2692 (Mahon and Turner 1989, 8–10, nos. 16–17, pls. 16–17); *Head Study*, Mahon Collection, on loan to the Ashmolean Museum, Oxford (Mahon and Ekserdjian 1986, no. 12).

3 Rome, Vatican Library, Ashby Collection, repr. Mahon and Turner 1989, figs. 3–4; Mahon Collection, on loan to the Ashmolean Museum, Oxford (Mahon and Ekserdjian 1986, no. 11).

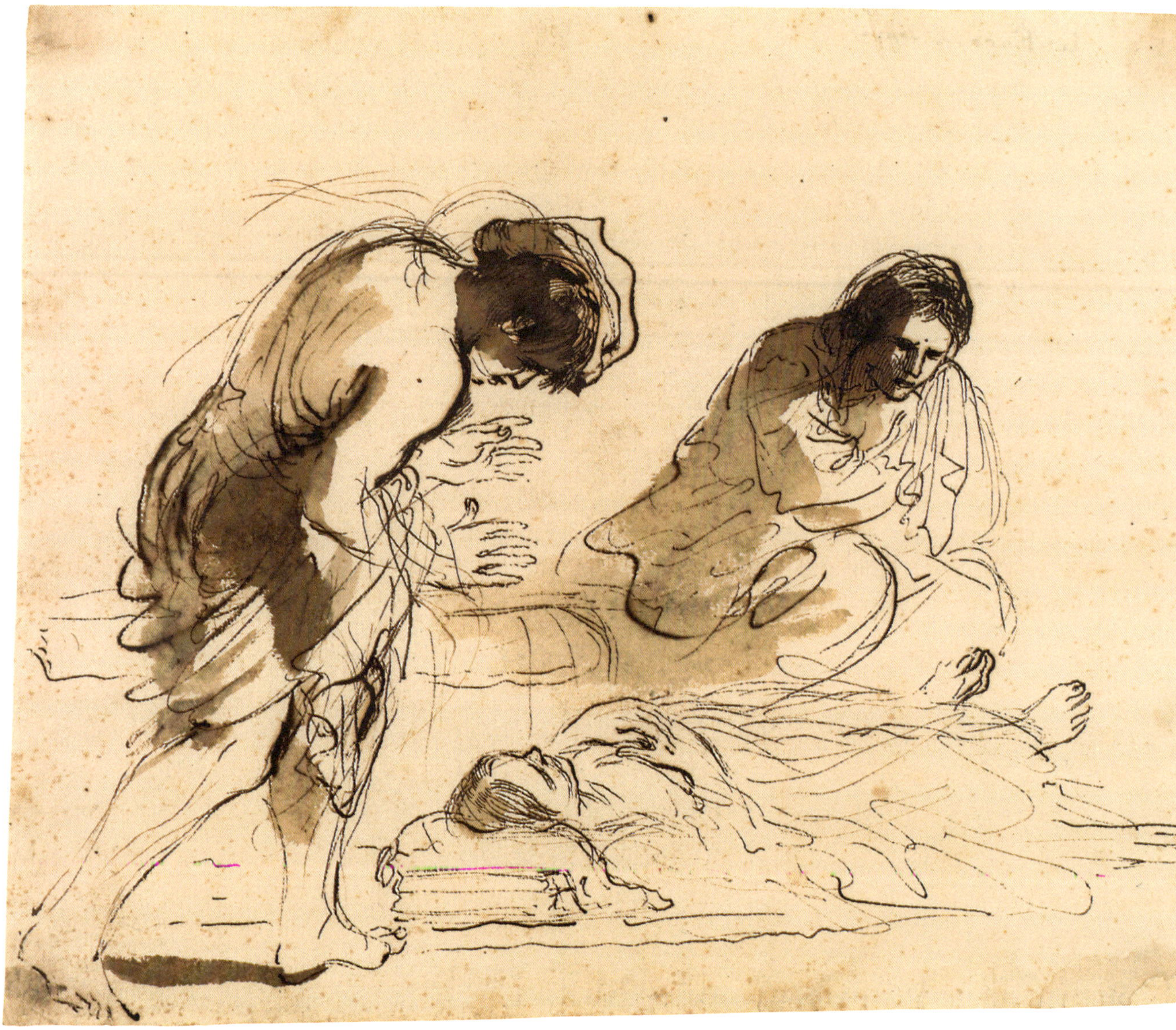

4.
THE MOURNING OF SAINT PETRONILLA

1621
Pen and brown ink, brush with brown wash
21.5 × 25.7 cm (8½ × 10⅛ in.).
Inscribed in brown ink on verso: *L. I. F. 200. di sopra*
London, Courtauld Institute of Art Gallery, D.1952.RW.1345

PROVENANCE Casa Gennari / Bouverie family / Sir Robert Witt (see p. 16).

EXHIBITIONS Bologna 1968, no. 87; London 1977, no. 20; London 1991, no. 38.

BIBLIOGRAPHY Blunt 1956, 76; Mahon *Disegni* 1969, 93, 95, 97, pl 87; Hammer et al. 1977, 13; Mahon and Turner 1989, 12; Turner 1991, 54, 56, fig. 18; Turner and Plazzotta 1991, 31n92, 32n108, 47, 60, 67–68, 279, fig. 38.

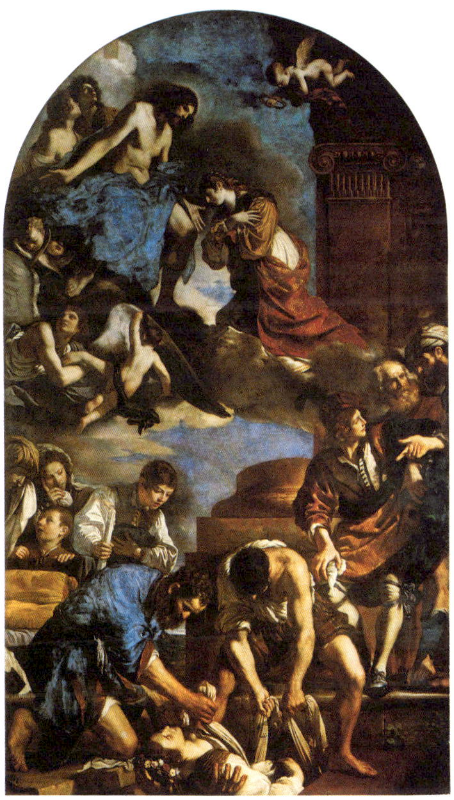

FIGURE 4.1
Guercino. *The Burial and Reception into Heaven of Saint Petronilla*, ca. 1621–23. Oil on canvas, 920 × 423 cm (362 × 166⅝ in.). Rome, Pinacoteca Capitolina. Photo: Erich Lessing/Art Resource, New York

THIS DRAWING IS ONE of a number of studies made for the most important commission of Guercino's early career. In December 1621, after Guercino's success with the decoration of the Casino Ludovisi (see cat. no. 3), Pope Gregory XV awarded him a commission for an altarpiece for Saint Peter's, the most important cathedral in Christendom. The significance of this moment was not lost on the artist, and a full sequence of drawings provides evidence that he worked diligently toward his solution. The large altarpiece (fig. 4.1) was delivered in spring 1623 and remained *in situ* until 1730, when it was replaced by a mosaic copy; the original was moved to the Pinacoteca Capitolina.[1]

Saint Petronilla was a legendary first-century martyr whom early Christian writers claimed was Saint Peter's daughter; her name derives from his. According to the *Golden Legend*, a book of Christian narratives compiled by Jacobus de Voragine in 1275, Peter was protective of her because she was so extraordinarily beautiful. He took the extreme measure of causing her to be permanently sick with a fever, until visiting apostles questioned him and he temporarily restored her to health. Flaccus, a young Roman nobleman, fell in love with Petronilla and pledged to marry her. But Petronilla instead assumed a life of prayer and fasting and died shortly afterward.

In catalogue number 4, the dead Saint Petronilla lies on the ground, and a female mourner sits by her feet. Her suitor, Flaccus, stands at her head in a classic pose of shock, with hands upheld. The composition relies on dramatic foreshortening, and the artist handles the sharp depth of space with great self-assurance. With her lank, parted hair—created by a superb set of lines—and her almost caricatured feet, the dead figure seems less like a saint and more like the women in Guercino's genre scenes (see cat. nos. 6 and 17). The drawing is made in the fluid, calligraphic lines typical of Guercino's early work. A number of pentimenti are visible: in particular, tentative lines postulate a higher positioning of the suitor's head, and in the figure of the mourner there is some uncertainty as to which hand should hold the handkerchief, the soft folds of which are delicately conveyed.

A drawing in the Royal Library at Windsor Castle shows the saint from the side, mourned by three figures.[2] Significantly, in that drawing she wears a wreath of leaves,

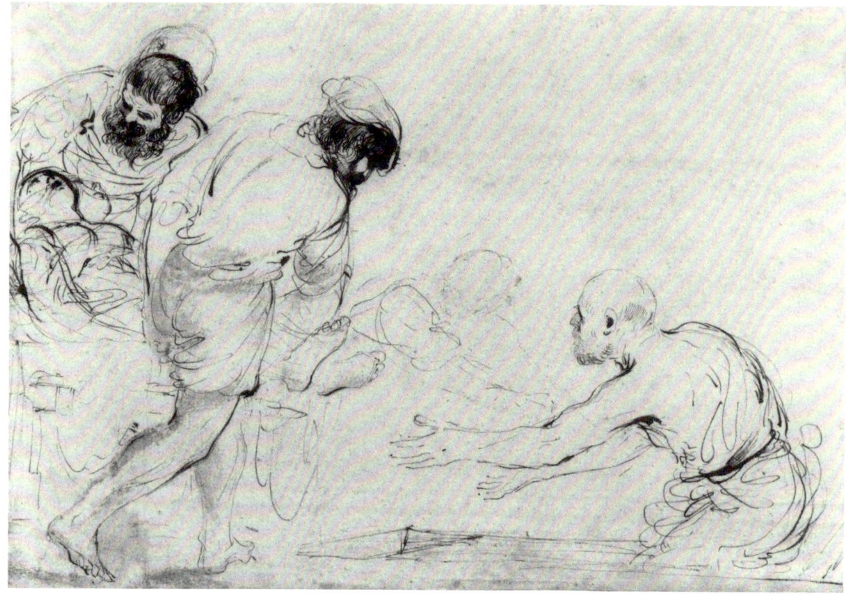

FIGURE 4.2
Guercino. *The Body of Saint Petronilla Raised from the Bier*, ca. 1621–23. Pen and brown ink, brush with gray wash, 21.1 × 30.9 cm (8¼ × 12⅛ in.). Windsor Castle, Royal Library, RL 2574

which anticipates the wreath of flowers in the final painting. At some stage, Guercino abandoned the idea of representing the saint's mourning, and all further drawings instead show Petronilla's burial. The decision to change the iconography of such an important commission is unlikely to have been made by the artist alone and would have involved the authorities at Saint Peter's; perhaps it was made when the upper half of the altarpiece was reconsidered, and the burial and reception were thought a fitting pair of subjects.

Initially, Guercino considered showing the saint's body raised from a bier, as in figure 4.2. In that sheet, the body is about to be passed to a man who stands on a ladder (indicated by two short diagonal lines at lower right) leading down to the catacombs, where she was buried. It must have been at some stage after this that Guercino made a highly finished large-scale *modello* of the project (fig. 4.3).[3] This sheet is the only *modello* by the artist that survives today. Guercino may have felt the need to make such a sheet because the commission was such an important one.

Typically, a final composition follows its *modello* closely, exhibiting only minor adjustments. In this case, however, surprisingly large differences exist between Guercino's *modello* and the altarpiece. Presumably Guercino or a church official decided major revisions were necessary. Sir Denis Mahon sees this as a pivotal moment in Guercino's career, in which the artist moves from a Baroque solution in the *modello* to a more classical one, with clearer spatial planes, in the painting.[4] In a large drawing now in Copenhagen (fig. 4.4), the artist experimented with the entire lower part of the work and included a stooping figure carrying Petronilla's feet whose pose and type are close to those of a figure in the final painting.[5] The body of the saint has been reversed and foreshortened in the painting, bringing it back to Guercino's original idea in catalogue number 4.

Guercino's drawings relating to the Saint Peter's altarpiece are made in all the media that were at his disposal: red chalk, black chalk, pen and ink, and brush and wash.[6]

NOTES

1 Mahon *Dipinti* 1968, 6n11. The painting was one of many looted by French troops and hung in the Louvre between 1797 and 1815, when it was returned. The series of drawings is discussed by Mahon (*Disegni* 1969, 93–98); Mahon and Turner 1989, 11–15; and Turner and Plazzotta 1991, 67–73.

2 Windsor Castle, Royal Library, inv. RL 2550 (M&T 21; Mahon and Turner 1989, 11–12, pl. 21).

3 Windsor Castle, Royal Library, inv. RL 2756 (M&T 23; Mahon and Turner 1989, 12–15, pl. 23).

4 Mahon and Turner 1989, 14–15, reflecting Mahon's earlier writings of 1947 and 1968.

5 Copenhagen, Thorvaldsen Museum, inv. D.473 (Roli 1972, pl. 28). As has been noted by Mahon and Turner (1989, 12–13), this sheet is very similar in style to a related drawing in Windsor Castle, Royal Library, inv. RL 2781 (M&T 25).

6 Two drawings in red chalk study the top part of the painting: Windsor Castle, Royal Library, inv. RL 2392 (M&T no. 24; Mahon and Turner 1989, 12); Darmstadt, Hessisches Landesmuseum, inv. AE 2110 (Mahon *Disegni* 1969, 94, no. 90, fig. 90). Other drawings for the lower section are: *Female Mourners*, Madrid, Prado, inv. FD 11 (Turner and Plazzotta 1991, 73, fig. 8), and *Study for Spectators*, Berlin, inv. KdZ 5184 (discussed in Turner and Plazzotta 1991, 73).

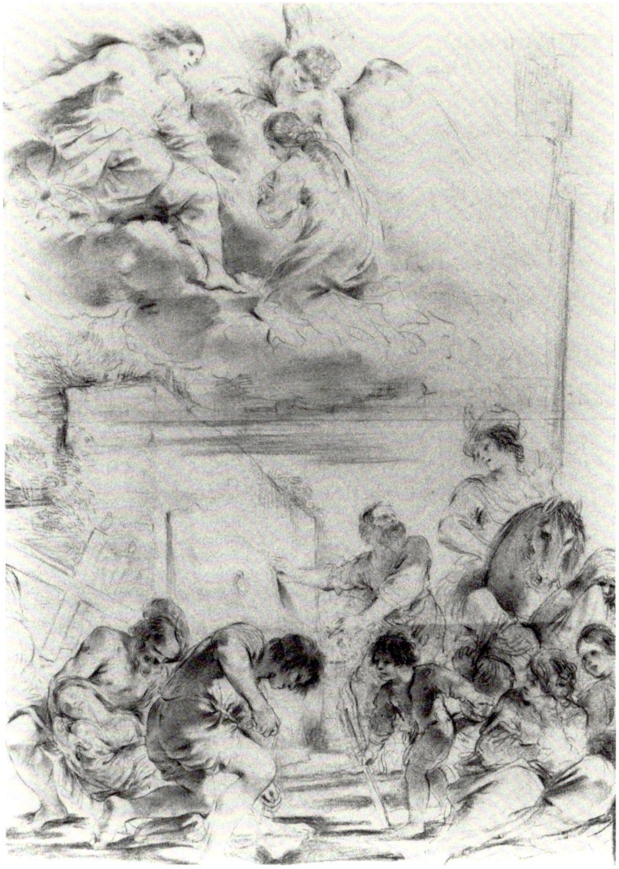

FIGURE 4.3
Guercino. *Modello* for *The Burial and Reception into Heaven of Saint Petronilla*, ca. 1621–23. Black chalk, stumping, some red chalk, 51.6 × 37.8 cm (20 5/16 × 14 7/8 in.). Windsor Castle, Royal Library, RL 2756

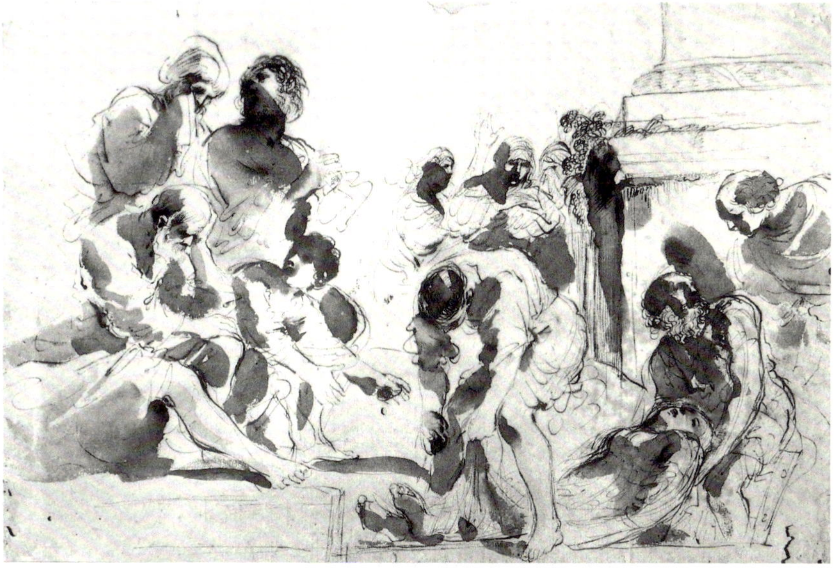

FIGURE 4.4
Guercino. Study for *The Burial and Reception into Heaven of Saint Petronilla*, ca. 1621–23. Pen and brown ink, brush with brown wash, 27.1 × 42.3 cm (10 5/8 × 16 5/8 in.). Copenhagen, Thorvaldsen Museum, D.473

While no doubt only a small percentage of the drawings made for this commission survive, those extant demonstrate the remarkable extent to which Guercino "thought through" compositional problems in full scale on paper, rather than in tiny jottings or in his head. One can see that he considered the scene from every conceivable angle before "picking and choosing" from the drawings he had made. □

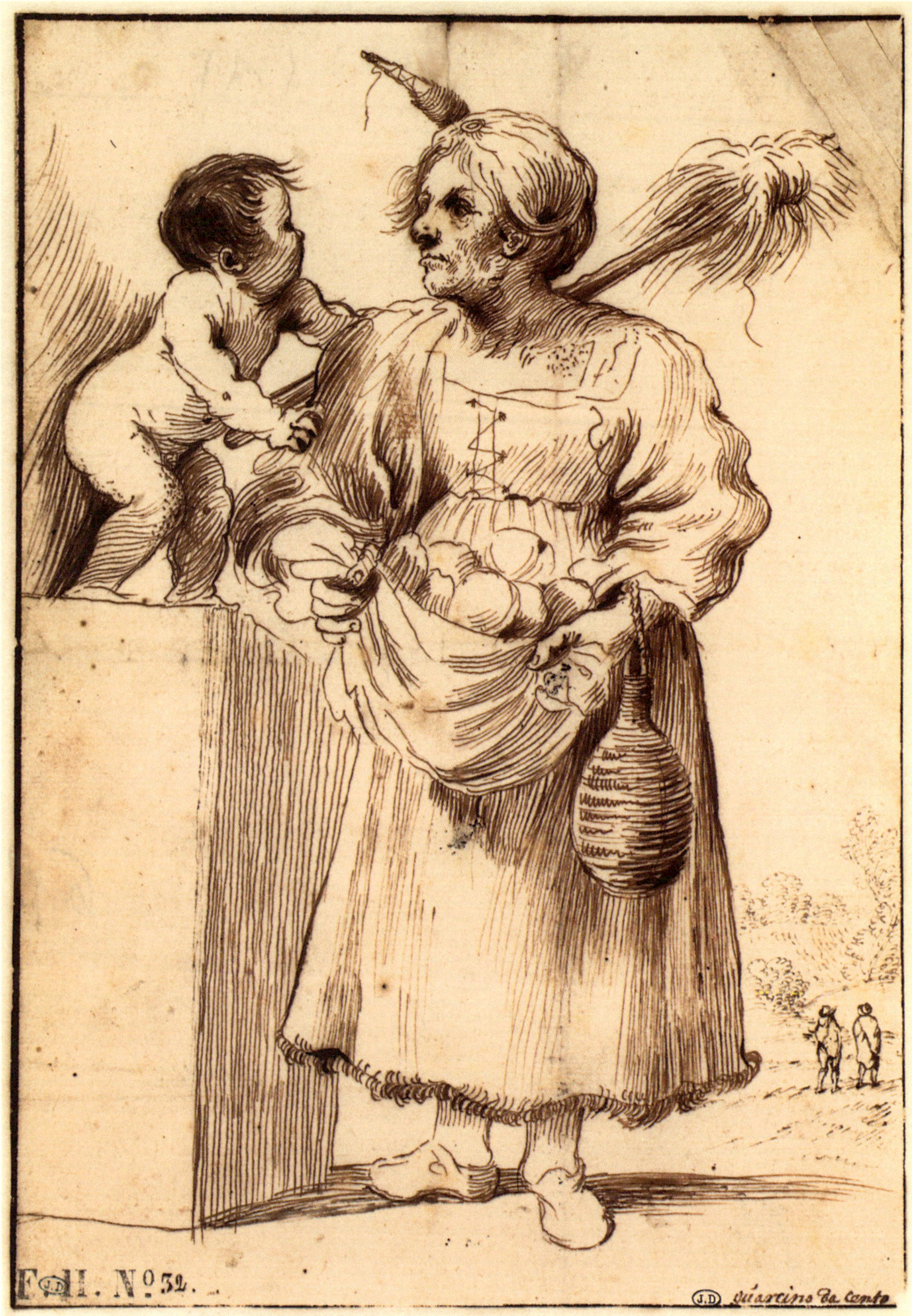
F. II. N° 32.
J.D

5.
AN OLD SEAMSTRESS WITH A SMALL CHILD

ca. 1623
Pen and brown ink
23.1 × 16.8 cm (9⅛ × 6⅝ in.)
Inscribed in brown ink at lower right: *guarcino da cento*
London, Courtauld Institute of Art Gallery, D.1952.RW.303

PROVENANCE Jules-Alexandre Duval le Camus (1814–1878), stamped *J.D.* bottom right (black) and bottom left (blue) (L.1441); Flury Hérard (ca. 1860), stamped bottom left *F.H. no. 32* (L.1015); F. R. Meatyard; Sir Robert Witt (1872–1952), L.2228B, *verso*, by bequest to the Courtauld Institute of Art, 1952.

EXHIBITIONS London 1977, no. 49.

BIBLIOGRAPHY Blunt 1956, 75; Hammer et al. 1977, 21.

THIS CHARMING DRAWING shows an imaginary encounter between an aged seamstress and a young child. The naked child stands on a handy stone block, and the two figures look at one another eye to eye. While the child is playful and active, the woman stands still and appraises the youngster uncertainly, as if suspicious of the trouble he might cause. She wears a spindle in her hair, bears a series of round objects—presumably balls of wool—in her apron, and carries a flask over her left wrist. The child seems to be holding the seamstress's distaff in his left hand and leans lightly on the woman for support. In the distance behind them, two men chat in a landscape. Although the subject matter would lend itself to an allegorical theme of youth and old age (a distaff also sometimes denoted a witch), in Guercino's hands it becomes a gentle, sympathetic caricature.

Throughout the composition, the artist employs an enormous variety of line to convey a wide range of textures. Long, straight pen lines create the stone block, while short ones mark the hem of the skirt. Dots suggest stubble on the old woman's face and a mole on her nose, while loose, curling strokes delineate the end of the distaff. A particularly skillful and sensitive touch is the series of tiny zigzagging lines on the flask's wicker covering, each of which peters out in the center to convey the impression of roundness.

The whole composition is drawn with the pen, without any use of brush and wash. Many lines resemble the precise hatching created by an engraver's burin, and in fact this seems deliberate. The tidy composition, intimate character, ink-line border, and "sweet" subject matter all suggest that this drawing was intended to be made into an engraving or etching, although no such print is now known. In style, it is similar to a number of drawings that Guercino produced for this purpose in the early to mid-1620s, including *Holy Family with Saints John the Baptist and Anne*; *Madonna and Child with Saint Anne*; and *Girl Looking at a Drawing of a Landscape*.[1] These sheets share the rich penwork of catalogue number 5 and convey a similar delight in texture and visual effects. □

NOTES

1 Windsor Castle, Royal Library, inv. RL 2754 (M&T 15; Mahon and Turner 1989, 8); London, British Museum, inv. Pp-4-62 (Turner and Plazzotta 1991, 65, no. 36, fig. 36); private collection (Turner and Plazzotta 1991, 212, no. 192, fig. 192). For Guercino's work for engravers, see Bagni 1985.

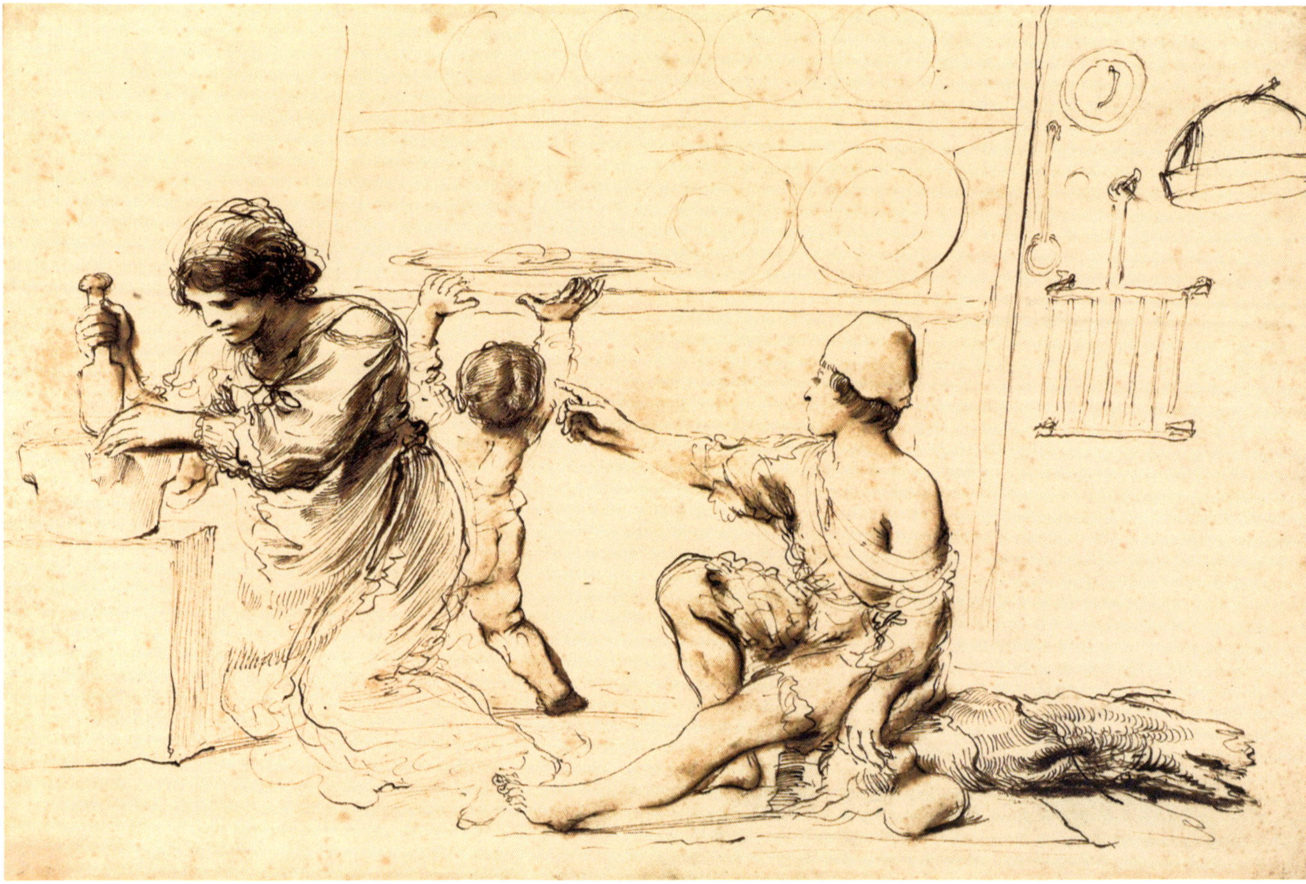

6.
INTERIOR OF A KITCHEN

ca. 1624
Pen and brown ink, brush with brown wash
26 × 40.3 cm (10¼ × 15⅞ in.)
Numbered in graphite at lower left: *3*
London, Courtauld Institute of Art Gallery, D.1952.RW.1347

PROVENANCE Casa Gennari / Bouverie family / Sir Robert Witt, L.2228B, *verso* (see p. 16).

EXHIBITIONS Bologna 1968, no. 216; London 1977, no. 46; London 1991, no. 189.

BIBLIOGRAPHY Blunt 1956, 76; Mahon *Disegni* 1969, 201, 205, 206, 207, 208; Hammer et al. 1977, 20; Turner and Plazzotta 1991, 31n92, 32n108, 89, 205, 210, fig. 189.

THIS INTIMATE DOMESTIC TABLEAU captures a particular moment, but the drawing provides few contextual clues about exactly what is going on. We can only guess at past and future events, but it seems likely that chaos will shortly ensue: the child reaching for a plate of food appears certain to drop it. His mother's attention is focused on her pestle and mortar, and the young man seated on a log, who seems to be lazily directing the child, gives no sign of being prepared to catch the dish or help.

In many artists' hands, such a scene would become a crude allegory of industry and indolence. But here, the numerous specific details combine with the lack of overall finish to present a simple and realistic genre scene. As ever, Guercino provides only enough cues for the visual brain of the viewer to discern the scene (for example, a few lines indicate the sideboard at the back), yet he includes specific, true-to-life details: the bunched-up shirtsleeves of the infant as he reaches up; the geomorphic depiction of the top of the infant's head and parted hair; the curls peeking out from beneath the young man's cap; and the suggestion of eyelashes in the man's profile. A contrast of draftsmanship typical of Guercino appears within the figure of the mother: her upper body is relatively finished, while her lower body remains just a flurry of lines (for drapery) and a discernible bare foot. □

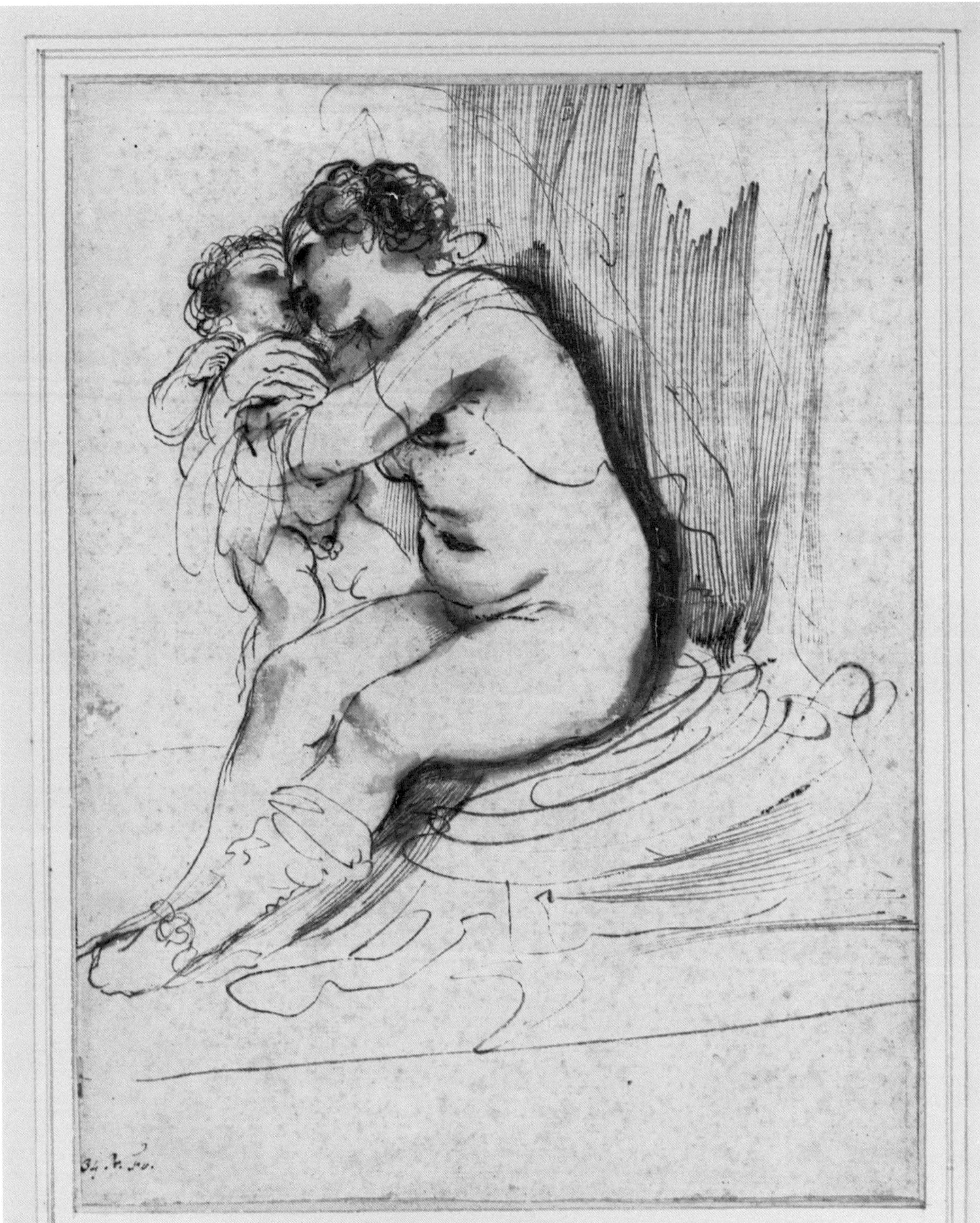

7.

A NUDE WOMAN, SEATED, EMBRACING A CHILD

ca. 1625
Pen and brown ink, brush with brown wash
23.4 × 18.1 cm (9¼ × 7⅛ in.)
Inscribed in brown ink at lower left: *34 Pr. Fo.*
London, Courtauld Institute of Art Gallery, D.1952.RW.1358

PROVENANCE Casa Gennari / Bouverie family / Sir Robert Witt (see p. 16).

EXHIBITIONS London 1923, no number; London 1937, no. 27; London 1938, no. 465; London 1943, no number; London 1953, no. 143; London 1953a, no. 55; Auckland 1960, no. 33; Bologna 1968, no. 220; London 1971, no. 13; Wellington 1973, no. 32; London 1977, no. 44; London 1991, no. 46.

BIBLIOGRAPHY Russell 1923, 21, 43, pl. X; Ragghianti 1938, XVI–XVIII, XX, fig. 5; Popham 1938, 19; Popham 1938a, 162; V. and A. 1943, 24; Arts Council 1953, 21; RA 1953, 40; Blunt 1956, 76; Marangoni 1959, 12, pl. 16; Horton 1960, 15n17; Troutman 1960, 14, pl. 1; Mahon *Disegni* 1969, 201, 207–8, pl. 220; Courtauld 1971, 3; Troutman 1973, 19; Hammer et al. 1977, 20; Turner and Plazzotta 1991, 31n92, 31n95, 32n108, 44, 75, fig. 46.

WITH A SEQUENCE of deft strokes, Guercino shows us a woman and child gently nuzzling in a quiet embrace. Scholars disagree about whether or not Guercino adapted this composition from a woodcut of Venus and Cupid by Nicolò Boldrini after Titian, as A. E. Popham suggested.[1] Boldrini's woodcut shows a similarly posed woman in a woodland setting; there, she reaches up to embrace a winged Cupid who crouches on a ledge. While Sir Denis Mahon is skeptical of the link, Nicholas Turner and Carol Plazzotta find it convincing. They see the drawing as a sensuous treatment of the subject and raise the possibility that Guercino's figures represent Venus and Cupid.[2]

This writer sees the subject as purely familial, and the relationship with Boldrini's print as coincidental or unconscious. It seems that here Guercino captures an intimate moment between a mother and a child. She has been interrupted by the infant while dressing or undressing and clutches the child to her; she tenderly presses her cheek to his nose. The nature of the space in which she sits is not clear, but it appears to be an interior; parallel lines create a "backing," while a single line in multiple loops makes up an undefined low bench, bed, or couch. The atmosphere seems to be natural, human, and spontaneous, as in catalogue number 9.

A date in the mid-1620s was suggested by Mahon and endorsed by Turner and Plazzotta. □

NOTES

1 *The Illustrated Bartsch*, vol. 48 [12]; *Italian Chiaroscuro Woodcuts*, 29 [126].

2 Turner and Plazzotta 1991, 75.

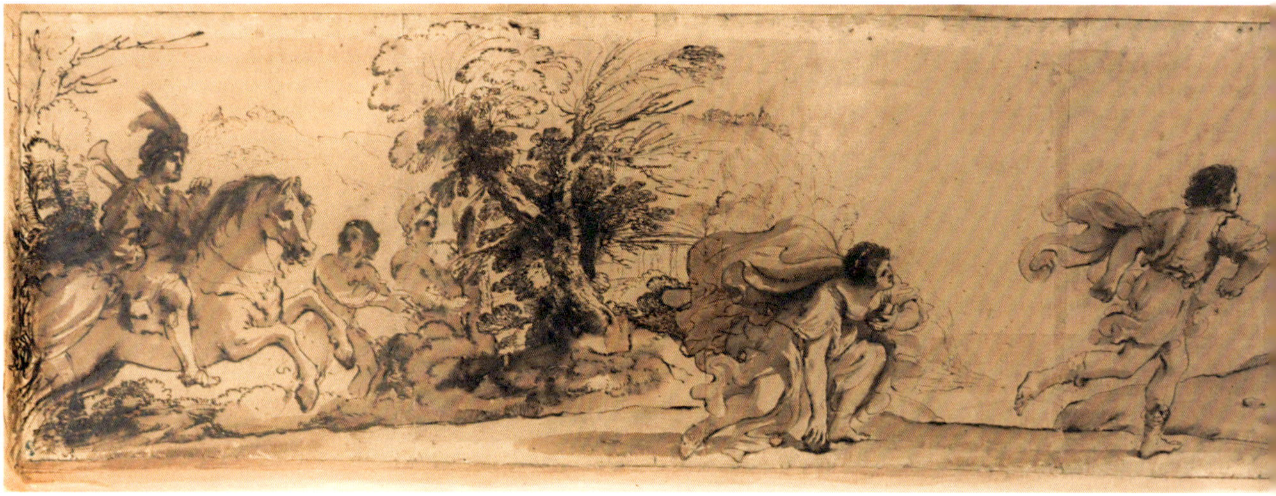

HERE GUERCINO PROVIDES a lively account of the race of Atalanta, a legend made popular by the Roman poet Ovid.[1] Atalanta was an athletic huntress with numerous suitors, but she was unwilling to marry. She challenged each prospective partner to a race on foot: the man who beat her would win her hand, but losers would be killed. Remaining unbeaten and a virgin, she was eventually challenged by Hippomenes. During the race, he distracted Atalanta by dropping three golden apples that Venus had given him. Atalanta could not resist pausing to pick up the apples and lost the race. Hippomenes and Atalanta later made love in a temple dedicated to Cybele, who became enraged and turned them into lions.

Guercino tells the story using a wealth of incidental detail. The two runners feature prominently, their frozen movement and airborne robes giving the impression of speed, but the artist has also taken obvious delight in the subsidiary figures. People follow the race on foot and horseback, and at the palace where the race ends, onlookers—including one animated character waving the victor's wreath—shout and encourage the runners. At the balustrade, two seated figures wearing turbans—perhaps Atalanta's parents—express

8.
THE RACE OF ATALANTA

ca. 1625
Pen and brown ink, brush with brown wash, over traces of black chalk on five joined pieces of paper, laid on canvas
28.5 × 159.5 cm (11¼ × 62¾ in.)
London, Courtauld Institute of Art Gallery, Witt Fund, D.1953.WF.4593

PROVENANCE G. Vallardi (1784–1863), L.1223; Sir Matthew Digby Wyatt (1820–1877); purchased by the Courtauld Institute of Art Gallery, 1953, Witt Fund.

EXHIBITIONS Leeds 1868, no. 2741; London 1953, no. 144; London 1958, no. 20; London 1965, no. 31; London 1977, no. 42; London 1991, no. 47.

BIBLIOGRAPHY Waring 1868, 155; RA 1953, 40; Blunt 1956, 76; Courtauld 1958, 8; Courtauld 1966, 10, 19; Hammer et al. 1977, 19; Turner and Plazzotta 1991, 76–78, figs. 47a–d.

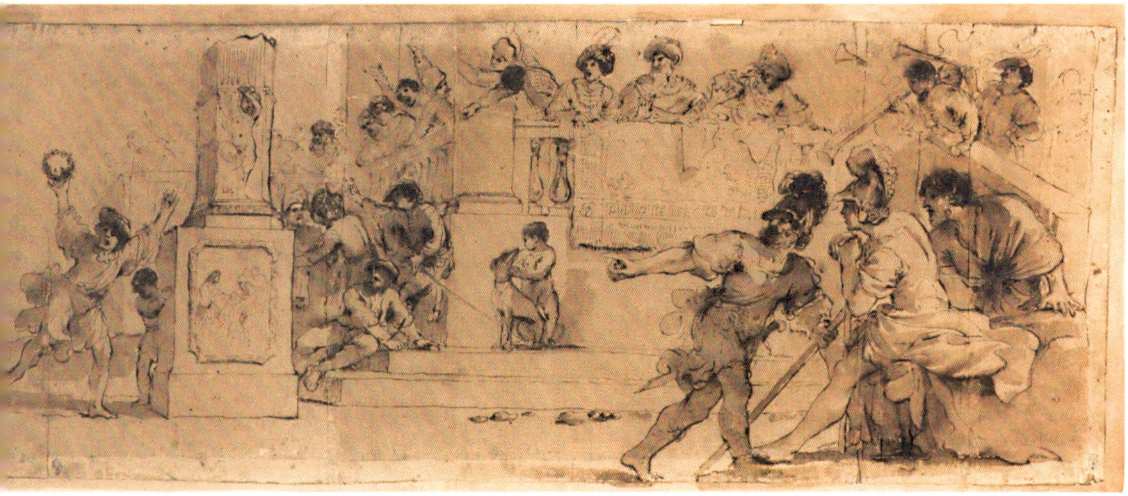

shock at the imminent result, while a third wipes away a tear. In front of them, a child playfully prepares to ride a dog.

Given its long format, the balance and symmetry of the scene are remarkable. Indeed, the scale and proportions of the drawing invite speculation as to its purpose. There are no known subsidiary studies for any of the figures or groups in the drawing, nor are there signs of pentimenti, and these factors suggest that it was made as a finished work of art rather than as a compositional preparatory study. Many of the figures are seen from below, indicating that the drawing might have been intended as a decoration to be placed over a doorway.[2] As Nicholas Turner and Carol Plazzotta also note, the discoloration of the paper and its canvas backing point to the fact that it was hung on a wall and exposed to light, in all likelihood along with many others recorded in the house of the artist's heirs. Turner and Plazzotta date the drawing to about 1621 to 1623, when the artist was working in Rome, "or possibly a little later"; the latter seems more likely, given the similarity in the handling of wash between catalogue number 8 and two genre scenes now at Windsor Castle.[3] □

NOTES

1 Ovid, *Metamorphoses*, 10.560–707.

2 Turner and Plazzotta 1991, 78; Mahon and Turner 1989, pp. xviii ff.

3 Windsor Castle, Royal Library, invs. RL 2570, RL 2515 (M&T 279 & 280; Mahon and Turner 1989, 111–12, pls. 256–57).

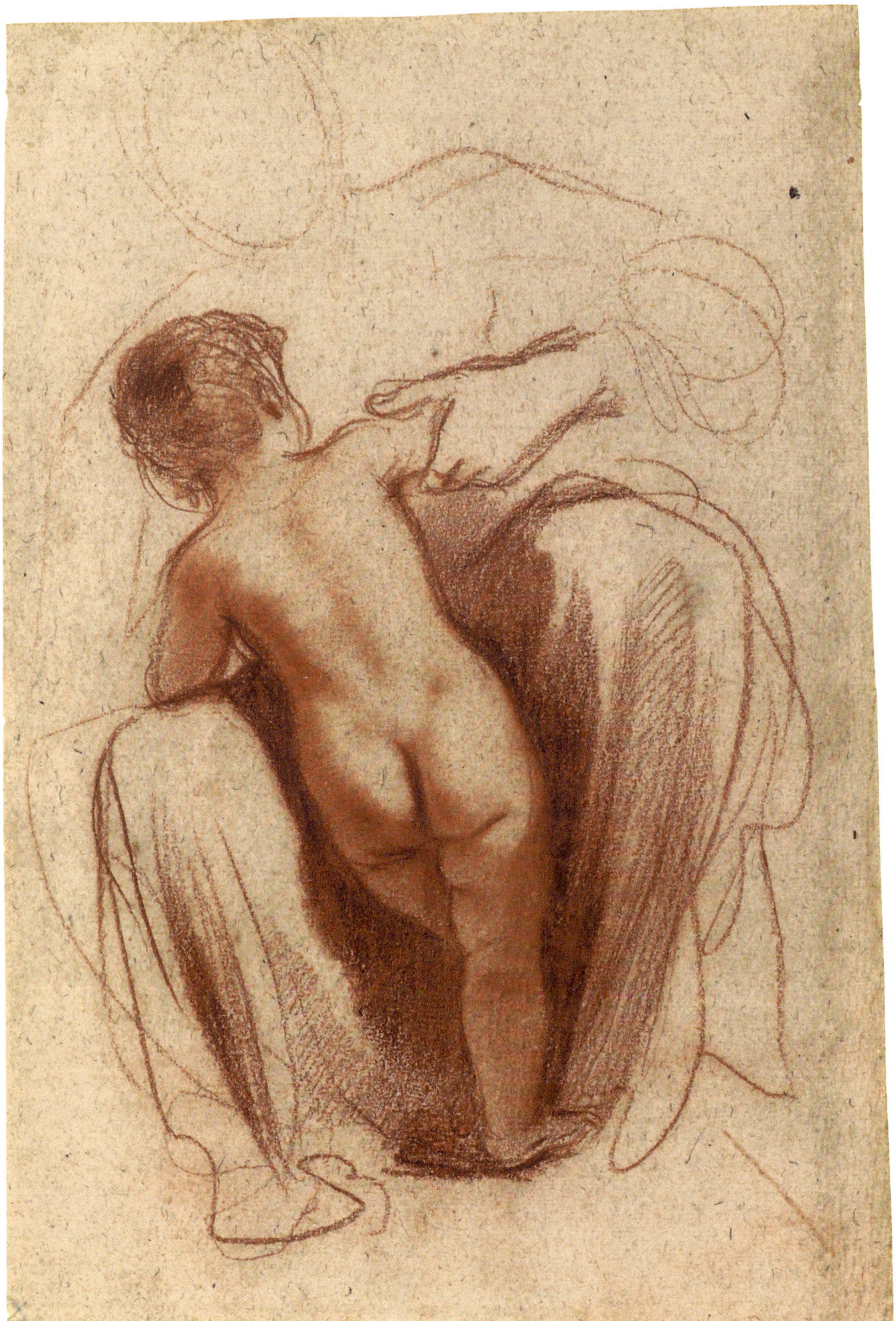

9.

A CHILD SEEN FROM BEHIND, STANDING BETWEEN HIS MOTHER'S KNEES

ca. 1625
Red chalk, stumping
30.1 × 21.1 cm (11⅞ × 8¼ in.)
London, Courtauld Institute of Art Gallery, D.1952.RW.1327

PROVENANCE Casa Gennari / Bouverie family / Sir Robert Witt, L.2228B, *verso* (see p. 16).

EXHIBITIONS London 1923, no number; London 1937, no. 26; London 1938, no. 452; Windsor 1939, no number; London 1943, no number; London 1953a, no. 53; London 1958, no. 28; Auckland 1960, no. 32; Manchester 1962, no. 81; Bologna 1968, no. 187; London 1971, no. 16; London 1977, no. 43; London 1991, no. 44; London 1991a, no. 42.

BIBLIOGRAPHY Russell 1923, 38, pl. VII; Popham 1938a, 160; V. and A. 1943, 24; Arts Council 1953, 21; Blunt 1956, 75; Courtauld 1958, 10; Troutman 1960, 14, pl. 1; Blunt and Troutman 1962, 37; Mahon *Disegni* 1969, 176, 207, 208, pl. 187; Courtauld 1971, 4; Hammer et al. 1977, 20; Bradford and Braham 1991, 92, 182, ill.; Turner and Plazzotta 1991, 18, 31n92, 31n95, 32n108, 74, 91, pl. 8.

THIS EXTRAORDINARY TESTAMENT to Guercino's use of red chalk is one of the most widely exhibited and compelling drawings in the Witt Collection. Guercino focuses on the infant and the space around him, while only summarily representing the mother. Such is the success of the artist in rendering the scene in three dimensions that it seems almost impossible to imagine that this was once a blank sheet of paper. Extremely sensitive use of the chalk creates the almost imperceptible shadow of the child's backbone in the midst of bright reserves of paper, even though the type of sheet used here is rougher than that generally employed by the artist. For the curvature of the side of the body, and in the legs, Guercino used a stump or his finger to spread the grains of chalk delicately. In contrast, he employed a thick, linear technique for the dark shadows in the drapery, creating a strong plastic effect. The line marking the *profil perdu* of the infant's face brilliantly represents the soft roundness of his cheek; a second line just inside it indicates that the artist initially thought to tilt the head more.

This drawing was clearly taken from life. Nicholas Turner and Carol Plazzotta have suggested that it relates to a drawing in Frankfurt, which shows a child standing between his mother's knees, but stretching up to suckle from her breast.[1] That sheet, in turn, seems to relate to a very highly finished drawing (at the Morgan Library, New York) of the Holy Family, in which the Christ child is also shown suckling.[2] While the link between the Frankfurt and Morgan sheets seems clear—the infant is in almost the same pose, but reversed—the role of the Courtauld drawing is debatable. The sturdy hand holding the child's upper right arm and the mother's stooping pose perhaps make it seem as if she is about to lift him into her lap.

Like so many of Guercino's chalk drawings, this sheet has had a counterproof taken from it (see p. 11), which slightly smudged the lines. The effect is most noticeable in areas of very delicate chalk work (for example, beneath the right buttock), where the counterproof's dampness creates the mistaken impression that the artist used a thin wash of chalk rather than dry media. This is also the case in some areas of catalogue number 15, yet in neither case does it diminish the extraordinary quality of the draftsmanship. □

NOTES

1 Turner and Plazzotta 1991, 74. Frankfurt, Städelsches Kunstinstitut, inv. 448 (Turner and Plazzotta, 1991, 74, fig. 9).

2 New York, Morgan Library, inv. I, 99 (Stone 1991, 57, no. 23, pl. 23).

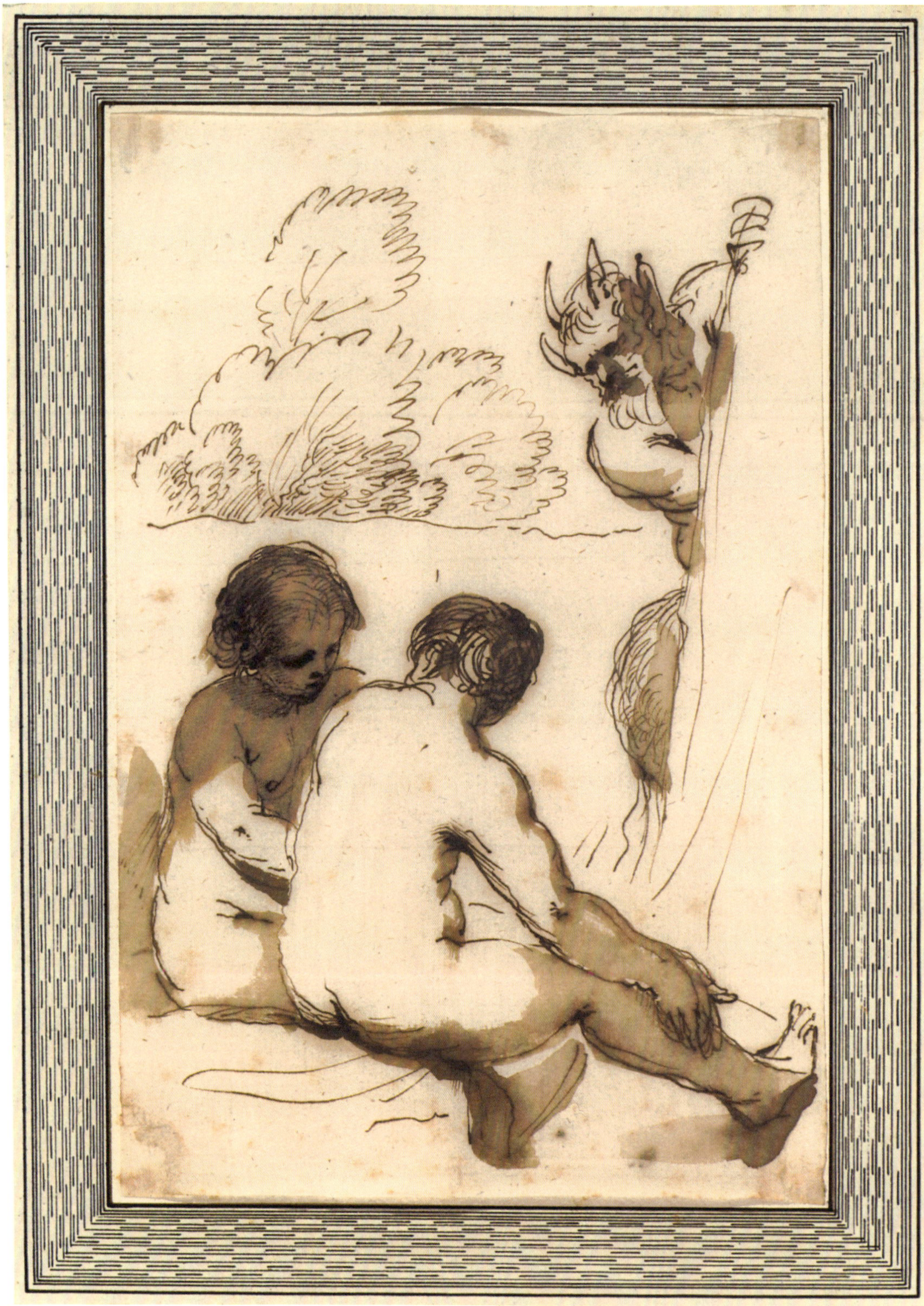

10.
TWO NYMPHS AND A SATYR

ca. 1625
Pen and brown ink, brush with brown wash
20.3 × 13.7 cm (8 × 5 3/8 in.)
London, Courtauld Institute of Art Gallery, D.1952.RW.1346

PROVENANCE Casa Gennari / Bouverie family / Sir Robert Witt, L.2228B, *verso* (see p. 16).

EXHIBITIONS London 1923, no. 5; London 1938, no. 454; London 1943, no number; Manchester 1962, no. 79; Bologna 1968, no. 245; London 1977, no. 40; London 1991, no. 203; Sydney 1999, no. 182.

BIBLIOGRAPHY Russell 1923, 21, 39, pl. VIII; Popham 1938a, 160; RA 1938, 103, pl. 454; V. and A. 1943, 24; Blunt 1956, 76; Marangoni 1959, 13, pl. 19; Blunt and Troutman 1962, 37; Mahon *Disegni* 1969, 201, 245, pl. 245; Hammer et al. 1977, 19; Turner and Plazzotta 1991, 25, fig. 4, 31n92, 32n108, 205, 220, pl. 30; Maloon and Raissis 1999, 178, 227, 239; Negro, Pirondini, and Roio 2004, 287, 292, fig. 292; Brugerolles and Strasser 2006, 39, 40n4.

ONE OF A NUMBER of drawings often called *capricci*, or imaginary scenes, this sheet seems to have been made for Guercino's own pleasure or the amusement of his friends. The mythological subject—a satyr spying on two nude nymphs in the countryside—belongs to a long art-historical tradition of such themes. In particular, Guercino most likely knew of prints of such scenes by the Carracci family in Bologna.

While other artists might revel in the opportunity to represent the nude female form, Guercino provides only a shadowy glimpse of one woman and the brightly lit back of the other. He arranges the figures so that the viewer, like the voyeuristic satyr, is watching as if hidden by nearby bushes. The two nymphs are deep in conversation and have not yet sensed the presence of the satyr.

Few sheets demonstrate so well Guercino's ability to evoke an outside space filled with brilliant sunshine. The white of the paper is left blank to represent various bright surfaces, and, because of the variety and subtlety of visual cues, mainly in the form of pools of dark wash, the human eye accepts this, and its pleasing effect. Indeed, as Nicholas Turner and Carol Plazzotta observe, the back of one nymph is completely blank, but, remarkably, the form does not appear flat. The delicate wash on her right arm and belly creates a convincing illusion of roundness and substance within a three-dimensional space.

The artist conveyed the basic elements of the composition with pen and ink, and a few pentimenti are visible in the fingers and thumb of the most prominent nymph. The pen was used little for description: only the pointy horns and ears of the satyr, the nymphs' hair, and the satyr's hairy leg are fully described. In the background, a number of quick, squiggly pen lines set the scene in a landscape.

The drawing has been placed on a distinctive "Casa Gennari" mount, also shown here (see p. 7 for details). □

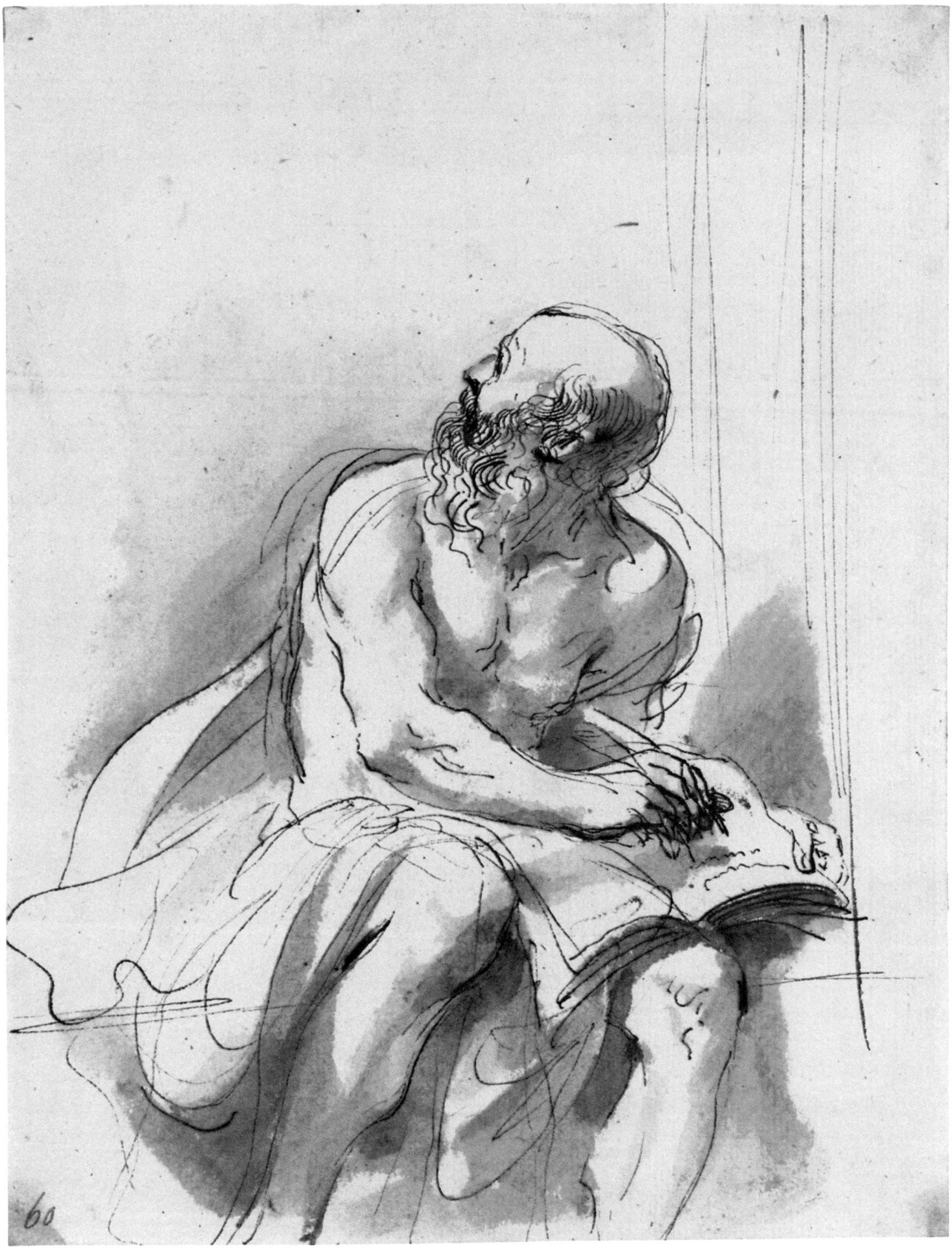
60

11.

SEATED FIGURE OF SAINT JEROME

1626
Pen and brown ink, brush with gray-brown wash
25.1 × 19.7 cm (9⅞ × 7¾ in.)
Numbered in graphite at lower left: 60
London, Courtauld Institute of Art Gallery, D.1952.RW.1365

PROVENANCE Casa Gennari / Bouverie family / Sir Robert Witt, L.2228B, *verso* (see p. 16).

EXHIBITIONS London 1991, no. 56.

BIBLIOGRAPHY Turner and Plazzotta 1991, 31n92, 32n108, 43, 79, 83–85, fig. 56; Boccardo 1992, 44.

IN MAY 1626, GUERCINO personally delivered an altarpiece for the Girolda Fiordibelli chapel in the Cathedral of Reggio Emilia.[1] The subject was the Assumption of the Virgin with Saint Peter as pope, and Saint Jerome. The artist clearly took particular care with the figure of Saint Jerome, who is the subject of seven of eight related drawings known today, including this one.[2]

This drawing shows Saint Jerome seated on a ledge. He writes in a book that rests on his left knee; his body faces the viewer, but his head is turned to look over his right shoulder. A vertical line near the figure's left hand seems to represent the artist's anticipation of the edge of the picture space. The location of the figures was specified in the contract for the painting, so it was clear to Guercino from an early stage that Saint Jerome would be positioned in the lower right-hand corner of the altarpiece.[3] Pentimenti appear on the figure's right shoulder, and, most noticeably, in the hand and pen of the saint, which were moved to a different position on the page. The artist has chosen to combine two separate iconographies for Saint Jerome: he wears few clothes, typical of his time as a penitent in the desert, and yet he is shown writing in a book, which recalls his role as a scholar.

Guercino's other preparatory drawings for Saint Jerome provide a fascinating insight into the artist's versatility and inventiveness. Nicholas Turner and Carol Plazzotta have established the drawings' approximate order.[4] Initially, the artist experimented with placing the saint kneeling as a supplicant with hands clasped and facing inward in the painting.[5] Then he created several drawings with the figure on one knee facing to the left, and the hands variously placed.[6] Catalogue number 11 seems to have come next, followed by two others where the saint also sits, facing outward. As Turner and Plazzotta have noted, the seated pose in the drawings echoes a Saint Jerome in a painting made by Guido Reni about 1620 to 1621 for the nearby church of San Prospero.[7] Finally, to study the disposition of light and shade, Guercino made a highly finished half-length drawing of Saint Jerome.[8]

Cathedral officials must have been pleased with Guercino's altarpiece, and in August 1626 they resolved to commission from him the chapel's lateral panels and vault decoration (see cat. no. 16).[9] □

NOTES

1 Artioli and Monducci 1982, 97f.; Salerno 1988, no. 113.

2 The eighth drawing, in pen and ink, relates to the upper part of the picture, with the Madonna, an angel, and putti. (Sold Christie's, London, December 9, 1949, part of lot 78, bought by the dealer Hans Calmann, as noted by Turner and Plazzotta 1991, 83. According to Salerno 1988, 194, it was located at that time in a U.S. private collection.

3 Artioli and Monducci 1982, 150.

4 Turner and Plazzotta 1991, 83.

5 Genoa, Palazzo Rossi, inv. 1683 (Turner and Plazzotta 1991, 83, fig. 10).

6 Sold Christie's, London, July 6, 1982, lot 40 (Turner and Plazzotta 1991, 83, fig. 12, recto only); U.S. private collection (formerly sold Christie's, London, April 1, 1987, lot 64) (Stone 1991, 37–39, no. 16).

7 A lost drawing engraved by Bartsch (*Recueil*, XXIII, 962b); a studio copy at Windsor Castle of a lost drawing (Mahon and Turner 1989, no. 458). Both drawings identified by Turner and Plazzotta.

8 Collection Alain Moatti, Paris (Stone 1991, 37–38, fig. 16b).

9 Mahon *Dipinti* 1968, 157; Artioli and Monducci 1982, 103.

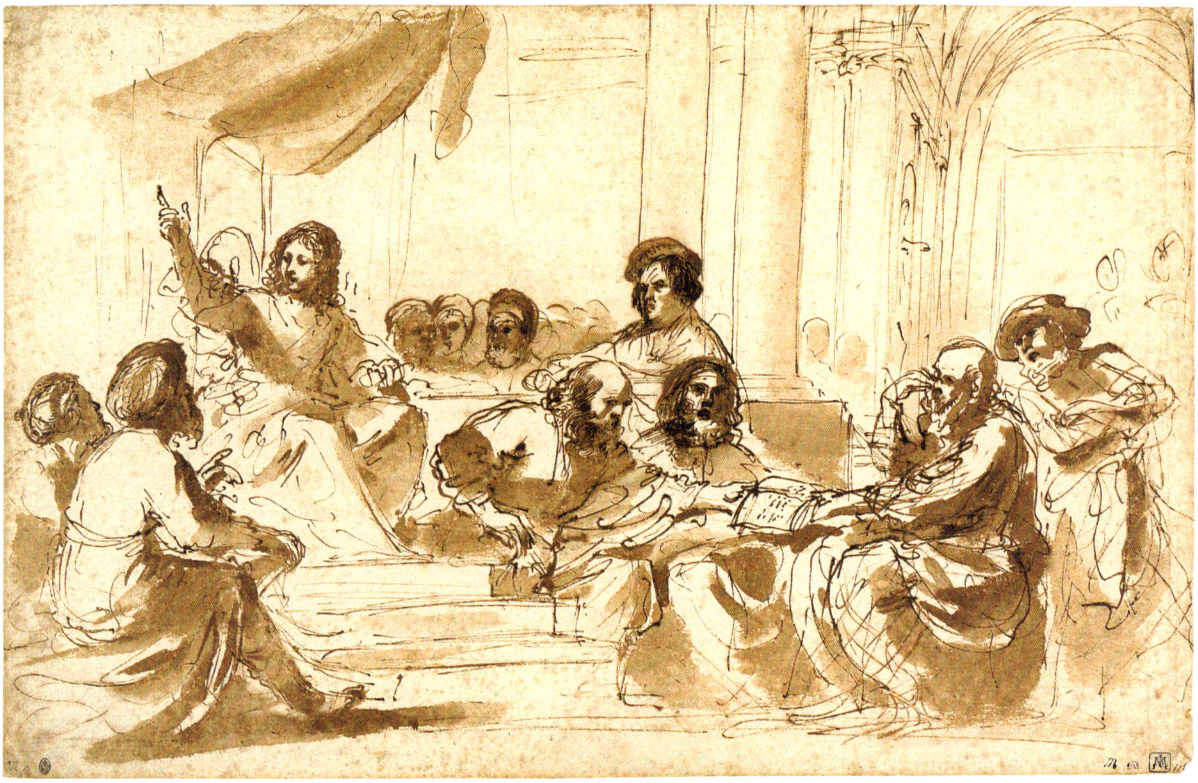

12.

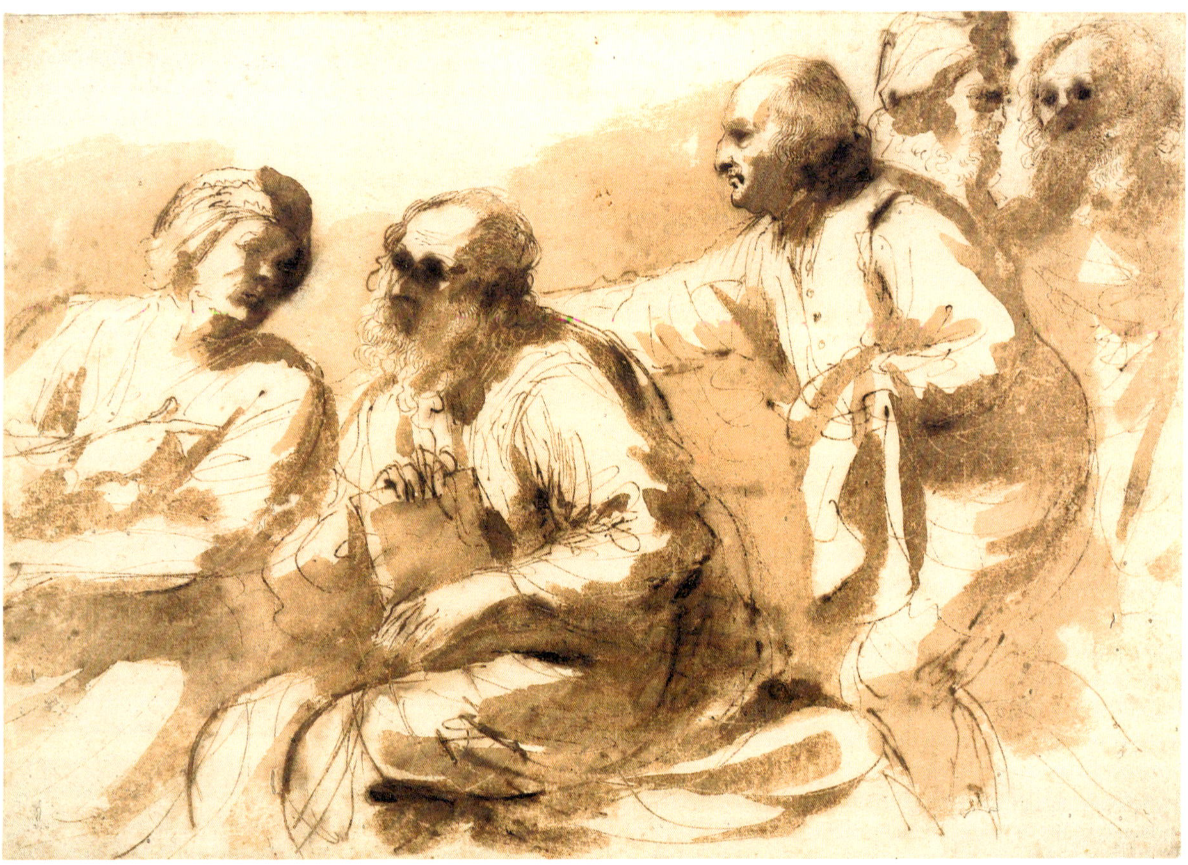

13.

12.
CHRIST PREACHING IN THE TEMPLE

ca. 1625–27
Pen and brown ink, brush with brown wash
26.8 × 42.4 cm (10 9/16 × 16 3/4 in.)
Los Angeles, J. Paul Getty Museum, 84.GG.23

PROVENANCE Baron D. Vivant-Denon, Paris (1747–1825), his sale, A. N. Pérignon, Paris, April 1–19, 1826, lot 443); Baron de Malaussena, Indre (ca. 1860), L. 1887; Marie Marignane, Paris, L.1848; Hubert Marignane (b. 1921); Jacques Petit-Horry, Paris.

EXHIBITIONS Monte Carlo 1966, no. 81; Paris 1971, no. 55; Cambridge 1991, no. 17; Bologna 1991, no. 47; Los Angeles 1998, no number; Paris 1999, no. 570; Los Angeles 2004, no number.

BIBLIOGRAPHY Duval 1829, no. 211; Caviggioli 1966, pl. 63; Bean 1967, 304, pl. 50; Riccòmini 1969, 38, no. 21a, fig. 21a; Vitzthum 1970, 44; Aubry 1971, unpaginated, under no. 81; Varriano 1973, 11, 13, 15, fig. 3; Varriano 1974, unpaginated, under no. 7; Feinblatt 1976, 78; Gibbons 1977, 111; Varriano 1984, 24; Getty 1985, 195, fig. 111; Goldman 1988, 32–33, unnumbered fig.; Goldner, Hendrix ,and Williams 1988, 52, no. 16; Turner and Plazzotta 1991, 286, 287; Mahon 1991, 19; Stone 1991, 40, 44, 213, fig. 17; Bicart-Sée 1999, 461; Negro, Pirondini, and Roio 2004, 58, 59, fig. 145.

13.
AN ASSEMBLY OF LEARNED MEN

ca. 1625–27
Pen and brown ink, brush with brown wash
27 × 39.1 cm (10 5/8 × 15 3/8 in.)
Los Angeles County Museum of Art,
Los Angeles County Fund, 64.24

PROVENANCE Paul Brandt, Amsterdam; Frederick Anthon Gallery, Beverly Hills; purchased by the Museum in 1964.

EXHIBITIONS Saskatchewan and Montreal 1970, no. 34; Los Angeles 1976, 94; Los Angeles 1984, no. 37; Cambridge 1991, no. 18.

BIBLIOGRAPHY Vitzthum 1970, 44; Roli 1972, 26, tav. 38; Varriano 1973, 13n5; Feinblatt 1976, 78, fig. 94; Davis 1984, 30, 60, no. 37, ill.; Stone 1991, 40, 44, 213, fig. 18; Davis 1997, 48–49, no. 17, fig. 17.

SINCE GUERCINO'S PREPARATORY drawings for larger paintings are generally sheets with either rough ideas or intense studies focused on a group of figures, relatively highly finished full compositional drawings such as catalogue number 12 are comparatively unusual. Guercino produced the particular type of sheet shown here because it served a very specific purpose: it was made to help his follower, Antonio Bonfanti, il Torricella (fl. 1620–30, Ferrara), with the design of the painting *Christ Preaching in the Temple* (fig. 12.2).[1] Catalogue number 13 is a "close-up" study toward the same composition.

The little-known Bonfanti seems to have been a pupil of Guercino's, and the two had a number of dealings, all concerning work done in Ferrara. Bonfanti acted as the agent in a commission for an altarpiece Guercino made between 1633 and 1636; Guercino provided drawings to Bonfanti for the subject of *Saint Charles Borromeo Surviving the Shot of an Assassin* around the same time; and, in 1661, Bonfanti acted as the intermediary for the retouching of the earlier altarpiece.[2] The exact circumstances surrounding their relationship

NOTES

1 Riccòmini 1969, 38, no. 49, fig. 19.

2 Mahon and Turner 1989, 45, 91.

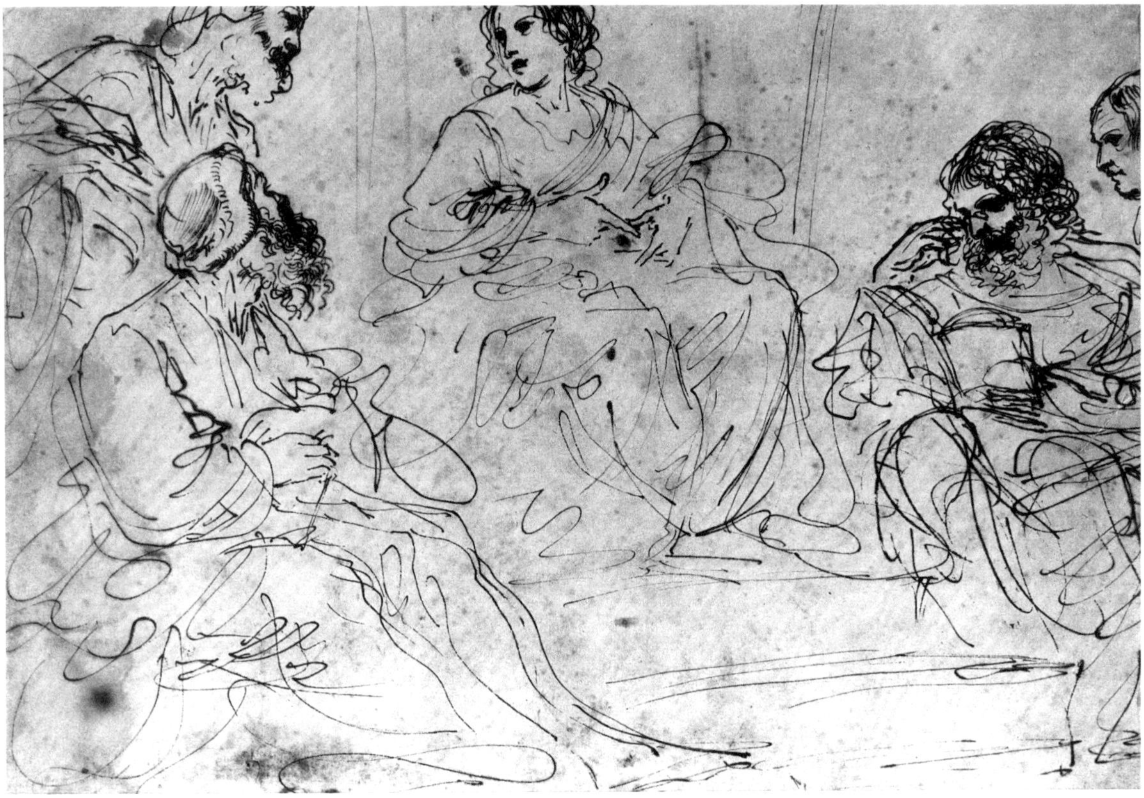

FIGURE 12.1
Guercino. *Christ Preaching in the Temple* (recto), ca. 1625–27. Pen and brown ink, 26.1 × 39.4 cm (10¼ × 15½ in.). South Hadley, Mass., Mount Holyoke College Art Museum, Museum Purchase: Nancy Everett Dwight Fund II, 1954, P.RIV.1.1954

for *Christ Preaching in the Temple* are unclear, but that painting was commissioned, along with *The Presentation of Christ in the Temple*, by Cardinal Bonifacio Bevilacqua (d. 1627). John Varriano and David Stone have reconstructed something of the preparatory process from the surviving drawings.[3]

Guercino first sketched his ideas on the recto of a sheet now at Mount Holyoke (fig. 12.1) and developed them further on the verso of that sheet and on catalogue number 12. The LACMA sheet (cat. no. 13) focused on a solution for the right-hand part of the composition, which was later rejected. Antonio Bonfanti must have known at least the Mount Holyoke (fig. 12.1) and Getty (cat. no. 12) drawings, and his final painted solution (fig. 12.2) takes ideas from both of them.[4]

The scene is taken from the Gospel of Luke (2:41–51) in which a youthful Christ debates with learned doctors in the temple at Jerusalem. In catalogue number 12 Guercino places Christ on a prominent seat in the temple, his position further emphasized by the canopy placed over it. On the lower left, a seated figure in a turban raises a finger to object, while the majority of the doctors are ranged across the right-hand side of the composition; one passes a book of law to another. Compared to the fluid and fast-changing nature of most of Guercino's drawings, this is an extremely measured sheet that gives the sense of a "fair-copy" solution. No doubt this impression derives partly from the composition's full architectural background. Yet there are areas of extremely fluid draftsmanship, such as the flurry of lines under the seated figure at right who touches his eye, and the deft precision with which the doctor handing the book to him is shown reaching forward into space.

NOTES

3 Varriano 1973, 11–15; Stone 1991, 40–44.

4 Bonfanti's painting closely follows his own drawing now at Princeton, inv. 48-730 (Stone 1991, 41, fig. 17c).

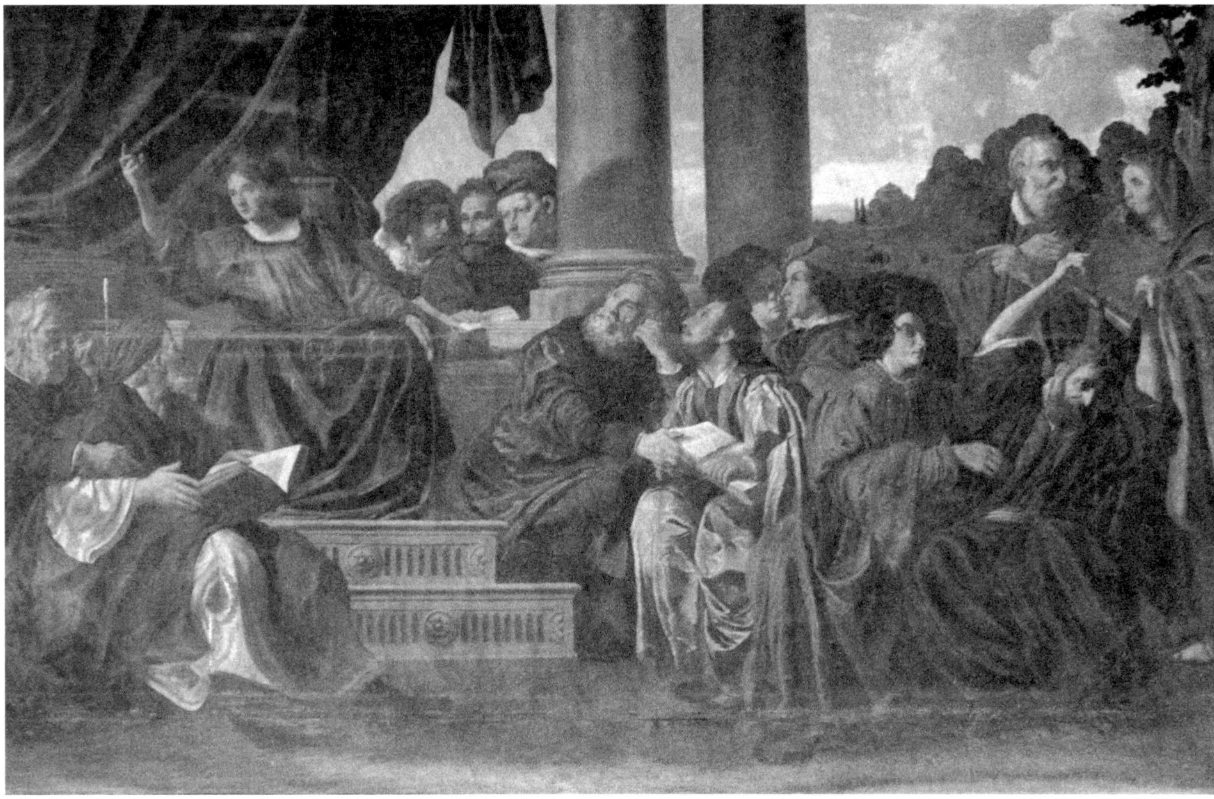

FIGURE 12.2
Antonio Bonfanti. *Christ Preaching in the Temple*, ca. 1625–27. Oil on canvas. Ferrara, San Francesco

Pentimenti are found only occasionally; for example, under the strongly drawn face of the central seated figure, one can see traces of an idea to show him conversing with the man on his right.

Catalogue number 13 studies the right-hand side of the composition. It centers the figures around the aged seated man, but with a new cast, animated differently. The doctors are characterized more fully than in catalogue number 12, with details such as the dotted bristles and combed locks of the figure in motion at the right. The corrosive action of the iron-gall ink in the dark dots of the figures' eyes today provides the characters with a strange disconnectedness that would not have been present when the drawing was made.

Bonfanti's finished painting (fig. 12.2) adopts the broad compositional strategy of catalogue number 12 and has some similar characteristics. It includes Christ's pose but differs in the poses of the doctors and the landscape setting. Yet the commission is a particularly interesting case of an artist providing drawings for another artist, a phenomenon that was not rare but for which very little documentation remains. Although Guercino is not known to have created many drawings for the benefit of other artists, the practice would be in keeping with his apparently low valuation of *invenzione* (he would charge a similar amount for a replica painting as for the original and would not increase or decrease the price over time).[5]

Nicholas Turner and Carol Plazzotta have published an inspired but faithful copy of catalogue number 12 by Francesco Bartolozzi (1727–1815) in the British Museum.[6] □

NOTES

5 Spear 1994, 596.

6 Turner and Plazzotta 1991, 286–87, no. 111.

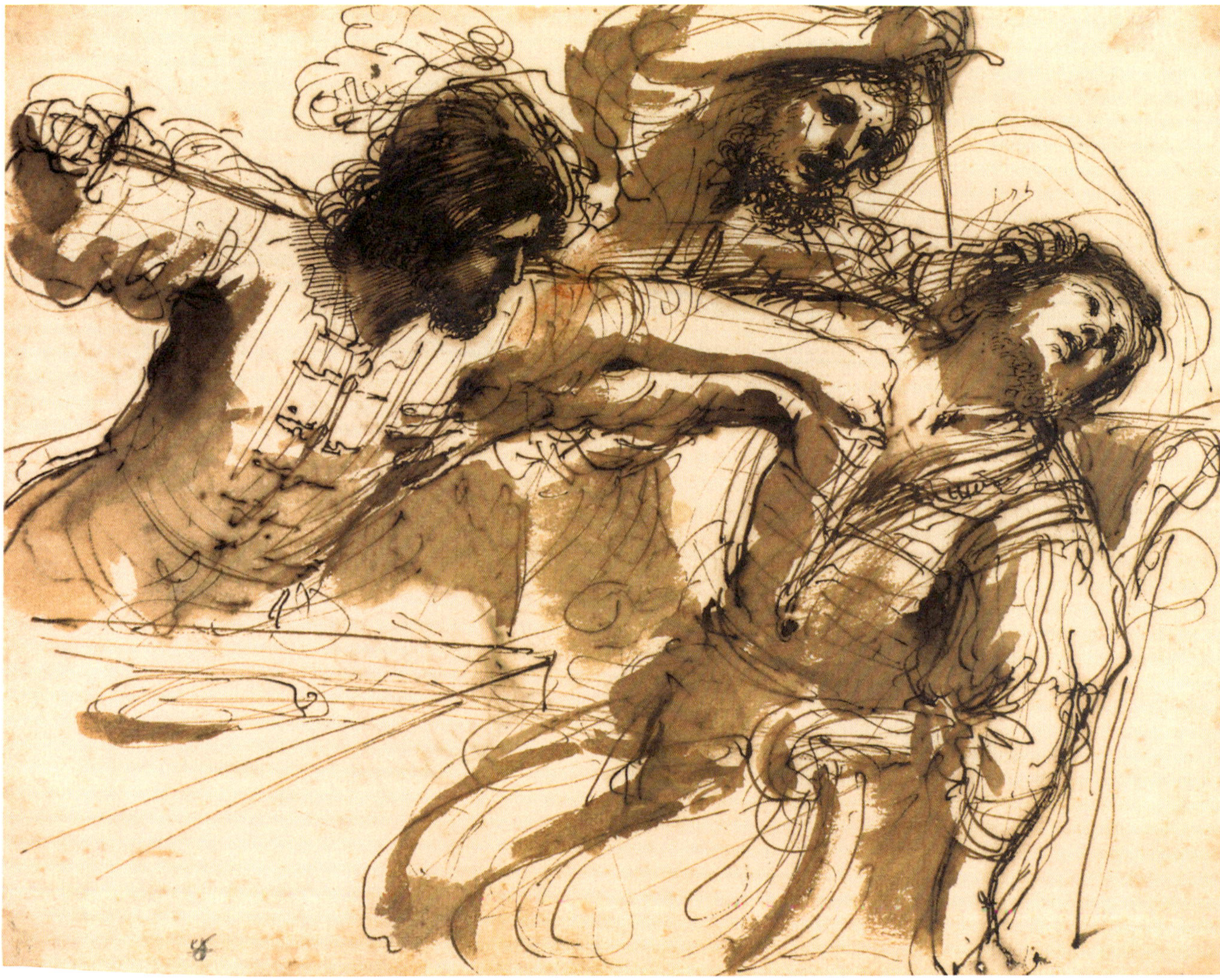

Recto

14.

THE ASSASSINATION OF AMNON (RECTO) STUDY OF TWO FIGURES (VERSO)

1628
Recto: pen and brown ink, brush with brown wash
Verso: pen and brown ink
20 × 26.3 cm (7⅞ × 10⅜ in.)
London, Courtauld Institute of Art Gallery, D.1952.RW.1344

PROVENANCE Casa Gennari / Bouverie family / Sir Robert Witt, L.2228B, *verso* (see p. 16).

EXHIBITIONS London 1943, no number; Bologna 1968, no. 118; London 1977, no. 21; London 1991, no. 71.

BIBLIOGRAPHY V. and A. 1943, 24; Blunt 1956, 76; Mahon 1967, 39; Mahon *Disegni* 1969, 31, 33n12, 116–118, pl. 118; Roli 1972, 26, tav. 38; Mahon and Ekserdjian 1986, 12; Ebert-Schifferer 1991, 426; Turner 1991, 78; Turner and Plazzotta 1991, 16, 19, 31n92, 32n108, 33, 99, 102, pl. 14; Adam et al. 2005, 98.

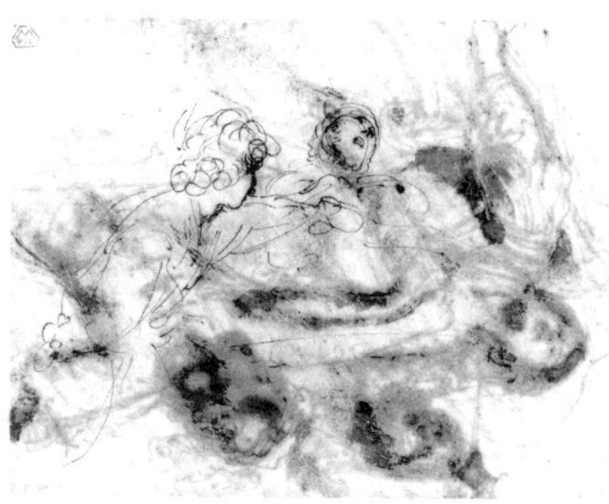

Verso (inverted)

THE SHEER ENERGY and directness of this drawing match the violence of the Old Testament subject (2 Samuel 13:1–29): Absalom's revenge on his half-brother Amnon for having raped their sister Tamar. Amnon, David's eldest son, had feigned illness and raped Tamar when she brought him food in bed. Absalom harbored a deep hatred for Amnon, and two years later he invited Amnon to a feast, made him drunk, and instructed his servants to kill him at the table.

In Guercino's drawing, Amnon is seated to the right of the table. One attacker (center) grasps the victim's head and pushes it back with his left hand while preparing to strike with a raised dagger in his right. Amnon desperately tries to push away a second attacker coming from the left, who prepares the way with one hand for his own poised dagger.

In drawings such as this, one can almost sense Guercino's pen scratching the paper, and the drama of the scene is conveyed partly through the energy carried by the flurry of lines. As the artist struggled to capture the changing image in his mind, his pen left indications of fleeting thoughts, such as the lines showing that he considered placing Amnon's right arm over the figure's head, and the ones suggesting a lower position for the chairback. As each idea hit the paper, it was assessed and either worked up or discarded. The verso of the Courtauld sheet contains one of the abandoned ideas: a few pen lines that indicate a different composition, with Amnon seen from directly in front, as if he were to be placed in the center of the picture, and an attacker at left. In contrast, the design on the recto is fully explored, with many of the strokes repeated several times for emphasis. Guercino added details—registered quickly by the human eye—that bring an indication of reality, such as the buttons and detailing on the front of one attacker's tunic. Contrasting with such details, the few bold lines used for the table in the left corner create a dramatic and unstable sense of context.

The whole composition is brought together by a fluid wash, which heightens the sense of space through the rhythmic disposition of light and shadow and, on occasion, delineates the composition, as in the areas around Amnon's legs and the central attacker's right arm. Guercino's bravura use of brown wash is evident in the tunic of the attacker at

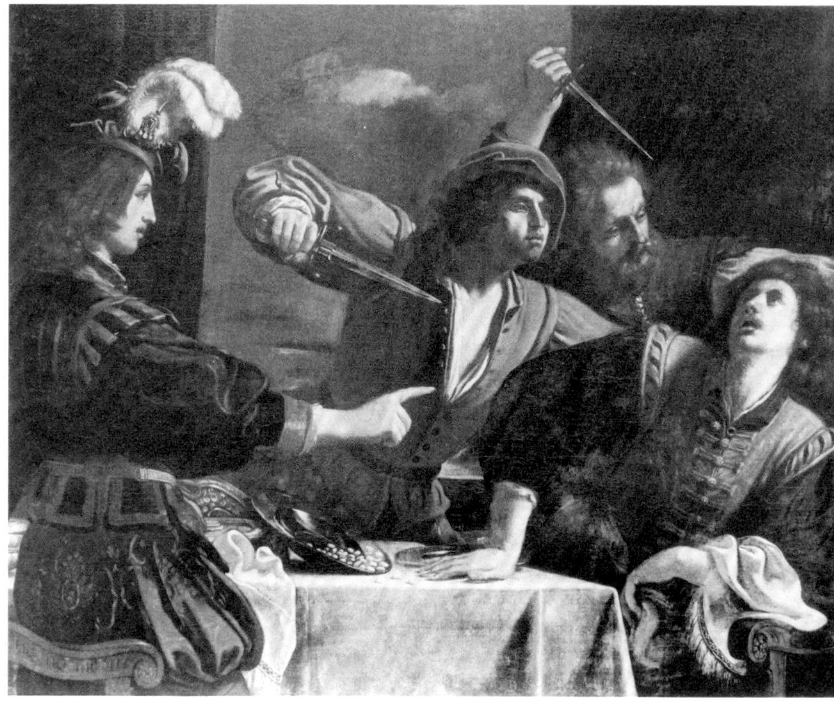

FIGURE 14.1
Follower of Guercino. *The Assassination of Amnon*, after 1628. Oil on canvas, 139 × 176 cm (54¾ × 69¼ in.). Bologna, Pinacoteca Nazionale, 932. Photo: Archivio Fotografico della Pinacoteca Nazionale di Bologna, by permission of the Ministero per i Beni e le Attività culturali

left: a light application across the stomach gently gives way to darker tones on the side of the body and under the sleeve, where a brushstroke with darker ink directly conveys the shadow under the arm.

This drawing is one of a sequence of studies made in preparation for a painting commissioned by a Bolognese patron, Lorenzo Fioravanti, in 1628.[1] Although that painting's whereabouts are now unknown, the composition survives in a number of early copies, reflecting its popularity (fig. 14.1).[2] The painting preserves many of the motifs found in the Courtauld drawing, but it shows Amnon trying to rise and escape from the table, and it includes Absalom (on the left), pointing out Amnon to his servants.

In his preparatory drawings, Guercino eschewed the contemporary practice of making numerous small-scale studies on a single sheet. Instead, he drew each new idea for the composition full scale on a clean sheet of paper. In this case, the artist used most of the drawings to work out how best to show Amnon and his attackers. His initial thought seems to have been to place Amnon with his back to the viewer and have the attackers reaching across the table, as in a drawing at Windsor Castle (fig. 14.2), which also features a figure fleeing at upper left, an idea Guercino soon dropped.[3] A drawing in the Mahon Collection (fig. 14.3) shows Amnon seated to the left of the table but seen from the front, with the attackers, daggers raised, behind the table.[4] Apparently satisfied with the figures' visibility in such a composition but aware of the awkward way that the principal attacker wielded the dagger in his right hand, Guercino reversed the composition, resulting in the smoother attack and cleaner diagonal axis seen in catalogue number 14. A similar drawing at Windsor Castle is the only one of this type to include Absalom; he is seated at the table.[5] A drawing in the Albertina in Vienna places Amnon and the attackers on the right behind

NOTES

1 Malvasia ed. 1841, 2:261.

2 For details of the commission and existing copies, see Salerno 1988, 215; and Mahon and Turner 1989, 29.

3 Windsor Castle, Royal Library, inv. RL 2399 (M&T 53; Mahon and Turner 1989, 29, pl. 55; Turner and Plazzotta 1991, 97, no. 69, fig. 69).

4 Mahon Collection, on loan to the Ashmolean Museum, Oxford; Mahon and Ekserdjian 1986, p. 12, no. 19 (Turner and Plazzotta 1991, 98, no. 70, fig. 70).

5 Windsor Castle, Royal Library, inv. RL 2398 (M&T 52; Mahon and Turner 1989, 28–29, no. 52, pl. 54; Turner and Plazzotta 1991, 100, no. 72, fig. 72).

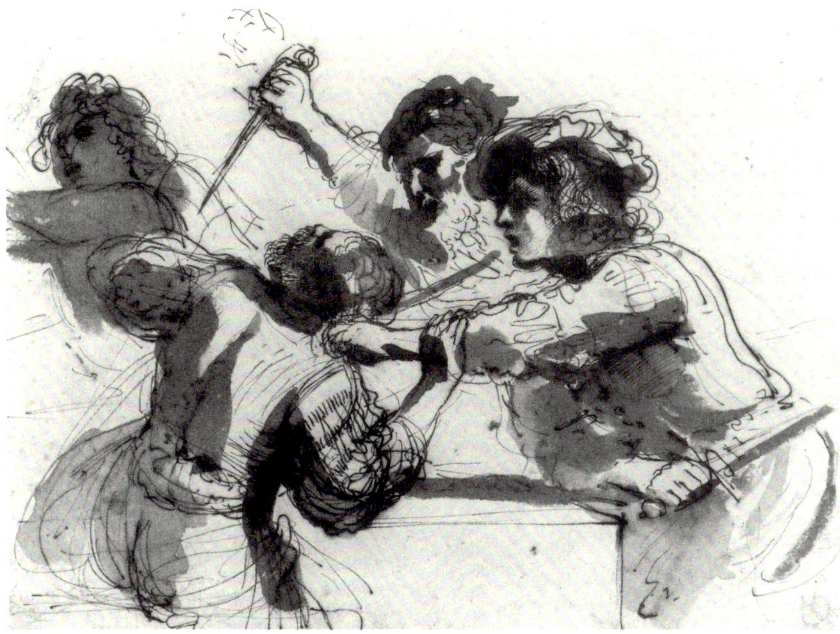

FIGURE 14.2

Guercino. *The Assassination of Amnon*, 1628. Pen and brown ink, brush with brown wash, 19.6 × 27.3 cm (7¾ × 10¾ in.). Windsor Castle, Royal Library, RL 2399. Photo: The Royal Collection, © 2005 Her Majesty Queen Elizabeth II

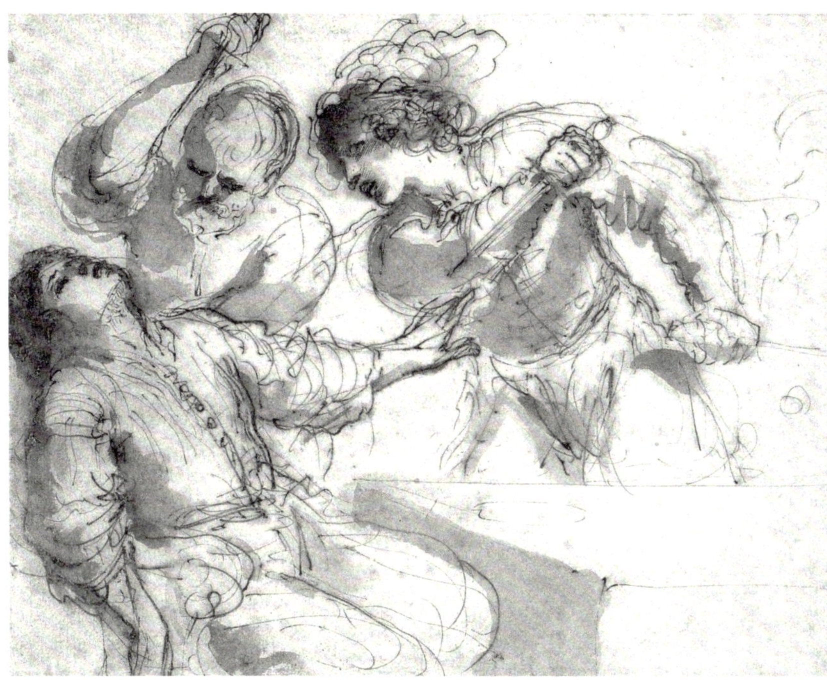

FIGURE 14.3

Guercino, *The Assassination of Amnon*, 1628. Pen and brown ink, brush with brown wash, 20.4 × 25.9 cm (8 × 10¼ in.). Mahon Collection, on loan to the Ashmolean Museum, Oxford

the table, and a drawing in a private collection has him rising from the table, something Guercino adopted in the final painting, instead of sitting with his head cast back, as in catalogue number 14 and figure 14.3.[6] A single red-chalk figure study of Absalom, whose pose seems to have been studied separately, is in the Pinacoteca di Brera in Milan.[7] Across this group of studies, it is significant that the two attackers and Amnon vary in age and type. Amnon is usually youthful, but in figure 14.2 he sports a beard; in most of the drawings, one assassin is older and one younger, but in the second Windsor Castle drawing they are both older. Clearly, Guercino resolved such matters only in the painting itself. □

NOTES

6 Vienna, Albertina, inv. 34-529; Saville Gallery 1929, p. 13, no. 35, fig. 35.

7 Milan, Pinacoteca di Brera, inv. 614 (Mahon and Turner 1989, 29; Emiliani 1959, no. 72, fig. 72).

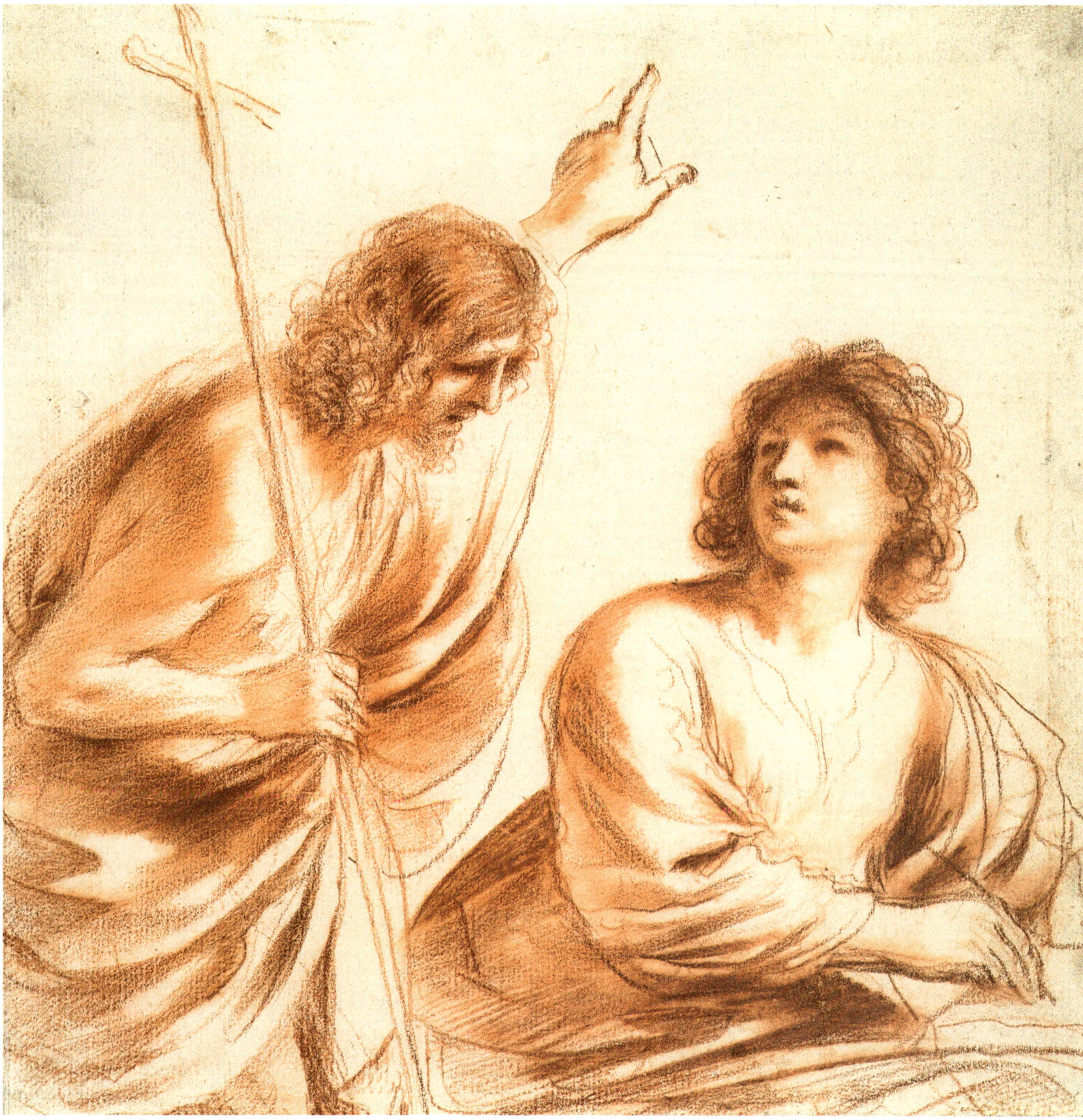

15.

SAINTS JOHN THE BAPTIST AND JOHN THE EVANGELIST

ca. 1631–32
Red chalk, stumping
27.5 × 27.3 cm (10 13/16 × 10 3/4 in.)
Los Angeles County Museum of Art, Graphic Arts Council Fund, M.78.25

PROVENANCE Henry Oppenheimer, London; his sale, Christie's, London, July 10, 1936, lot 102b; Denis Mahon, London; Baron P. Hatvany; his sale, Christie's, London, November 27, 1973, lot 346; Thomas Agnew and Sons, London; purchased by the Museum in 1978.

EXHIBITIONS Los Angeles 1984, no. 38; Cambridge 1991, no. 27.

LITERATURE Mahon 1967, 46; Bisogni 1975, 342, fig. 6; Davis 1984, 30, 31, 60, no. 38, ill.; Mahon and Ekserdjian 1986, 15; Salerno 1988, 234; Mahon and Turner 1989, 184; Davis 1997, 52–53, no. 19, ill.; Stone 1991, 68, 213, color pl. 27; Adam et al. 2005, 106.

THIS IS ONE OF A NUMBER of studies for an altarpiece (now destroyed) commissioned in 1631 by Giovanni Mosca for the church of San Giovanni Battista at Pesaro.[1] The subject of the altarpiece was the Madonna and Child with Saints Lucy, Francis, John the Evangelist, and John the Baptist, and only a fragment, with a figure of Saint Lucy, survives.[2] Catalogue number 15 represents an unusual type of study, but one that Guercino used a good deal: an intense, large-scale, "close-up" drawing of a few figures removed from the larger composition. Guercino made such drawings while he was still resolving the composition, and they not only informed the figures' characterization but also often affected the final resolution of the painting (see p. 11).

In catalogue number 15, the artist explores the spatial and human relationship between the two figures, and works out details of their individual facial expressions. Saint John the Baptist stands at left, pointing upward, while Saint John the Evangelist looks up at him, interrupted from his writing. As throughout Western art, the Evangelist—identified with the New Testament character "the disciple whom Jesus loved"—is somewhat effeminate. While Guercino has not indicated a background, he has set the two figures clearly in space: the Baptist's cross and his pointing left hand, for example, are perfectly placed above and behind his head. The plasticity of the outlines of the Baptist's left hand also recalls the draftsmanship of Lodovico Carracci, whose work Guercino studied. A turbulent mass of bushy lines conveys the Baptist's hair, and a swift series of long strokes creates the loose hanging folds of drapery. Guercino used stumping on Saint John the Baptist's shoulder and forearm to convey deftly the effect of light across the skin. A counterproof (see p. 11) was taken from the drawing some time after it was made, possibly by the artist himself or his nephews.[3] In areas of thin stumping, the moisture on the damp secondary sheet liquefied the chalk to give the impression of a very thin wash (see also cat. no. 9).

Judging by the location of the Virgin in the remaining canvas fragment, it seems as if Guercino intended to place Saints John the Baptist and John the Evangelist in the lower left corner of the picture and Saint Francis in the center. An ink drawing in the Mahon Collection that shows the seated Evangelist with Saint Francis on the right supports this view.[4] □

NOTES

1 Bisogni 1975, 338–42.

2 Salerno 1988, 234, no. 141.

3 Windsor Castle, Royal Library, inv. RL 3174 (M&T 625); Mahon and Turner 1989, 184, where a counterproof of a similar drawing to the LACMA sheet is M&T 624, and two other related drawings are identified: Frankfurt, Städelsches Kunstinstitut, inv. 449, and Stockholm, Nationalmuseum, inv. 1113/1863 (repr. Stone 1991, 68, fig. 27a).

4 Mahon Collection, on loan to the Ashmolean Museum, Oxford (M&E 24; Mahon and Ekserdjian 1986, 15, no. 24). A black-chalk drawing with two studies of Saint John the Evangelist (in the Teylers Museum, Haarlem) has been linked with the Pesaro altarpiece, but Carel van Tuyll argues convincingly that it dates from later in the artist's career (Mahon and Turner 1989, 184; van Tuyll 1991, 162, no. 71). The saint holds a similar pose to other sheets for the project, but the black chalk lacks the "attack" of drawings of this period.

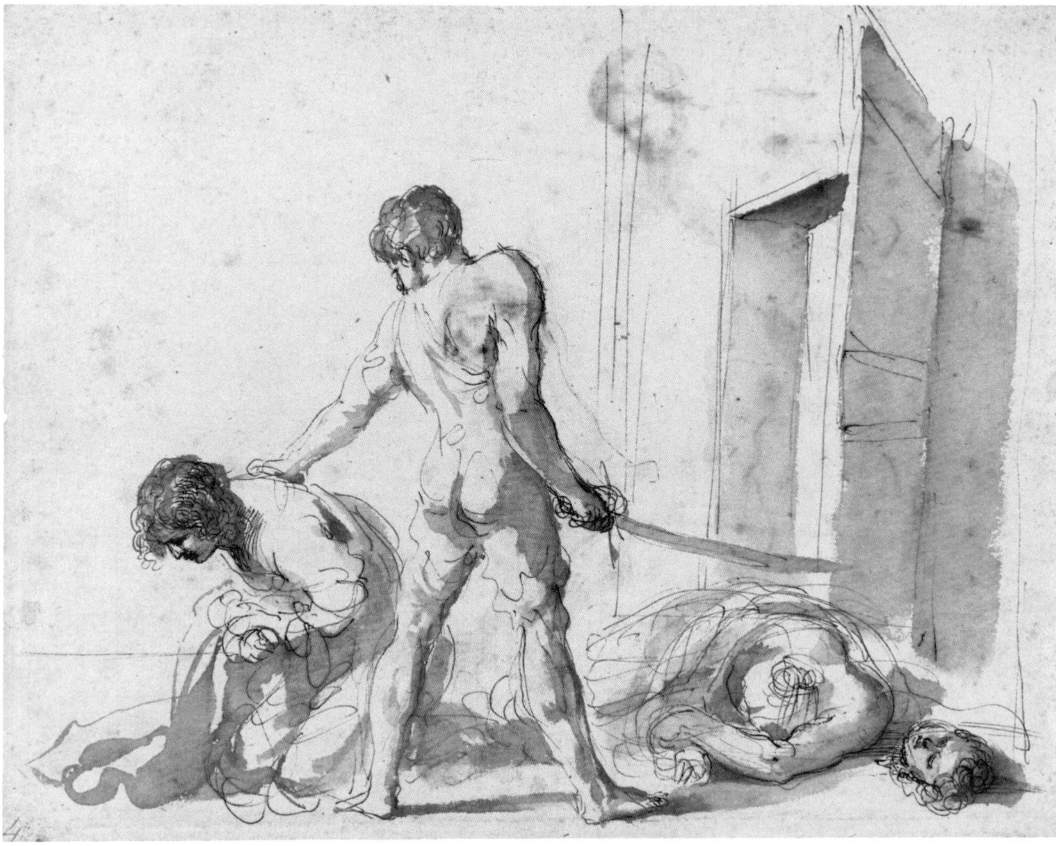

Recto

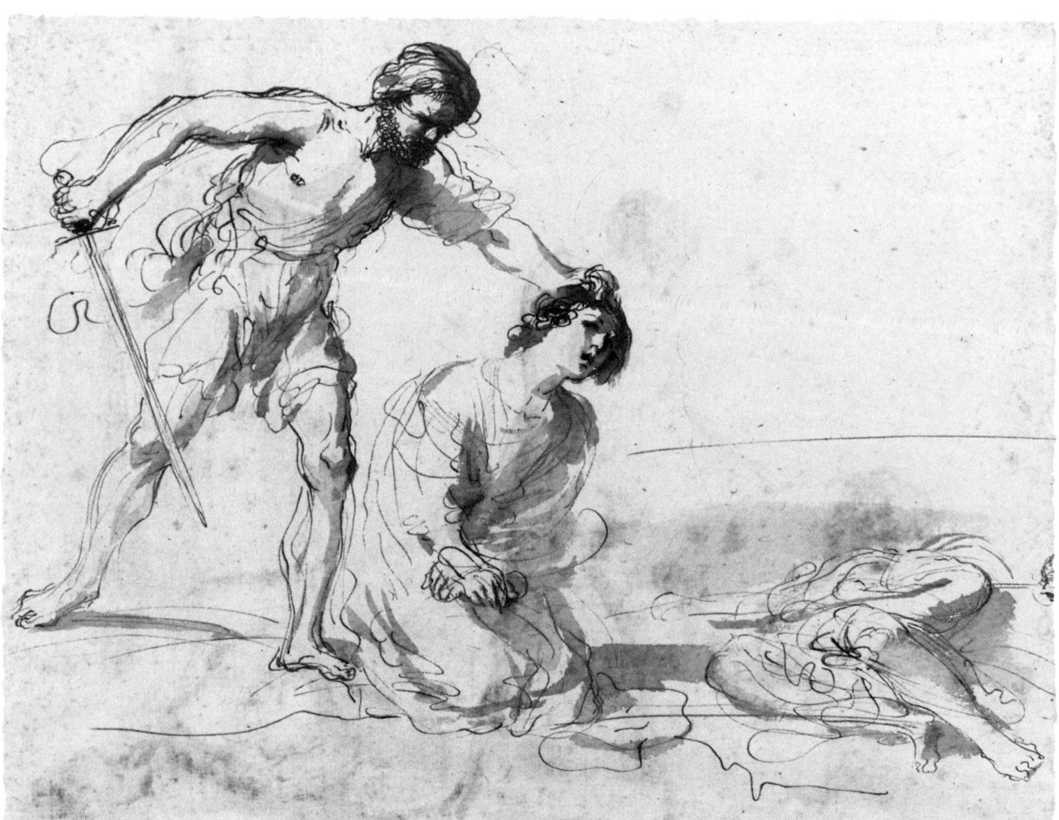

Verso

16.

THE MARTYRDOM OF SAINTS JOHN AND PAUL

(RECTO AND VERSO)

1630–32
Pen and brown ink, brush with brown wash
23.9 × 31 cm (9 3/8 × 12 1/4 in.)
Numbered in graphite at lower left: *4*
London, Courtauld Institute of Art Gallery, D.1952.RW.1341

PROVENANCE Casa Gennari / Bouverie family / Sir Robert Witt, L.2228B, *verso* (see p. 16).

EXHIBITIONS Bologna 1968, no. 130; London 1977, no. 23; London 1991, no. 88.

BIBLIOGRAPHY Blunt 1956, 75; Mahon 1967, 44; Mahon *Dipinti* 1968, 159; Mahon *Disegni* 1969, 36, 126, 127–28, pl. 130; Hammer et al. 1977, 14; Artioli and Monducci 1982, 105, pl. 53; Salerno 1988, 232; Stone 1991, 58, 66; Ebert-Schifferer 1991, 434; Turner and Plazzotta 1991, 31n92, 32n108, 43, 102, 112, 114, 115, 116–17, fig. 88.

OF THE MANY PROJECTS for which sequences of preparatory drawings survive, Guercino's sheets for *The Martyrdom of Saints John and Paul with the Madonna and Child Above* (fig. 16.1) best illustrate the extraordinarily inventive way he choreographs the main characters. Unlike other artists of his time, Guercino would place each possible arrangement on its own clean, standard-size sheet of paper and work it through fully, rather than sketching a series of tiny alternative solutions on one sheet and then working up only the best ones.

Saints John and Paul were brothers, both Roman officers, who were beheaded for their faith in A.D. 362 during the reign of Emperor Julian the Apostate. In a sequence of drawings, Guercino studied the method of their execution and, in particular, the relative positions of the three figures. The artist's attention to detail makes it clear that he was attempting to imagine what would have happened at a beheading.

The surviving drawings constitute a homogenous group and seem to have been made in a relatively short span of time, perhaps only a few hours or days. However, the way Guercino jumps around the subject makes it difficult to reconstruct their exact order.[1] The most gruesome of the studies, a drawing in Amsterdam (fig. 16.2), was probably an early idea for a solution.[2] In it, the executioner, having made the decisive stroke and placed his sword on the ground, uses his dagger to finish severing the head, which bleeds copiously from the mouth and neck, while the saint's hands still cling to the executioner's block. The decapitated body of the other saint lies to the right of the block. The executioner's block also appears faintly in a drawing at Windsor Castle (fig. 16.3), a "close-up" of a decapitated body with arms tied behind his back (throughout the sequence of drawings, the artist considered several options for the hands).[3] To emphasize the low viewpoint of the composition, Guercino sketched a dramatically foreshortened wall with a column.

On the next drawing in the series, the verso of catalogue number 16, Guercino considered having the executioner walk up to a kneeling saint.[4] Here the violence is strikingly implicit in the way the executioner exposes the saint's neck by pulling up his hair. Pentimenti in the executioner's right arm add to a sense of motion, and Guercino has

NOTES

1 Mahon *Disegni* 1969, 127–28; Mahon and Turner 1989, 37–39; Turner and Plazzotta 1991, 112–17; Stone 1991, 58–64; and van Tuyll 1991, 76.

2 Amsterdam, Rijksmuseum, Rijksprentenkabinet, inv. 1964.38 (van Tuyll 1991, 76, no. 23).

3 Windsor Castle, Royal Library, inv. RL 2849 (M&T 63; Mahon and Turner 1989, 37, pl. 67).

4 Guercino studies this approach from a different angle on the recto of the drawing in the Morgan Library, inv. I, 101h (Stone 1991, 58–64, no. 24).

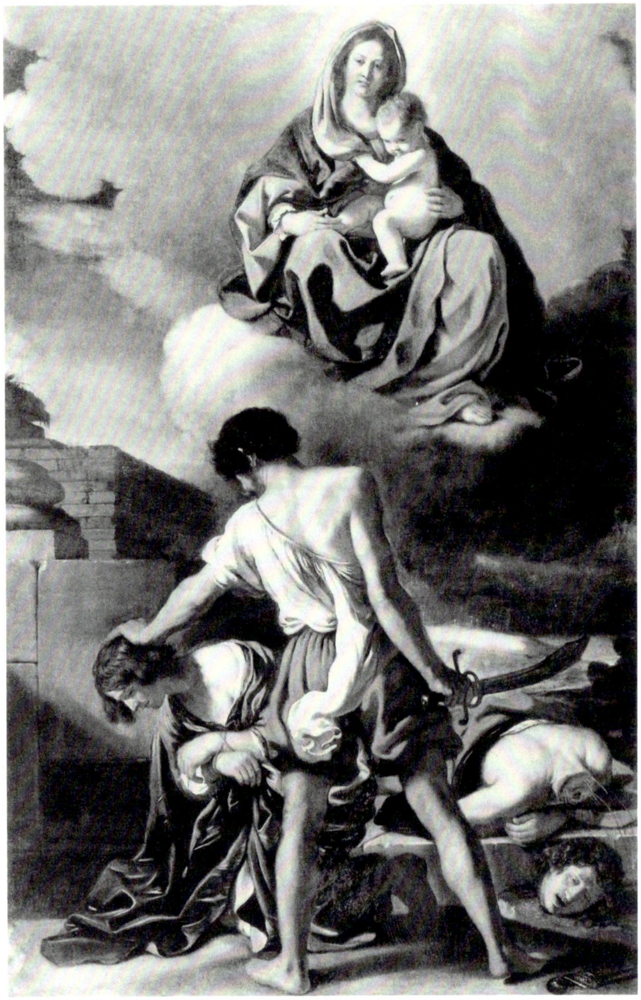

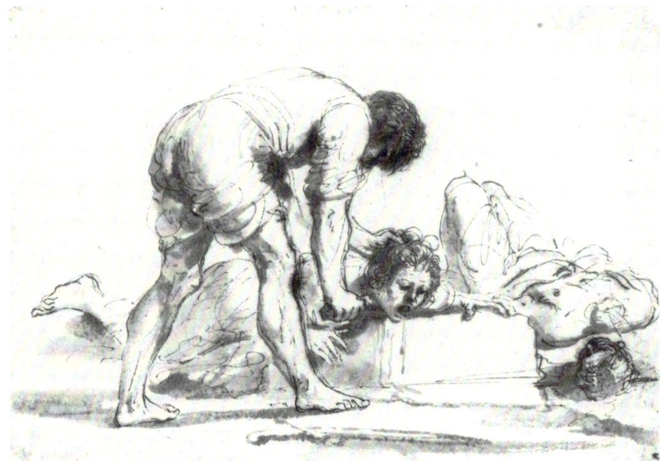

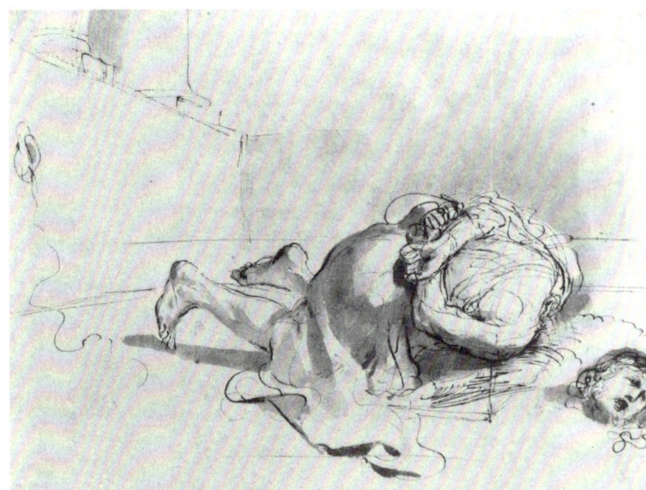

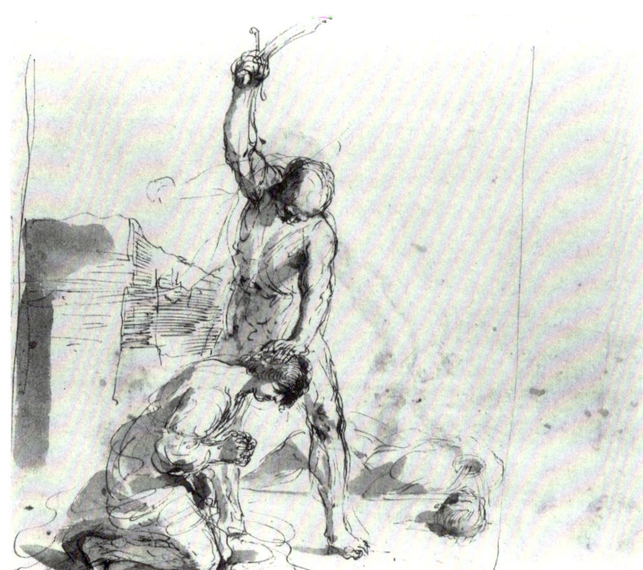

FIGURE 16.1
Guercino. *The Martyrdom of Saints John and Paul with the Madonna and Child Above*, 1632. Oil on canvas, 308 × 203 cm (120⅛ × 80 in.). Toulouse, Musée des Augustins

FIGURE 16.2
Guercino. *The Martyrdom of Saints John and Paul*, ca. 1631. Pen and brown ink, brush with brown wash, 20.7 × 30.2 cm (8⅛ × 11 ⅞ in.). Amsterdam, Rijksmuseum, Rijksprentenkabinet, 1964.38. Photo: © Rijksmuseum-Stichting Amsterdam

FIGURE 16.3
Guercino. *The Body of a Man with a Severed Head*, ca. 1631. Pen and brown ink, brush with brown wash, 19.1 × 25.9 cm (7½ × 10¼ in.). Windsor Castle, Royal Library, RL 2849. Photo: The Royal Collection, © Her Majesty Queen Elizabeth II

FIGURE 16.4
Guercino. *The Martyrdom of Saints John and Paul* (verso), ca. 1631. Pen and brown ink, brush with brown wash, 25.1 × 30.1 cm (9⅞ × 11⅞ in.). New York, Morgan Library, I, 101h

taken the time to characterize him with a bushy beard. Guercino initially positioned the figure of the other saint lying on the ground so that his bent legs were toward the viewer; he made a few lines with the point of the brush to indicate spurting blood, and on the far right he drew part of the severed head (truncated by the trimmed edge of the page). Then the artist changed his mind: with a few circular squiggles, he suggested that the prone saint's neck, not his legs, should be nearest the viewer; a single descending line on the edge of the platform seems to show blood dripping toward the bottom of the composition, marked by a long horizontal stroke.

In a drawing that instead shows the executioner standing behind the kneeling saint,[5] Guercino took the unusual step of attaching a small flap of paper on which he sketched an alternate resolution for that part: he changed the angle of the tormentor's head and gave him a different hat. This drawing seems to have been the catalyst for Guercino to make a more vertical, static composition; he did so, apparently, by turning over the two sheets on which he had already drawn and sketching on the other sides. In these two drawings (fig. 16.4 and the recto of cat. no. 16), Guercino approaches the solution he used in the painting. In figure 16.4, the executioner stands behind the kneeling saint with sword raised, while two striking pentimenti show that the artist considered other positions for the arm.[6] A wall along the left side of the composition, and the other martyr's decapitated body on a ledge at the right are both in positions similar to those in the painting, the borders of which Guercino indicates with vertical lines. Catalogue number 16 recto shows the two principal figures in positions close to those of the painting. Wash applied with the point of the brush has been used with great effect to create soft, languid forms of drapery; these contrast with brief lines in the figure and curly spirals of hair (retained in the painting). The executioner is shown with only little in the way of a tunic, and a pentimento reveals an alternate position for his right arm.

As his work on the composition progressed in these drawings, it is noticeable that Guercino gradually reined in his imagination. His treatment of the subject became less violent and macabre, and the final painting is certainly fitting for its ecclesiastical location. In addition, Guercino seems to have conceived the lower part of the painting as almost a completely separate project from the upper part, which shows the Madonna and Child. Although there are several studies for the Virgin and Child, there are no surviving drawings that study the relationship between the two of them and the scene of martyrdom below. In the painting, only the Christ child looks down with curiosity at the scene beneath him; the Madonna looks out at the viewer.[7] A study for the Madonna's drapery (fig. E) must have been made very late in the preparatory process. Such drawings of drapery are not widely found and seem not to have been scattered; the largest group is now at Stuttgart.[8]

The Martyrdom of Saints John and Paul with the Madonna and Child Above was made as a lateral panel for the Girolda Fiordibelli chapel in the Cathedral of Reggio Emilia. Although the commission followed the successful completion of the main altarpiece for the chapel in 1626 (for which see cat. no. 11), the two laterals (the other was *The Visitation*) were not delivered until the early summer of 1632.[9] □

NOTES

5 Mahon Collection, on loan to the Ashmolean Museum, M&E 23; Mahon and Ekserdjian 1986, 14, no. 23. A lost drawing known through an engraving by William Hebert, discussed by Turner and Plazzotta 1991, 115, seems to belong to the same stage of the process as the Mahon sheet.

6 New York, Morgan Library, inv. I, 101h verso (Stone 1991, 58–64, no. 24). At this stage in the sequence, Guercino also created a drawing, now lost, engraved by Bartolozzi (discussed by Turner and Plazzotta 1991, 115). A drawing in the British Museum, London, inv. 1943-11-13-20 (Turner and Plazzotta 1991, 245, no. 18, ill.), showing just the upper body of the kneeling saint, was made at a late stage to decide the position of the drapery, hands, and the fall of light. It is noticeably Leonardesque.

7 For analyses of the studies of the Virgin and Child in this painting, see Mahon and Turner 1989, 36–39; Turner and Plazzotta 1991, 112; Stone 1991, 58–64; and van Tuyll 1991, 76.

8 See Mahon *Disegni* 1969, 14; Turner and Plazzotta 1991, 244–45.

9 Artioli-Monducci 1982, 97f.; Salerno 1988, no. 113; best summarized by Mahon and Turner 1989, 37–38.

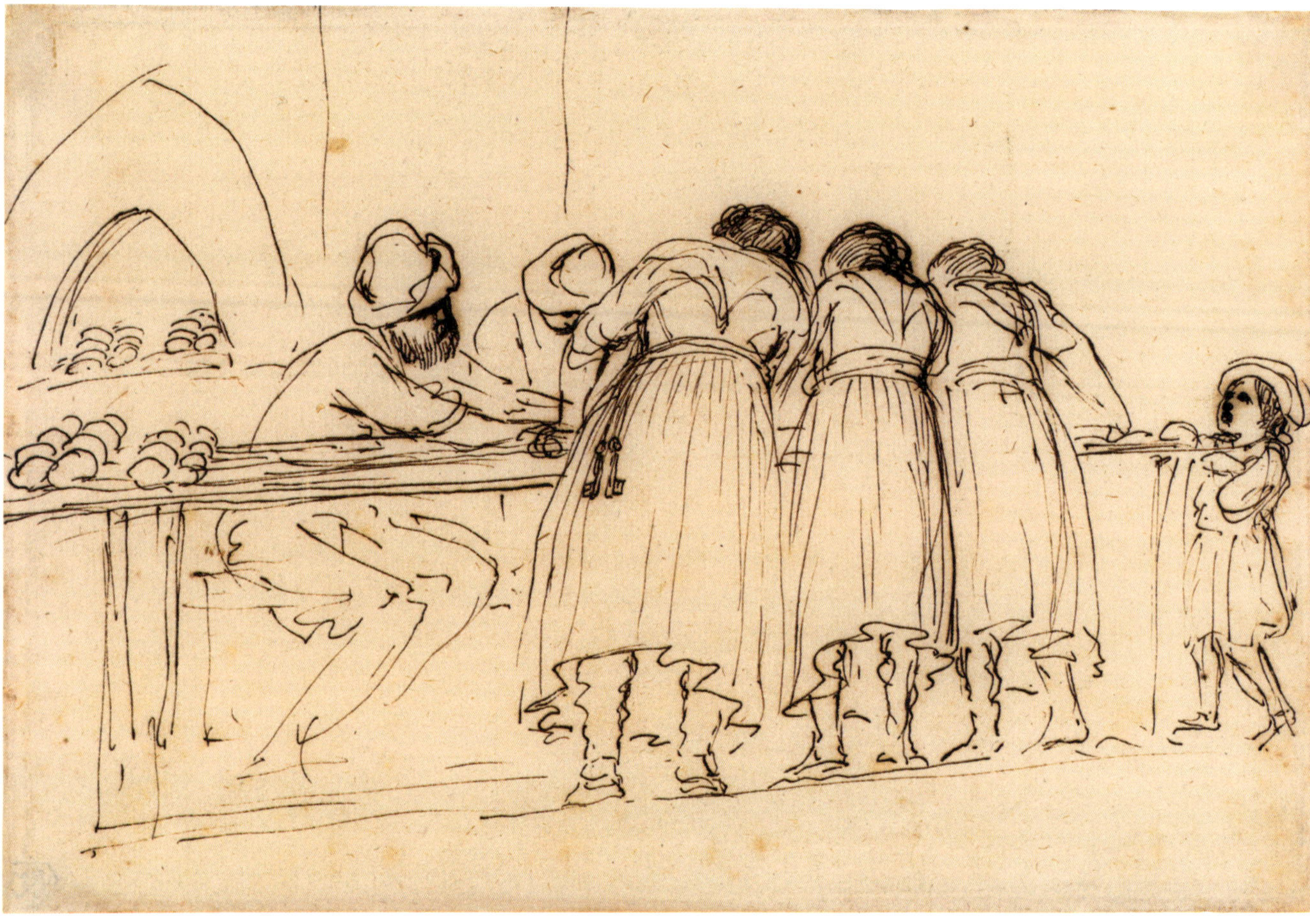

17.
INTERIOR OF A BAKER'S SHOP

ca. 1630–35
Pen and brown ink
17.7 × 26.5 cm (7 × 10$^{3}/_{8}$ in.)
London, Courtauld Institute of Art Gallery, D.1952.RW.1342

PROVENANCE Casa Gennari / Bouverie family / Sir Robert Witt, L.2228B, *verso* (see p. 16).

EXHIBITIONS Windsor 1950, no number; London 1953, no. 141; Bologna 1968, no. 215; London 1977, no. 47; London 1991, no. 190.

BIBLIOGRAPHY RA 1953, 40; Blunt 1956, 75; Mahon *Disegni* 1969, 201, 205, 206, 207, 208; Hammer et al. 1977, 21; Turner and Plazzotta 1991, 31n92, 32n108, 205, 210–12, 222, 276, fig. 190.

HERE GUERCINO PRESENTS—with typical detached amusement—the interior of a baker's shop. Rows of *panini* in the oven echo the ones waiting at the end of the long table. Another batch of bread is being prepared by a group of three women facing away from the artist (and viewer), the weight held in the top of their backs evident as they knead the dough. The three wear similar clothes, with long dresses tied at the waist, and the exaggeratedly low vantage point from which they are seen gives a view of their disheveled stockings. At the far end of the table, a small boy in a hat struggles to be seen, hoping a *panino* might come in his direction.

The drawing exemplifies Guercino's use of minimal lines to suggest a scene; could one possibly draw a wall with an oven containing multiple *panini* in fewer lines? Yet while there is very little suggestion of the setting of the shop or the background, the scene is given credibility by an emphasis on a few details, such as the keys hanging from the waist of the most prominent woman, the dense beard of the man on the left (presumably the baker), and the expectant expression on the boy's face. The eye registers these details and understands the scene through them, subconsciously filling in the blanks, such as the legs of the man sitting at the table. □

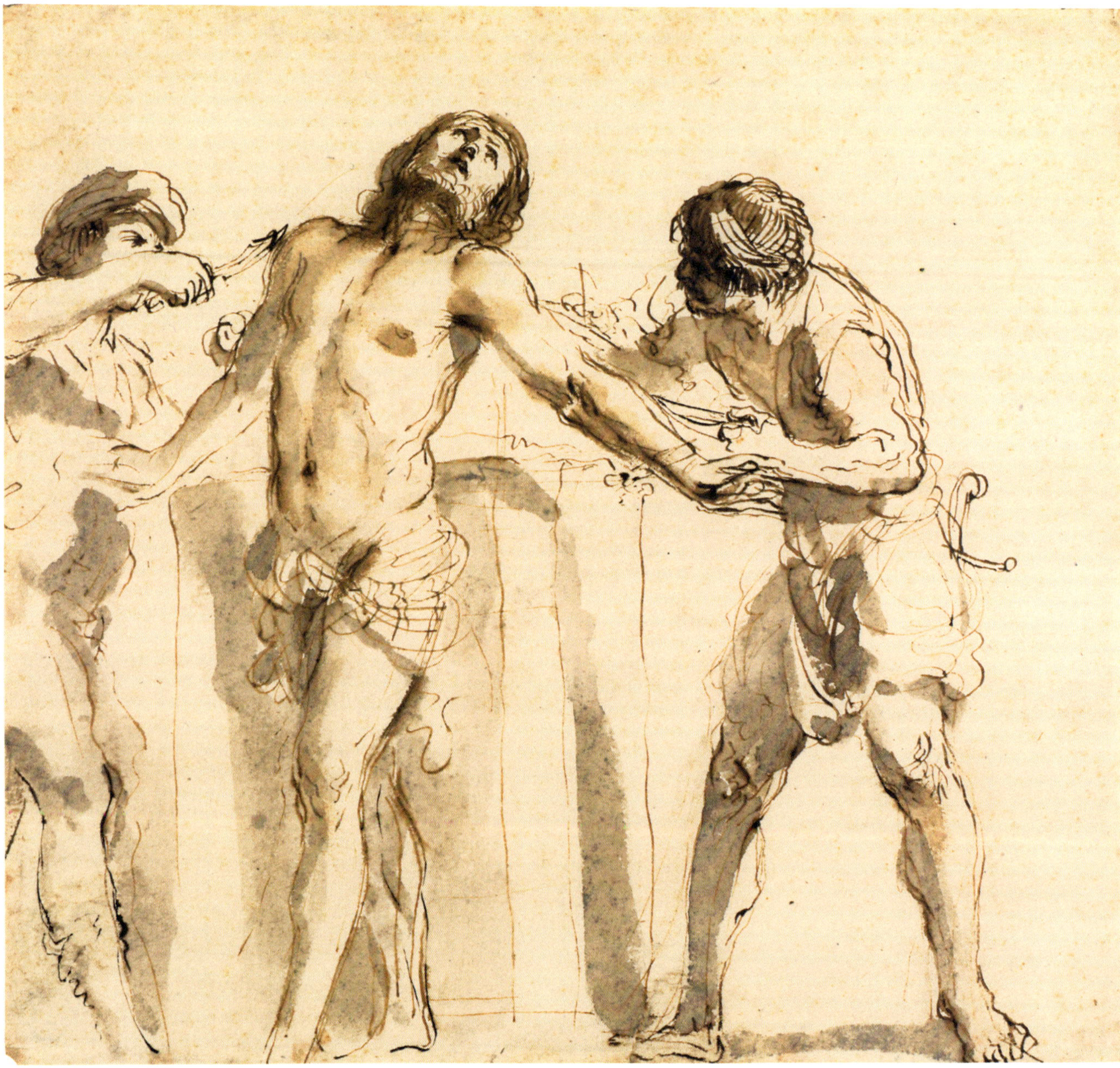

18.
THE MARTYRDOM OF SAINT BARTHOLOMEW

1635
Pen and brown ink, brush with brown and gray washes
23.4 × 25.6 cm (9¼ × 10⅛ in.)
London, Courtauld Institute of Art Gallery, D.1952.RW.1337

PROVENANCE Casa Gennari / Bouverie family / Sir Robert Witt, L.2228B, *verso* (see p. 16).

EXHIBITIONS London 1977, no. 25; Bologna 1991, no. 91; London 1991, no. 111.

BIBLIOGRAPHY Blunt 1956, 75; Hammer et al. 1977, 15; Stone 1991, 82; Mahon 1991, 29; Turner and Plazzotta 1991, 31n92, 32n108, 117, 136–38, 231, fig. 111.

SAINT BARTHOLOMEW was martyred by being flayed—having his skin stripped from his body—alive. In a series of preparatory drawings for an altarpiece in the church of San Martino in Siena, Guercino has, with great inventiveness, explored a variety of alternatives for the saint's pose, his relationship to his executioners, and the nature of the support to which he is attached. As David Stone has observed, the sequence of drawings for the altarpiece illustrates well the artist's process: he moved not in a linear progression in his drawings—from more-general to more-specific studies—but rather looked "close-up" at particular parts of the composition and let this dictate the entire design.[1]

Knowing that his commission for the altarpiece specified that it should include six full figures, the artist apparently first made a rough stab at the composition in which he positioned Saint Bartholomew in the center, an executioner at each side, and a group of spectators in the background, all in a classical architectural setting (fig. 18.1).[2] In the next drawing in the series (fig. 18.2), Guercino focused on the central group, and the saint stands with one knee on the gallows.[3] The executioner on the right concentrates on his grisly task with his back to the viewer, while the one on the left faces forward, his body partially obscured by the gallows. As in figure 18.1, a small crowd in the background's right side watches the gruesome scene.

Evidently unsatisfied with the way one executioner has his back turned, and seeking a greater vertical emphasis and rhythm across the figures, the artist rechoreographed his characters. In catalogue number 18 and in a drawing at Princeton University Art Museum, Guercino makes the executioner at left more prominent. He places the executioner on the right slightly behind the saint, and he has both executioners facing the saint (and each other).[4] As he worked on *The Martyrdom of Saint Bartholomew* drawings, Guercino apparently paid little attention to how the saint would be restrained, but in catalogue number 18 he placed a binding around the saint's left wrist and linked it to the block. In this sheet, he also dealt particularly with the positions of the executioners' right legs—attested to by pentimenti—as if he were working out how much the force of the flaying action would cause the weight of their bodies to shift. At about this stage in the sequence,

NOTES

1 Stone 1991, 82.

2 New York, Morgan Library, inv. I, 101e (Stone 1991, 83).

3 London, British Museum, inv. 1989-6-17-278 (Turner and Plazzotta 1991, 136, pl. 17).

4 Princeton University Art Museum, bequest of Dan Fellows Platt, inv. 48-734 (Stone 1991, 82–84, no. 32). The Princeton drawing adds action to the background by incorporating a soldier restraining a restless crowd.

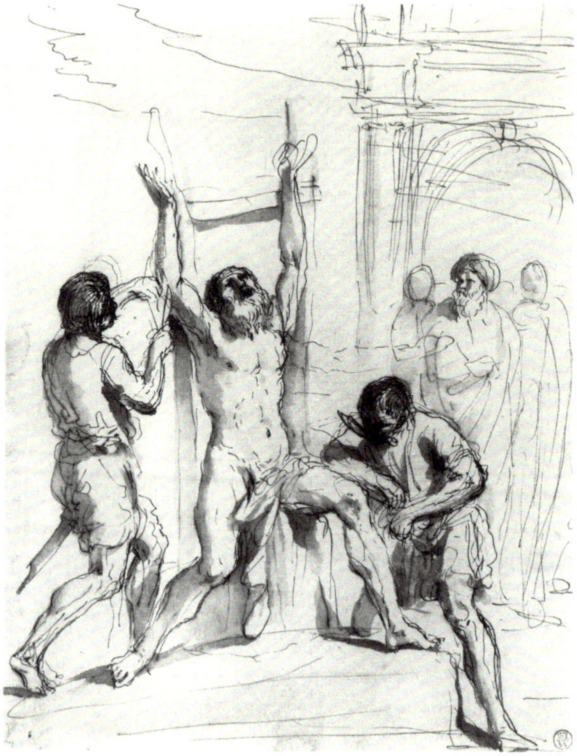

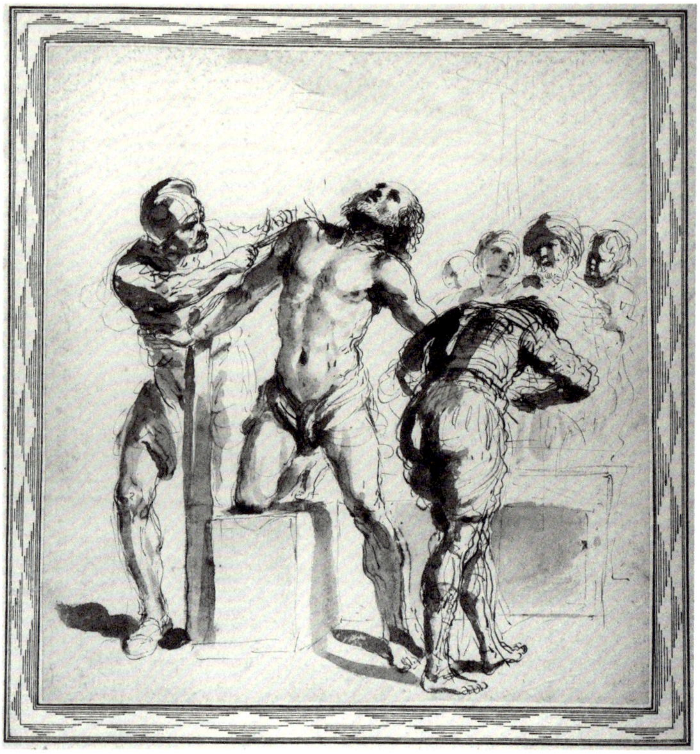

FIGURE 18.1
Guercino. *The Martyrdom of Saint Bartholomew*, 1635.
Pen and brown ink, brush with brown wash, 24.7 × 19.3 cm (9 11/16 × 7 9/16 in.). New York, Morgan Library, I, 101e

FIGURE 18.2
Guercino. *The Martyrdom of Saint Bartholomew*, 1635.
Pen and brown ink, brush with brown wash, 24.9 × 23.6 cm (9 3/4 × 9 1/4 in.). London, British Museum, 1989-6-17-278

Guercino must have made several "close-up" studies of the relationship between the saint and executioner on the right; in one of these (fig. 18.3), he contrasts the executioner's intense concentration on causing harm with Bartholomew's steadfast resignation to his fate.[5]

The commission was one of those for which Guercino was most highly paid in the 1630s, and he received payment in several installments between January 1635 and December 1636. Further, a copy of the painting was made by Giacinto Campana (and apparently retouched by Guercino himself). Malvasia's prediction that this would one day be used as the "original" is somewhat true: the canvas in the church is a wreck, and most authors reproduce the copy instead (fig. 18.4).[6]

Despite the saint's range of active poses in the preparatory drawings—in many, he is struggling vigorously against the executioners—the final painting shows him in a passive pose with closely crossed legs (fig. 18.4). While to modern eyes the saint appears improbably nonchalant given his situation, Guercino presumably intended to convey Bartholomew's supreme faith. This treatment of the subject, which probably derived partly from Guercino's "close-up" studies for the commission, also reflects the artist's understanding that the altarpiece was destined for a church setting. Likewise, several of the drawings are more explicitly gory than the final painted rendition. For example, in catalogue number 18 the executioner on the right pulls down the skin he is cutting from the top of the saint's arm. Although the executioner holds his knife in his right hand, Guercino, with a single quick line, toys with the possibility of having him wield it more vertically, like a pen, for more precision. In the altarpiece, the executioner holds the knife in

NOTES

5 The Art Institute of Chicago, inv. 1960.832; another is in a U.S. private collection (formerly Korda Collection); Stone 1991, nos. 33–34.

6 Salerno 1988, 247; Stone 1991, 82.

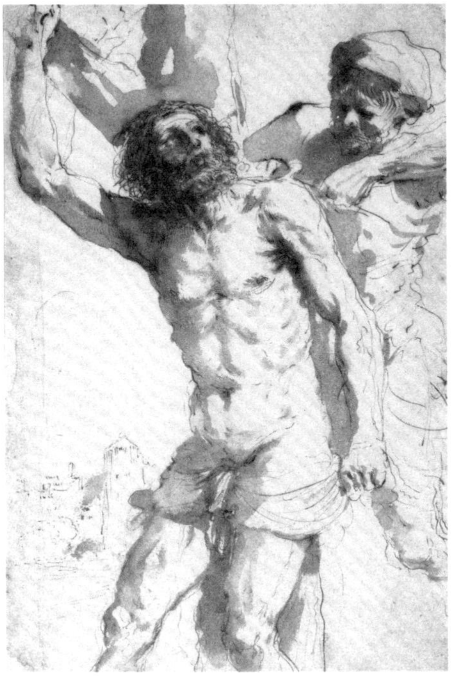

FIGURE 18.3
Guercino. *The Martyrdom of Saint Bartholomew*, 1635.
Pen and brown ink, brush with brown wash, 29.6 × 20.4 cm (11⅝ × 8 in.). The Art Institute of Chicago, Gift of Marie Louise Pritchard, 1960.832

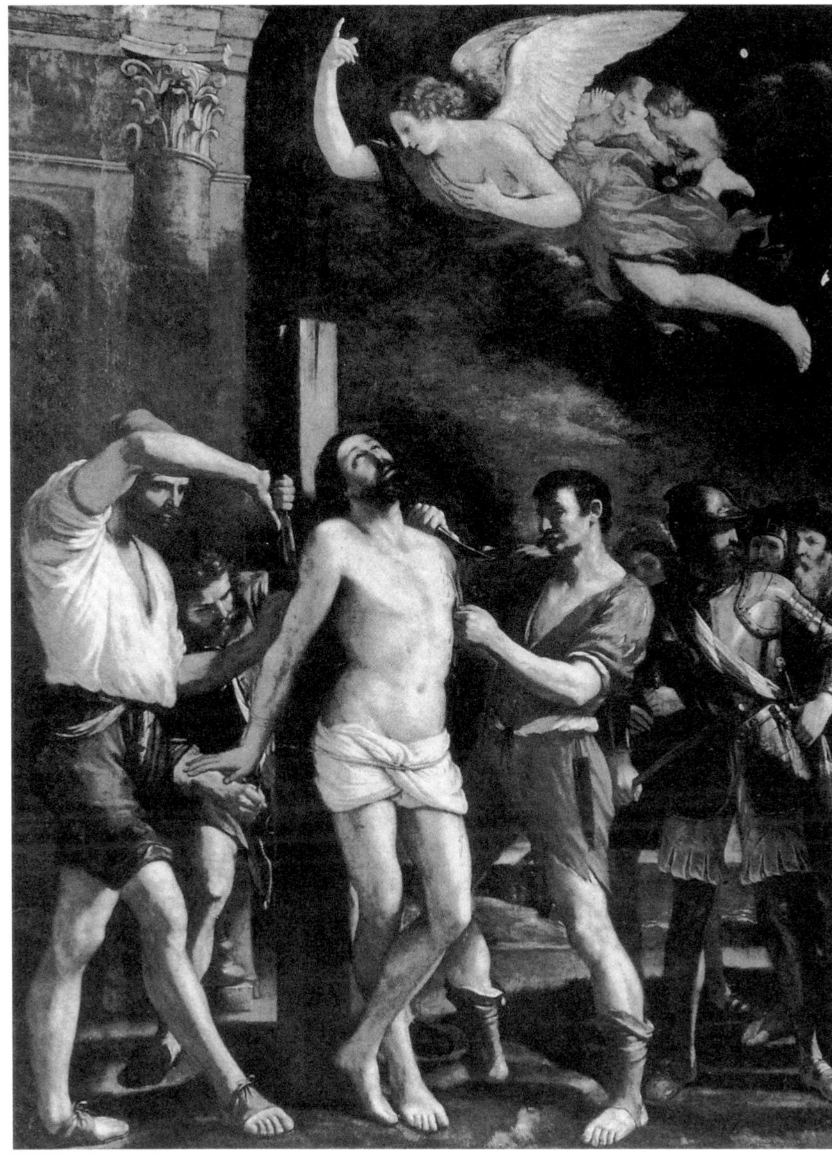

FIGURE 18.4
Giacinto Campana (Italian, ca. 1600–1650) (after Guercino). *The Martyrdom of Saint Bartholomew*, 1635. Oil on canvas. Marino Laziale, church of San Barnaba

the more traditional horizontal pose, and Guercino refrains from showing skin pulled away from flesh.

A sheet in red chalk of a seated, struggling saint has been convincingly identified by David Stone as a figure study for Saint Bartholomew made during an early stage of the process, and it fits well with a dating in the 1630s.[7] Another drawing of a bearded saint in pen and ink has been tentatively related by Nicholas Turner and Carol Plazzotta to the Saint Bartholomew altarpiece, but it represents an older man than the one featured in the drawings studied here. It seems sensible to revert to an earlier idea that it relates to a project for a Saint Jerome.[8] □

NOTES

7 Stone 1991, 83. The sheet is not similar enough to Guercino's early figure studies to relate to comparable figures in *The Martyrdom of Saint Peter* or *Raising of Lazarus* of ca. 1619 (Salerno 1988, 129, 133, nos. 152, 156).

8 Turner and Plazzotta 1991, 254–55, no. 34.

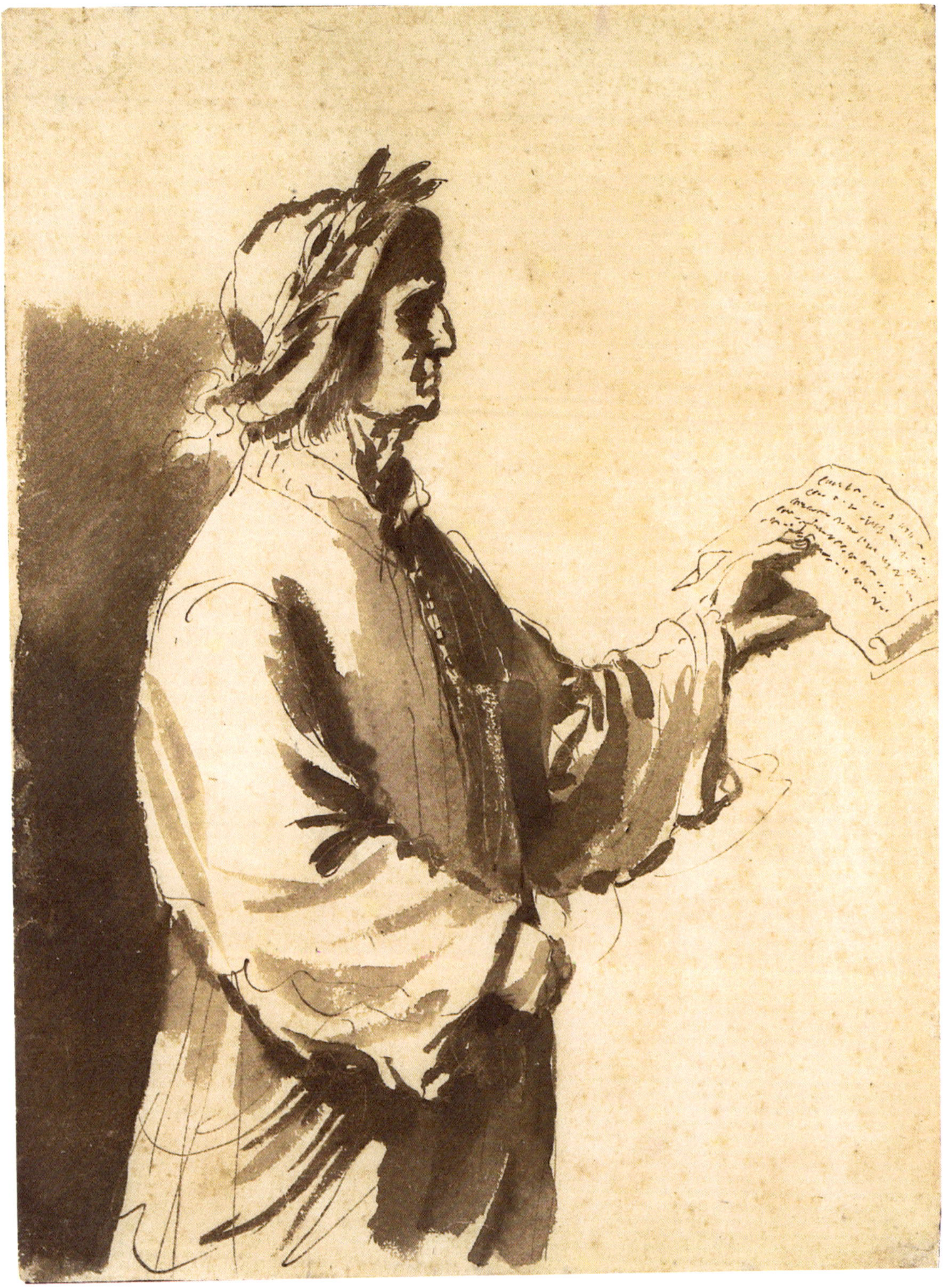

19.
DANTE STANDING IN PROFILE TO THE RIGHT

ca. 1635
Pen and brown ink, brush with brown wash
27.5 × 20.5 cm (10⅞ × 8⅛ in.)
Los Angeles, Collection of Gifford Combs

PROVENANCE Sotheby's, New York, January 28, 1998, lot 132; Christie's, London, July 6, 2004, lot 46.

EXHIBITIONS Not previously exhibited.

BIBLIOGRAPHY Unpublished.

THIS STANDING FIGURE holding up a poem in his left hand probably represents the Florentine poet Dante Aligheri (1265–1321). Although Guercino does not show him with the prominent nose and chin found in many representations, the profile view, robes, and laurel wreath echo Raphael's famous depiction of the poet in his fresco of the Parnassus (Vatican, Stanza della Segnatura). The drawing is a classic example of Guercino's use of wash with the point of the brush: several different shades are subtly employed to mimic the flowing folds of the poet's robes, to set the figure in a three-dimensional space, and to bathe the scene in strong sunlight. While brown wash defines the scene, many traces of the penwork that Guercino used to quickly map out the composition still remain.

The poet is shown in a profile view, a classical format revived in the Renaissance and rich in historic association. The drawing does not relate to any painted composition or subject by Guercino now known to us, and this makes it difficult to guess its purpose. The broad use of wash makes it likely that the drawing dates from the 1630s, and it can be compared to a number of drawings from that period, including *Joseph with the Flowering Staff* at Princeton, and drawings relating to the canvas of Sisyphus (see cat. no. 23).[1] □

NOTES

1 Princeton University Art Museum, inv. 49–40 (Stone 1991, 94–95, no. 39). The *Standing Man in Profile* in the Seattle Art Museum is also similar (Stone 1991, 221, no. 158, pl. D158).

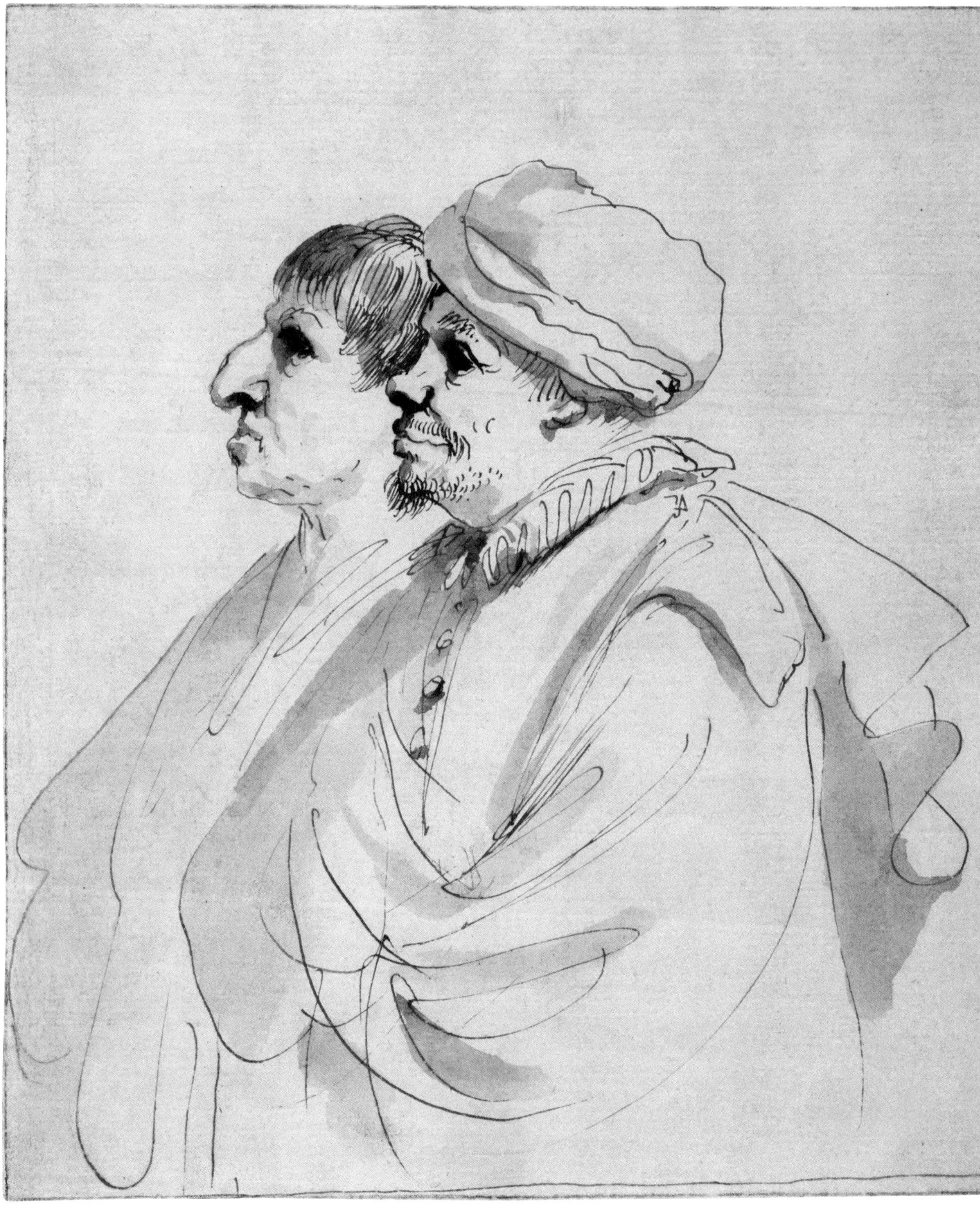

20.
CARICATURE OF TWO MEN SEEN IN PROFILE

ca. 1635
Pen and brown ink, brush with brown wash
20.4 × 17.3 cm (8 1/16 × 6 13/16 in.)
Los Angeles, J. Paul Getty Museum, 94.GA.75

PROVENANCE Private collection, Germany; art market, Hamburg, 1990; art market, London.

EXHIBITIONS Los Angeles 1998, no number; Los Angeles 2002, no number; Los Angeles 2003, no number.

BIBLIOGRAPHY Turner 2001, 60–61, no. 21, ill.

WHILE A PROFILE VIEW was normally chosen for its historic associations and to convey nobility, as in Guercino's depiction of Dante (see cat. no. 19), here the artist subverts the format to lampoon his subjects. Instead of evoking the dignified, "classical" portraits of the sitters, the view here accentuates the very different shapes of each character's nose and chin. Guercino no doubt was aware of Leonardo da Vinci's famous profile caricatures; like Leonardo, Guercino was an avid observer of human temperament and physiognomy, and he produced numerous caricatures.[1]

Here, Guercino started with the foreground figure, swiftly drawing ink lines that emphasize the man's abundant robes, thin moustache, and wispy beard. He gave the second figure—who seems more of an ecclesiastical type—a protruding lower lip and a large nose; its convex outline contrasts with the "ski-jump" nose of his companion. Guercino seems to have placed his caricatures in pairs on the sheet when this would provide a subtle emphasis of the exaggerated forms.[2] Many of Guercino's other sheets of caricatures show only single figures.

In the case of catalogue number 20, a line drawn by the artist freehand along the lower edge suggests that he "framed" his composition with ink lines on the page, as one would a finished work. This reflects the fact that Guercino seems to have made his caricatures as independent works of art, which he would keep in albums for his own delight and that of his friends. In fact, the 1719 inventory of Guercino drawings in the house of his heirs lists an album of 298 sheets "raprasentanti tutti delle Caricature diverse."[3]

A free copy of catalogue number 20 exists in the Metropolitan Museum of Art, New York. Apparently made by an anonymous seventeenth-century draftsman and with a more heavily applied wash, it reproduces the drawing faithfully, with a few small differences (for example, the copyist has added whiskers to the chin of the man on the left).[4] □

NOTES

1 The 1719 inventory of the Casa Gennari lists a notebook of 24 sheets with studies said to be by Leonardo; the subjects are not given (Mahon and Turner 1989, xx). Guercino also owned a copy of Leonardo's *Trattato della Pittura*; see Gozzi in Adam et al. 2005, 38–47.

2 Other examples are cited by Nicholas Turner in Turner 2001, 60, including Windsor Castle, Royal Library, inv. RL 2748 (M&T 321; Mahon and Turner 1989, 119, no. 321, pl. 288).

3 Mahon and Turner 1989, xxi.

4 Not noted in the literature; inv. 80-3-453; pen and brown ink, brush with brown wash, over traces of black chalk, on cream paper, 21.4 × 17.3 cm; Gift of Cornelius Vanderbilt, 1880.

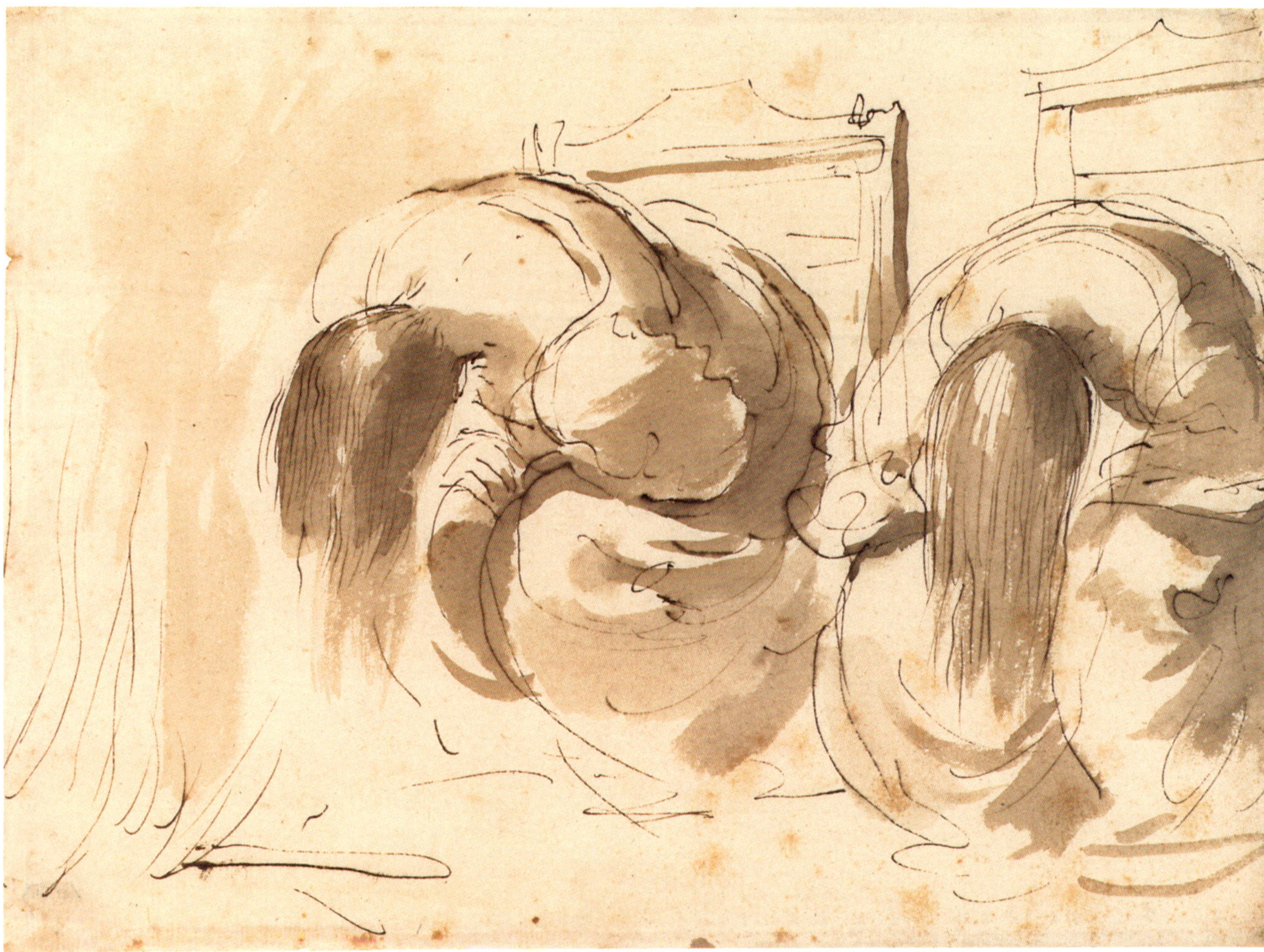

21.

TWO SEATED WOMEN DRYING THEIR HAIR IN FRONT OF A FIRE

ca. 1635
Pen and brown ink, brush with brown wash
18.9 × 26.6 cm (7⁷⁄₁₆ × 10½ in.)
London, Courtauld Institute of Art Gallery, D.1952.RW.1359

PROVENANCE Casa Gennari / Bouverie family / Sir Robert Witt, L.2228B, *verso* (see p. 16).

EXHIBITIONS Auckland 1960, no. 35; Bologna 1968, no. 217; London 1971, no. 15; Wellington 1973, no. 34; London 1977, no. 48; London 1991, no. 191; London 1991a, no. 42; Sydney 1999, no. 174.

BIBLIOGRAPHY Blunt 1956, 76; Troutman 1960, 15; Mahon *Disegni* 1969, 201, 205, 208; Courtauld 1971, 4; Troutman 1973, 20; Hammer et al. 1977, 21; Bradford and Braham 1991, 41, 182, ill.; Turner and Plazzotta 1991, 31n92, 32n108, 205, 212, fig. 191; Maloon and Raissis 1999, 182, 226, 239.

THIS SCENE IS SO UNUSUAL as to be difficult to "read" at first glance. Two women sit on chairs, leaning forward to expose their wet hair to a drying fire. It is an extreme example of Guercino's acute observation of everyday life and of his willingness to record it as an exercise in draftsmanship. Most of all, the drawing is a testament to the squint-eyed artist's extraordinary ability to convey texture using ink lines and wash. In particular, the roundness of the women's scalps and the softness and density of their falling, sodden hair are spectacularly drawn. In fact, Guercino applied the wash in those areas so thickly that it soaked through the sheet of paper to the other side. In contrast, the drying ends of the women's tresses consist of strokes of the brush "starved" of wash. The artist used arching lines and expansive brown wash to show the voluminous drapery of the figures' skirts and a series of short strokes to represent one hand of the woman on the left.

The two chair backs and thin wash at left provide the only clues of setting, and the fire is simply conveyed by a few scratchy quill-pen lines that curl back on themselves. A drawing identified by Sir Denis Mahon in the collection of Signora Valentina Latini at Jesi shows the same scene, with one woman sitting slightly behind the other; this makes it unlikely that catalogue number 21 represents two studies of the same woman.[1] Yet, William Bradford has insisted that this is the case, citing the overlapping of the foreground forms by those of the background and the fact that the figure on the right does not angle her head toward the fire's warmth.[2] However, the setting of the two figures seems entirely convincing, and the placement of the fire is clearly only schematic. Furthermore, two different shapes of upper chair back are also apparent.

In 1969, Mahon dated the drawing to before 1621, when Guercino departed for Rome, but Nicholas Turner and Carol Plazzotta suggest a more likely date in the 1630s.[3] □

NOTES

1 Mahon *Disegni* 1969, 206.

2 Bradford in Bradford and Braham 1991, 90.

3 Turner and Plazzotta 1991, 212.

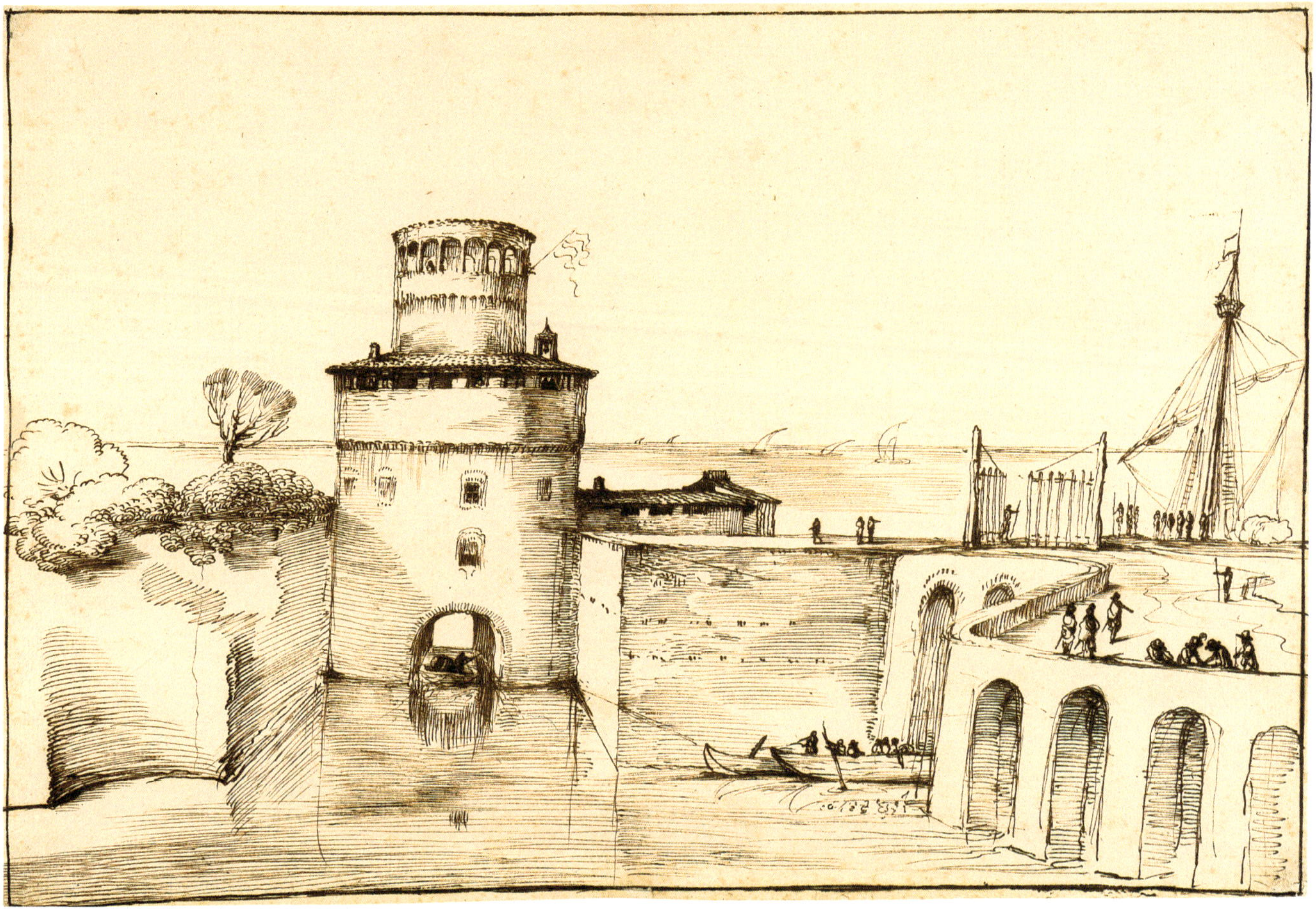

22.

LANDSCAPE WITH A VIEW OF A FORTIFIED PORT

ca. 1635
Pen and brown ink
29 × 43.2 cm (11⁷⁄₁₆ × 17 in.)
Los Angeles, J. Paul Getty Museum, 85.GA.408

PROVENANCE Art market, Amsterdam; sale, Sotheby's, London, March 23, 1972, lot 121; art market, New York.

EXHIBITIONS Cambridge 1991, no. 70; Bologna 1991, no. 176; Los Angeles 1998, no number; Los Angeles 1998a, no number.

BIBLIOGRAPHY Bagni 1985, 36, no. 18; Getty 1986, 236, no. 175; Goldner, Hendrix, and Williams 1988, 54, no. 17; Griswold 1991, 643; Mahon 1991, 46; Stone 1991, xxi, 162–63, 213, fig. 70.

THE PALPABLE SENSE OF LIGHT and space in this airy landscape impresses the viewer immediately. Large areas of blank paper evoke a scene in bright sunlight, while careful ranks of pen hatching create the numerous types and shapes of surface with uncanny sensitivity. A round tower dominates the scene, surrounded by other coastal fortifications, and with a view out to sea beyond. Yet on close examination, the sense that this is an actual place yields slowly to the realization that it is a creation of the artist's imagination. Faint pentimenti reveal that Guercino considered various placements for his buildings, choreographing them like the characters in his figure compositions. For example, a long diagonal line to the right of the tower's base at the waterline and a parallel line near the top of the wall indicate that he considered extending the blocklike wall in the center of the composition further into the foreground. On the right, a barely visible dotted line follows the top of the curving, S-shaped wall but then deviates at the apex to delineate an alternative configuration. It becomes apparent that the horizon has been deliberately aligned with the architectural molding on the tower and that the figures have been carefully placed.

Guercino made many landscape drawings, yet none are preparatory to the country scenes that he occasionally used as backgrounds in his paintings. Making drawings of landscapes seems to have been principally a pleasurable activity for him, and he was no doubt proud to show large and impressive sheets like this one to his friends and acquaintances.[1] On many of the landscapes, including this one, Guercino made carefully lined borders that preserve the extent of the blank sky. Clearly, his drawings were informed by a close observation of nature, but only a small number of his many landscapes are known to have been drawn on the spot or to represent local landmarks.[2]

It is striking that Guercino, who applied wash so adeptly to create effects of light and space, used only pen for most of his landscape drawings. A single sheet, at Windsor Castle, is made with brush and wash as well as pen, and the attributions of a small group of landscapes are not universally accepted.[3] Perhaps the artist intended for his landscape drawings to be engraved at some stage, and his nephews' later efforts in that direction (see pp. 5–6) were a natural conclusion of this thought. □

NOTES

1 The 1719 inventory of the Casa Gennari (see p. 16) lists a large album with 92 landscapes and a small one containing 69; Mahon and Turner 1989, xxi.

2 For an overview of Guercino's activity in this area and the influences on him, see Mahon and Turner 1989, 101–3. For a discussion of the large number of eighteenth-century forgeries of Guercino's landscape drawings (a testament to their popularity), see Bagni 1985.

3 Windsor Castle, Royal Library, inv. RL 2765 (M&T 263; Mahon and Turner 1989, 109, no. 263, pl. 246). For examples of the small group of dramatic wash landscapes (in the manner of Claude Lorrain), see Stone 1991, 168–71, nos. 73 and 74.

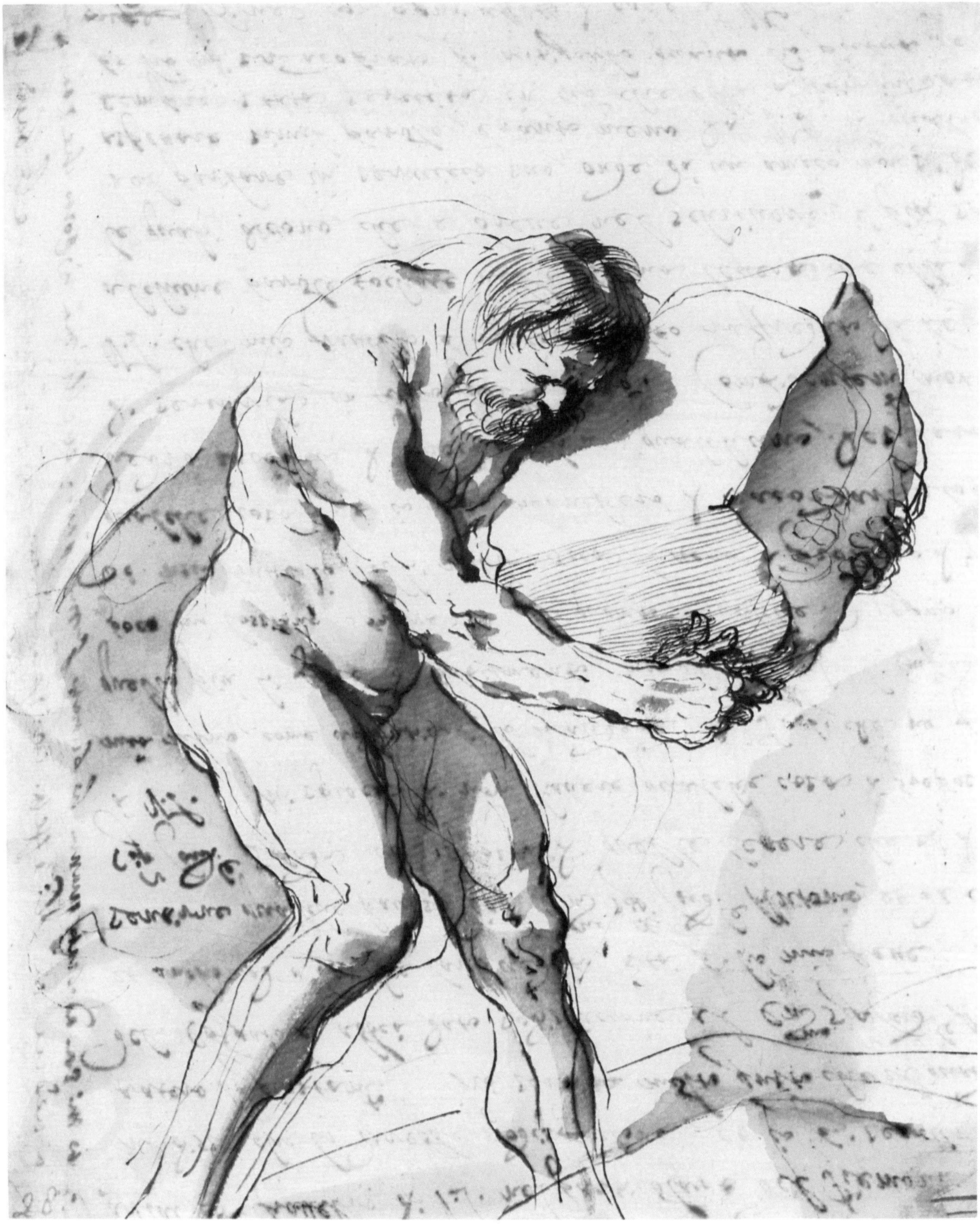

23.
SISYPHUS

1636
Pen and brown ink, brush with brown wash
23.2 × 19.2 cm (9⅛ × 7½ in.)
Numbered in graphite at lower left: *28*
London, Courtauld Institute of Art Gallery, D.1952.RW.1366

PROVENANCE Casa Gennari / Bouverie family / Sir Robert Witt, L.2228B, *verso* (see p. 16).

EXHIBITIONS London 1977, no. 33; Bologna 1991, no. 86; London 1991, no. 107.

BIBLIOGRAPHY Blunt 1956, 76; Hammer et al. 1977, 17; Mahon and Turner 1989, 49; Stone 1991, 92; Mahon 1991, 28; Turner and Plazzotta 1991, 18, 19, 31n92, 32n108, 43, 134–35, fig. 107.

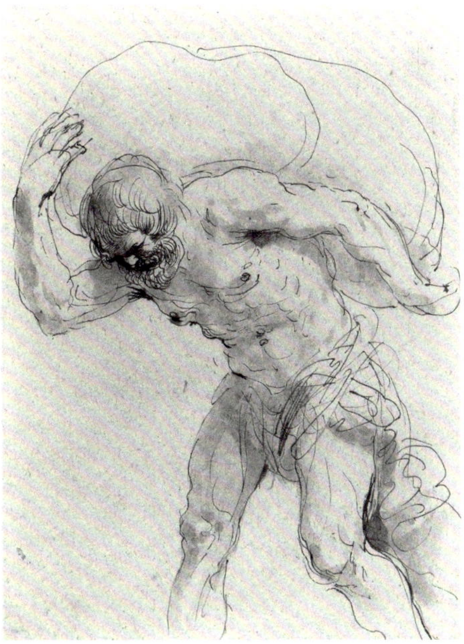

FIGURE 23.1
Guercino. *Sisyphus*, ca. 1636. Pen and brown ink, brush with light gray wash, 26.6 × 19.8 cm (10½ × 7¾ in.). Windsor Castle, Royal Library, RL 2882

ACCORDING TO GREEK MYTHOLOGY, Sisyphus was the founder of Corinth. Although cunning, he was also deceitful and double-dealing. When he reached the Underworld, he was condemned to push a boulder perpetually to the top of a hill; each time the stone reached the summit, it would roll down again. In *Sisyphus*, the former king struggles with the weight of a block of stone held precariously in front of him. Pentimenti show that the artist toyed with the idea of Sisyphus supporting the rock on his left knee: abandoned lines show his left knee raised and his left hand closer to his body. Different strengths of wash are used effectively to create a variety of shadows.

As can clearly be seen, *Sisyphus* has been drawn on the back of a draft of a letter turned upside down. This is unusual for the artist, who almost always seemed to have a supply of clean paper at hand. The letter was written by Guercino's brother, Paolo Antonio Barbieri, about a canvas painted by the artist in 1636, *Abigail Appeasing the Wrath of David*.[1] This fact provides additional evidence for the suggestion that catalogue number 23 was made as a study for a painting of Sisyphus commissioned by Conte Girolamo Ranuzzi of Bologna, and delivered by Guercino in 1636; the painting does not survive today.

In a number of studies, Guercino explored a range of ideas for how Sisyphus was to move the boulder up the hill.[2] They are particularly intriguing because we do not know which solution Guercino finally adopted. Catalogue number 23 is the only drawing in the series where Sisyphus carries his burden in front of him. Three drawings, including figure 23.1, show him carrying the boulder on his back. Notably, in figure 23.1 Guercino altered the position of the load, making it look like Sisyphus is carrying two stones. Three other drawings record compositional solutions with Sisyphus pushing the rock uphill rather than carrying it, including an interesting double-sided sheet in the Teylers Museum, the only one drawn in black chalk.[3] It is unique in featuring youthful characters in the role of Sisyphus and—as van Tuyll has suggested—probably records early ideas for the composition; it may even have been drawn quickly from life.

Guercino seems to have reused some of his ideas in these drawings when, ten years later, he dealt with the subject of Atlas struggling under the weight of the world.[4] □

NOTES

1 Mahon and Turner 1989, 49.

2 Discussed in Mahon and Turner 1989, 49; Turner and Plazzotta 1991, 134–35; Stone 1991, 92.

3 Haarlem, Teylers Museum, inv. H.29 (van Tuyll 1991, 102–3, no. 37).

4 For example, compare Sisyphus in the drawing sold Christie's, London (Stone 1991, 92, fig. 38a), and Atlas in Windsor Castle, Royal Library, inv. RL 2815 (Mahon and Turner 1989, 67, no. 118, pl. 123).

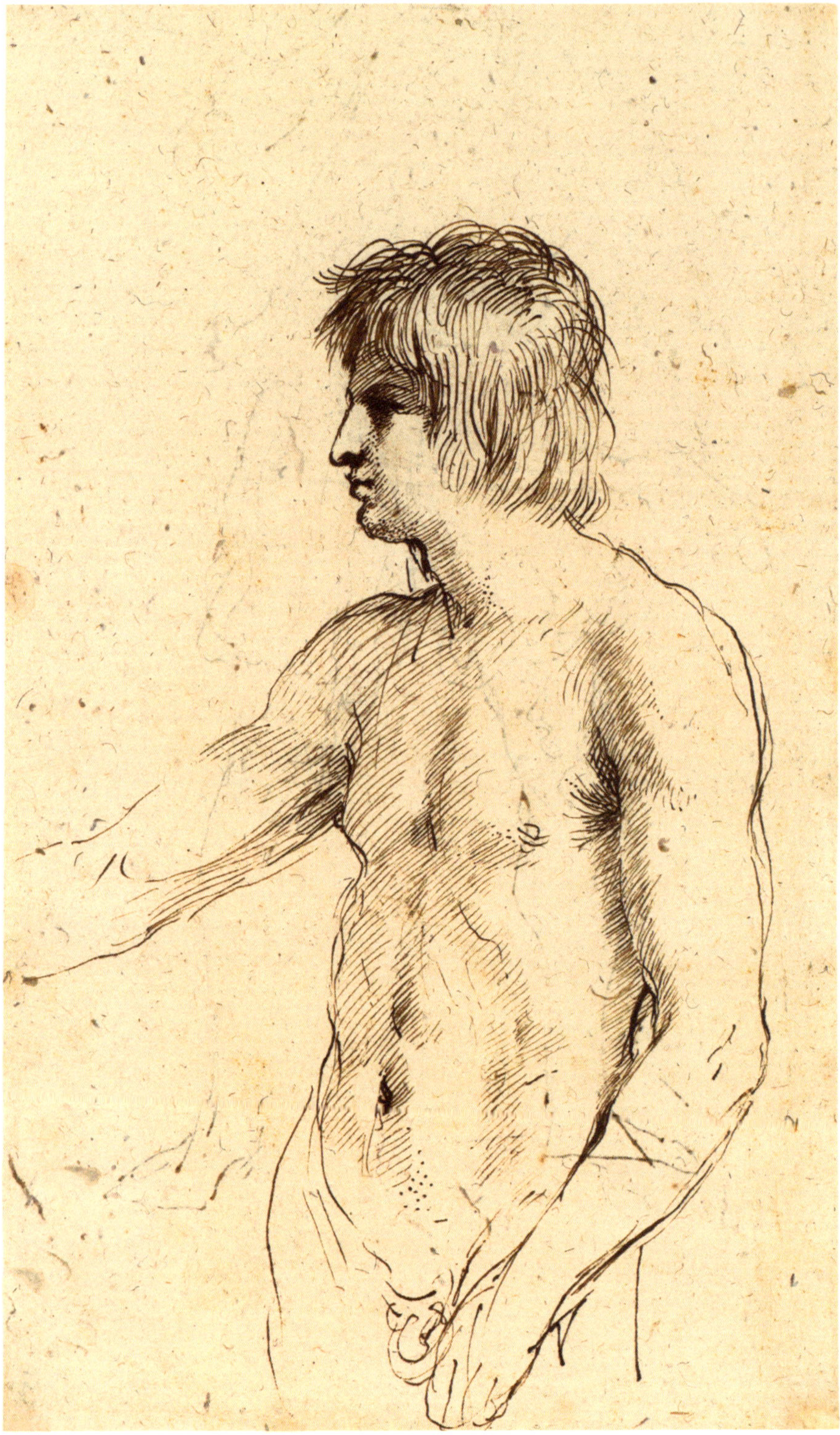

Recto

24.

STUDY OF A STANDING NUDE MAN, THREE-QUARTER LENGTH, IN PROFILE TO THE LEFT (RECTO) TRUNCATED STUDY OF A STANDING FIGURE (VERSO)

ca. 1637
Pen and brown ink
29 × 17.5 cm ($11^{3}/_{8}$ × $6^{7}/_{8}$ in.)
London, Courtauld Institute of Art Gallery, D.1952.RW.1364

PROVENANCE Casa Gennari / Bouverie family / Sir Robert Witt, L.2228B, *verso* (see p. 16).

EXHIBITIONS Not previously exhibited.

BIBLIOGRAPHY Blunt 1956, 76.

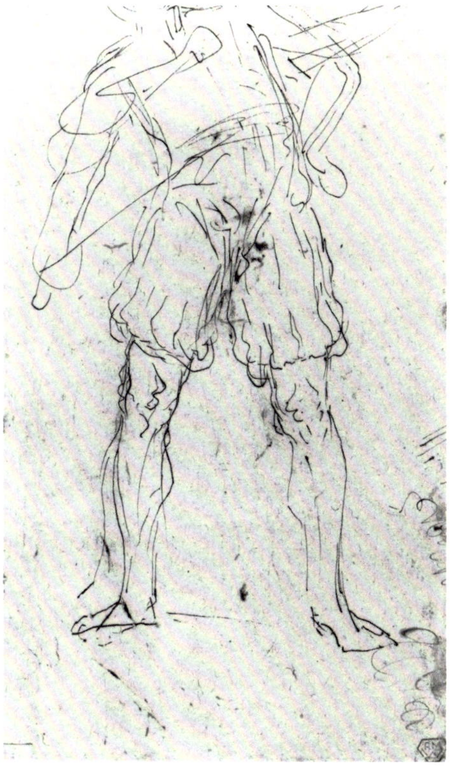

Verso

DRAWN ON COARSE PAPER, this brief study shows a nude man in profile, reaching out with his right arm. Guercino has taken care to characterize the figure, and most of the focus is on the face and hair. The rounding and profile of the head are well captured, and numerous dots populate an unshaven chin. Sequences of lines of different lengths give a curling sense of space and spikiness to the man's hair; tidy parallel lines form the shadow on his forehead. The torso is represented schematically, and sections of its outline have been gone over several times. A pentimento on the front of the man's neck reveals that Guercino initially thought about placing it lower.

Although the figure is of a fairly generic type, the drawing may be an early study for the executioner who gives Salome the head of Saint John the Baptist in a painting of 1637 in Rennes.[1] That figure is in a broadly similar pose and naked to the waist, although seen from the back. A dating in the late 1630s would certainly fit with the drawing.

On the verso of the sheet, Guercino quickly sketched a man in breeches. A pentimento for the right arm explores the possibility of positioning it down at the figure's side or up to his neck; likewise, the left arm is shown both raised and placed on the hip. The figure's head was "cut off" at a later date, when the edge of the sheet was trimmed. Although Guercino abandoned this sketch rather than working it up, the drawing demonstrates well the sort of preliminary lines from which he brings forth his characters. A few squiggles at the right edge show the artist testing his pen. □

NOTES

1 Salerno 1988, 256, no. 169, fig. 169.

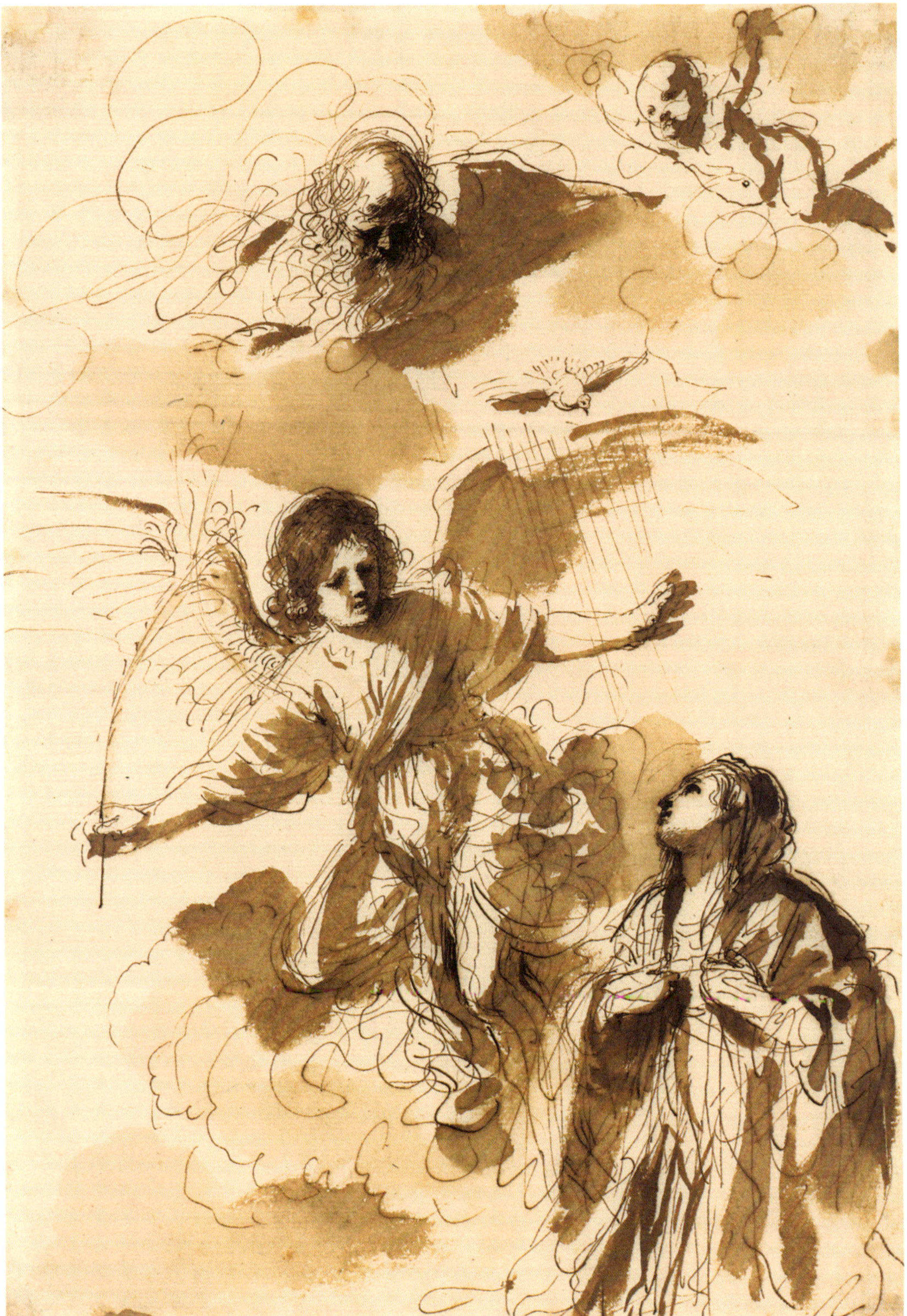

25.
THE ANNUNCIATION

1638–39
Pen and brown ink, brush with brown wash
30.3 × 21.2 cm (11⅞ × 8⅜ in.)
London, Courtauld Institute of Art Gallery, D.1952.RW.1339

PROVENANCE Casa Gennari / Bouverie family / Sir Robert Witt, L.2228B, *verso* (see p. 16).

EXHIBITIONS London 1977, no. 19; Bologna 1991, no. 103; London 1991, no. 121.

BIBLIOGRAPHY Blunt 1956, 75; Hammer et al. 1977, 3, 13; Czére 1989, 90; Mahon and Turner 1989, 57; Mahon 1991, 32; Turner 1991, 120; Turner and Plazzotta 1991, 31n92, 32n108, 146, fig. 121.

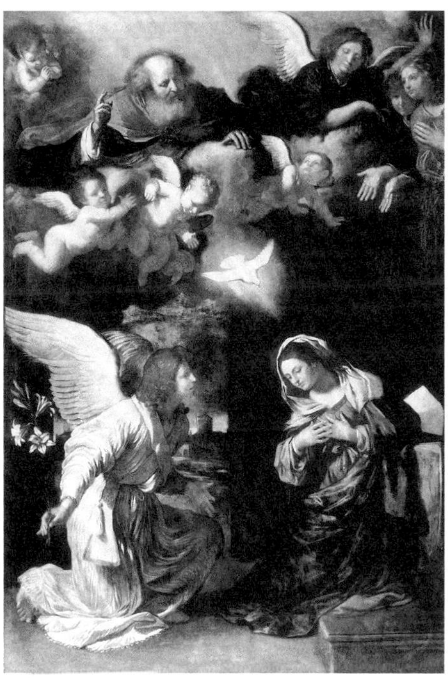

FIGURE 25.1
Guercino. *The Annunciation*, 1638–39. Oil on canvas, 305 × 211 cm (120 × 83 in.). Milan, Ospedale Maggiore, SS. Annunziata

THIS EXTRAORDINARILY vibrant sheet is a compositional study for Guercino's painting made for the high altar of the church of SS. Annunziata in the Ospedale Maggiore (called the Ca'Granda), Milan (fig. 25.1).[1] The sketch is built on a base of swirling pen lines applied with maniacal enthusiasm. The figure of God the Father, of whom we see only a head with wiry beard and hair, is given majesty and importance by a series of extended looping lines to the left, which also serve to push him forward on the page. At lower right, the artist has studied the Virgin Annunciate, and he experiments with different positions for her hands, including a set clasped over her heart. In the center is the archangel Gabriel, with numerous suggestions of billowing drapery as he flies down. An ink line remains from an earlier idea to have Gabriel's right arm reaching upward, above his head.

The most compelling aspect of this sheet is the subtlety of the artist's application of brown washes. These are not only used in the drapery to bring the figures into relief but also create a sense of light, air, and space within the composition. Different "layers" of wash give an impression of foreground, middle ground, and distance. Close examination reveals other elements delineated with wash rather than ink lines: the putto at top right is drawn with lines made with the tip of the brush, and in Gabriel's left wing the "starved brush" technique renders a flurry of movement in the feathers.

As often (for example, see cat. nos. 16 and 18), Guercino decided on a less dramatic composition for the final painting. In this case, he may have felt that the Virgin Annunciate was not prominent enough. Instead of placing Gabriel as if arriving from behind the kneeling Virgin and surprising her, as in the drawing, the painting follows a time-honored convention and shows them kneeling—facing each other—on the left and right. An intermediate compositional drawing in the Museum of Fine Arts, Budapest, shows them both kneeling but with the Virgin looking up at God the Father and the dove, rather than at Gabriel.[2] Other drawings are individual studies of God the Father, the archangel Gabriel, and one of the putti.[3] □

NOTES

1 Salerno 1988, 262, no. 177.

2 Budapest, Museum of Fine Arts, inv. 2315; Czére 1989, 90–91, no. 41, fig. 41.

3 Windsor Castle, Royal Library, invs. RL 2856 (M&T 96); RL 2794 (M&T 94); RL 2801 (M&T 95); RL 2711 (M&T 97; Mahon and Turner 1989, 57; Turner and Plazzotta 1991, 146–51); Washington, D.C., National Gallery of Art, inv. 1984.3.10 (Milkovich 1970, no. 125).

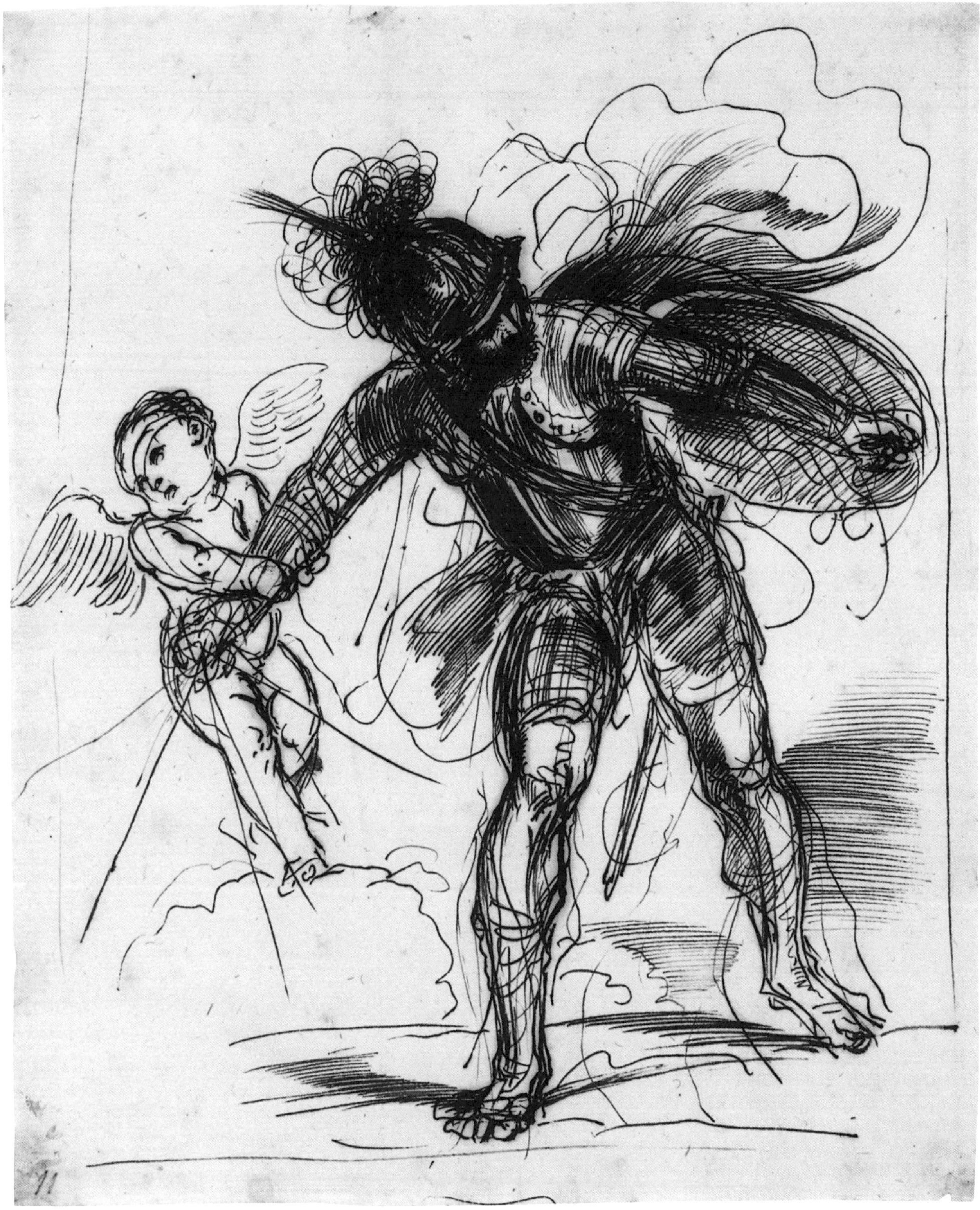

26.
CUPID RESTRAINING MARS

ca. 1640
Pen and brown ink
22.7 × 18.8 cm (9 × 7⁷⁄₁₆ in.)
Numbered in graphite at lower left: *11*
London, Courtauld Institute of Art Gallery, D.1952.RW.1349

PROVENANCE Casa Gennari / Bouverie family / Sir Robert Witt, L.2228B, *verso* (see p. 16).

EXHIBITIONS London 1977, no. 36; Bologna 1991, no. 114; London 1991, no. 132.

BIBLIOGRAPHY Blunt 1956, 76; Horton 1960, 7, 10, 13, 16n21, fig. 5; Hammer et al. 1977, no. 36; Mahon and Turner 1989, 30, 194; Mahon 1991, 34; Turner and Plazzotta 1991, 26, 31n92, 32n108, 43, 79, 158–61, 165, 171, 253–54, 262, 264, fig. 132; Stone 1991a, 633, 634, fig. 77.

THIS DRAWING WAS MADE as a preparatory study for a painting that Guercino's biographer, Malvasia, recorded as remaining in the artist's house when he died. Although the painting is not now known, an engraving by Giacomo Giovannini (1667–1717) preserves the composition.[1] In the drawing, the enraged god of war is restrained by peace-loving Cupid, who—in a comic touch—desperately seeks leverage from a cloud. The drawing is notable for its energy and speed of execution, two attributes that go hand in hand. Rapid penwork excavates the figures from the page, and the forceful, repeated lines of the god's unyielding armor contrast with the seemingly random, meandering lines of his billowing drapery. The beard is created from dozens of tiny swirls, echoed by the larger whorls of the helmet plume. Three lines at the right, left, and bottom of the page plot the borders of the composition, anticipating the canvas.

The sense of speed in the drawing also derives from numerous pentimenti, including several trials for Mars's left leg, two placements for the shield, and even an alternate position for Cupid's head. Apparently, Guercino considered having Cupid look directly at Mars instead of averting his eyes to the left; the lines below Cupid's left cheek would have been his mouth, and those going boldly through his forehead would have been the top of his head. By far the most dramatic and appealing pentimenti are the numerous lines radiating from Mars's right hand, where the artist explored alternative ideas for his sword.

With its brainstorm of ideas, catalogue number 26 seems to have been made as an early preparatory study.[2] In the series of less spontaneous drawings that followed, Guercino explored the possibility of twisting the god's body dramatically and showing him from the side; he also drew two half-length studies, with Mars's left arm variously raised and resting on his hip.[3] This latter configuration appears in the final painting, where the artist showed the god from the front, but in a more static pose than the one in catalogue number 26.

It is not known when Guercino executed the painting, but Nicholas Turner and Carol Plazzotta situate it around 1640. Such a dating is convincing given the swirling calligraphy on both catalogue numbers 26 and 25. □

NOTES

1 Malvasia ed. 1841, 2:273; print repr. Salerno 1988, 415, no. 364.

2 A drawing at Allen Memorial Art Museum, Oberlin College, Oberlin, Ohio (inv. 58.154), was probably drawn shortly after cat. no. 26 (Stone 1991, 221, no. 148, fig. B148).

3 (1) Composition, London, British Museum, inv. Ff.-2-135 (Turner and Plazzotta 1991, 161, no. 133, fig. 133); (2) composition, Paris, Louvre, inv. 6893 (Turner and Plazzotta 1991, 165, fig. 21); (3) *Mars*, red chalk, Frankfurt, Städelsches Kunstinstitut, inv. 6895 (Mahon and Turner 1989, 193–94, fig. 35) (retouched offset at Windsor, inv. RL 3022; Mahon and Turner 1989, 193–94, no. 661, pl. 367); (4) *Mars*, full-length, pen and ink, private collection (sold Christie's, New York, January 13, 1993, lot 33); (5) *Mars*, half-length, red chalk, lost but known through retouched offset at Windsor, inv. RL 3065 (Mahon and Turner 1989, 194, no. 662); (6) *Mars*, half-length, pen and ink; private collection (Turner and Plazzotta 1991, 161–65, no. 134, fig. 134; convincingly linked); (7) *Mars*, pen and ink, wash, Switzerland, David Koetser; (8) *Cupid*, Boston, Museum of Fine Arts, inv. 1891.161; Macandrew 1983, no. 133 (retouched offset at Windsor, inv. RL 2990; Mahon and Turner 1989, 201, no. 716).

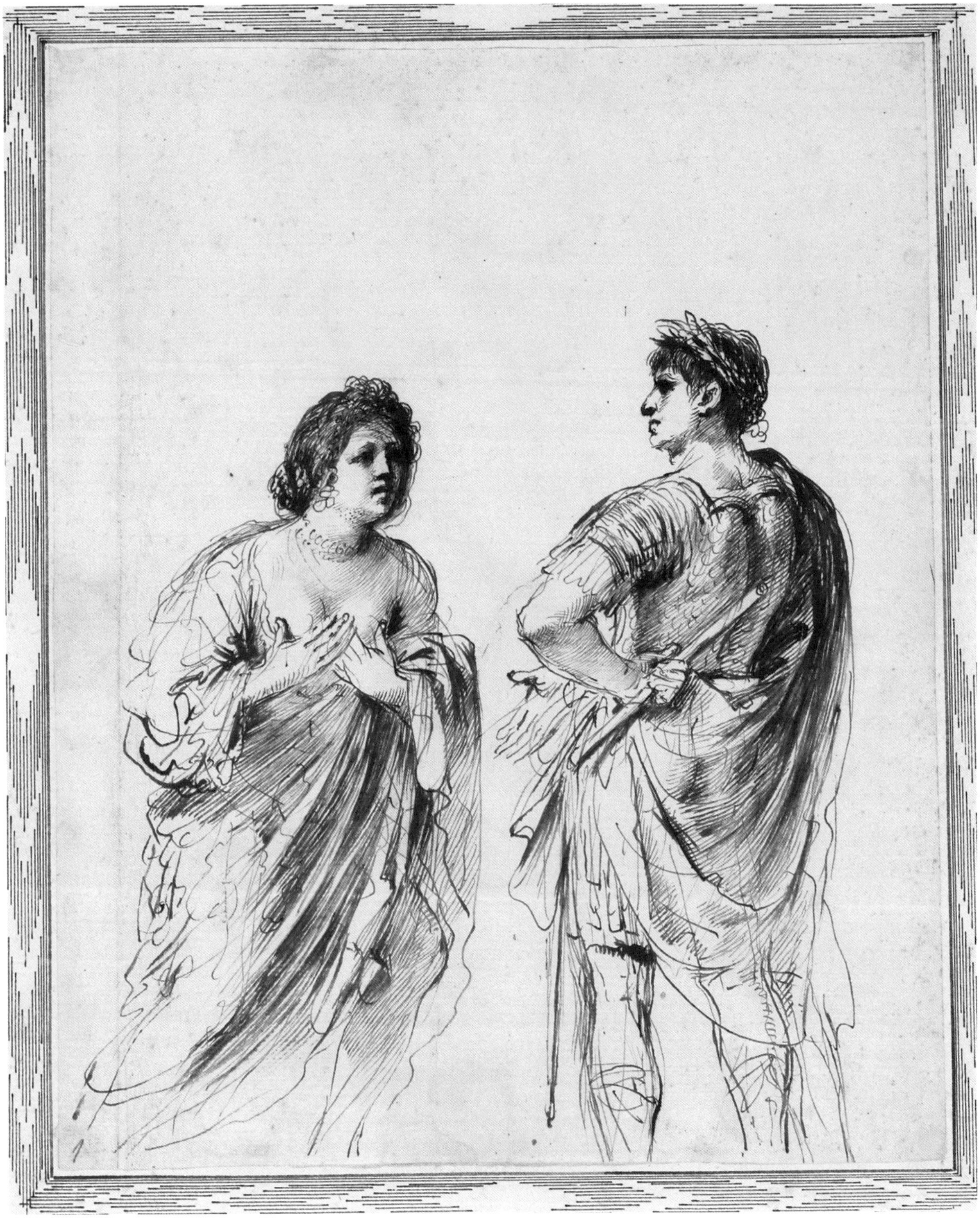

27.
CLEOPATRA AND AUGUSTUS

1640
Pen and brown ink, brush
26 × 21.3 cm (10¼ × 8⅜ in.)
Numbered in graphite at lower left: *1*
London, Courtauld Institute of Art Gallery, D.1952.RW.1348

PROVENANCE Casa Gennari / Bouverie family / Sir Robert Witt, L.2228B, *verso* (see p. 16).

EXHIBITIONS London 1943, no number.

LITERATURE V. and A. 1943, 24; Blunt 1956, 76; Mahon and Turner 1989, 59.

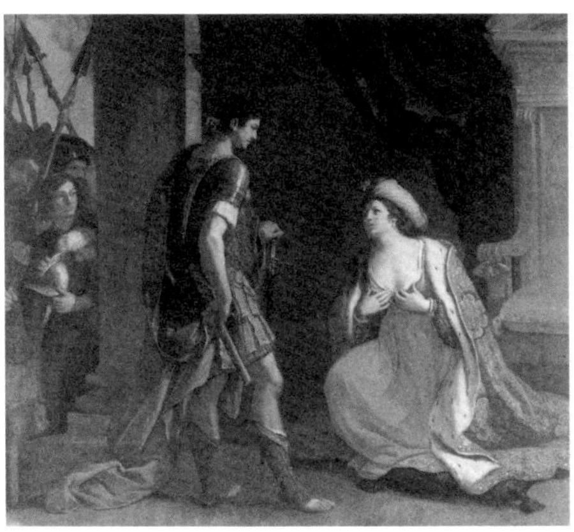

FIGURE 27.1
Guercino. *Cleopatra before Augustus*, 1640. Oil on canvas, 250 × 277 cm (98⅜ × 109 in.). Rome, Pinacoteca Capitolina

THIS DRAWING IS A STUDY for *Cleopatra before Augustus*, a painting now in the Pinacoteca Capitolina in Rome, which Cardinal Giulio Sacchetti commissioned from Guercino and paid for in 1640 (fig. 27.1).[1] The subject illustrates a meeting between the Roman emperor Octavian (Caesar Augustus) and Cleopatra, queen of Egypt. In the first century B.C., Augustus had defeated the fleet of Mark Antony and Cleopatra at the Battle of Actium. Augustus then invaded Egypt, where Antony committed suicide. According to the ancient Roman biographer Plutarch (44.83), Augustus then visited Cleopatra to comfort her.

In this drawing, Guercino captures the psychological intensity of the moment: the queen, perhaps concerned for her own safety, is supplicant before the victorious general, who tries to reassure her. The artist has given no indication of background, but he has taken care to study details of clothing and hair that bring the characters to life. Planes of parallel hatching show the reflective nature of Augustus's armor; the light shimmers off it. The hatching contrasts with the long, flowing lines used for the figures' drapery, some of which have been gone over with the tip of the brush to provide density. Very soft, delicate lines model Cleopatra's neck and collarbone. Here, as in so many of his drawings, Guercino played with hair texture: Cleopatra's is formed by a multitude of spidery curls, while that of Augustus consists of many short strokes, contrasting well with the spiky, light-filled (and less dense) laurel wreath.

Perhaps concerned that the drawing made Cleopatra appear too humble, in the final painting Guercino dressed the queen in a turban and long robe. He also reversed the positions of the two figures, placing Cleopatra on the right. Another preparatory study at Düsseldorf shows both figures as in catalogue number 27, but Cleopatra is kneeling; it was presumably made afterward. An oiled-charcoal drawing at Windsor Castle focuses on the head of Augustus; as in the painting, he is seen in profile to the right, but his shoulders are in a different position and he has the suggestion of a beard.[2]

The Roman commander in the painting has been variously identified as Mark Antony, Julius Caesar, and Augustus; modern scholarship has settled on Augustus, given Cleopatra's supplicant nature. □

NOTES

1 Ghelfi 1997, 102 (July 25, 1640), listed as a "Cleopatra." The painting entered the Pinacoteca Capitolina, Rome, in 1748 directly from the Sacchetti Collection (Salerno 1988, 268, no. 184, fig. 184).

2 Windsor Castle, Royal Library, inv. RL 2594 (M&T 99; Mahon and Turner 1989, 59, no. 99, pl. 104, where the Düsseldorf drawing [inv. 25/190] is first noted.)

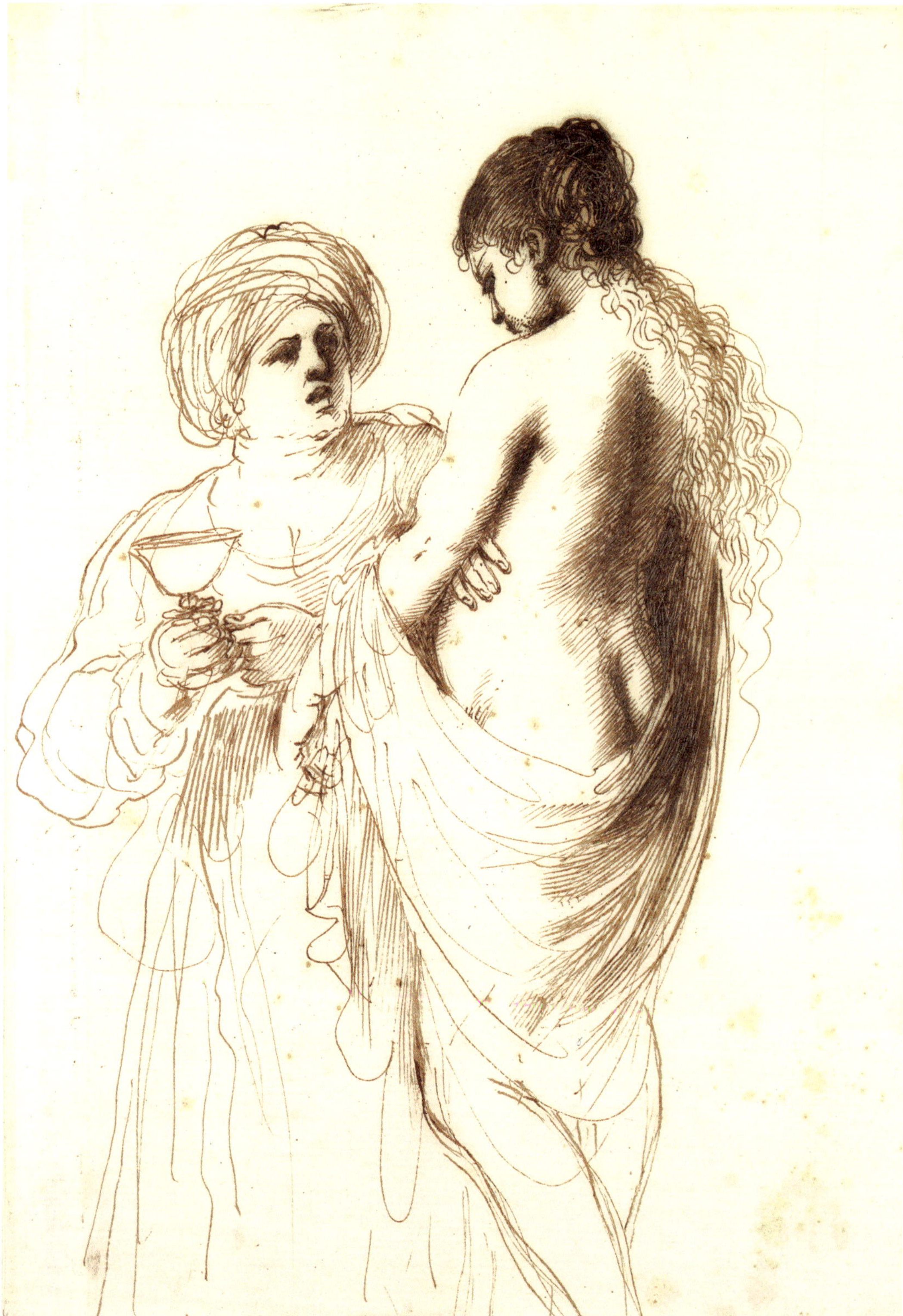

28.
BATHSHEBA ATTENDED BY HER MAID

1640
Pen and brown ink
25.5 × 17.9 cm (10 × 7 in.)
Mr. and Mrs. Edward D. Baker

PROVENANCE Christie's, London, July 8, 2003, lot 37.

EXHIBITIONS Not previously exhibited.

BIBLIOGRAPHY Unpublished.

GUERCINO PAINTED the Old Testament subject of Bathsheba only once in his career—according to the artist's detailed account book—and that was in 1640 for the Conte Astorre Ercolani. Although that painting apparently does not survive, its price, 375 *scudi*, suggests that the composition contained about three figures (given Guercino's practice of charging a set price per figure; see p. 4). A painting in Pesaro that has been identified as an old copy of Guercino's painting features a naked Bathsheba sitting just to the right of center, facing the viewer; two attendants are on the right, and on the left is a view into a courtyard with King David on a balcony.[1]

Although catalogue number 28 reflects a very different approach to the subject, it was probably made by Guercino as an early study for the 1640 painting. The drawing concentrates on the form of Bathsheba, which is conveyed through scintillating sequences of parallel hatching, especially in the small of her back. Focused details, such as the tiny curling lines of her cascading hair, give the drawing a realism and efficiency, making the human visual brain forget that the figure's lower body is incomplete and accept that a blank section of paper topped by a single line represents a shoulder. The figure of the maid is less intensively studied, and the focus of the drawing seems to be the characterization of the two figures and the relationship between them.

Sir Denis Mahon and Nicholas Turner identified a number of drawings relating to the painted composition, none of which provides such a sensuous solution as cat. no. 28. A pen-and-ink study of Bathsheba formerly on the London art market, showing her seated with drapery and looking to the left, comes closest. A drawing in the Weld-Blundell Collection at the Walker Art Gallery studies the horizontal composition as a whole, with Bathsheba looking to the left, while a School drawing at Windsor Castle reflects a design closer to the final painted version.[2]

Guercino seems to have appreciated the challenge of studying the three-quarter profile from behind. A red-chalk drawing in the Metropolitan Museum of Art of a boy holding a bowl shows the youth in an almost identical pose to Bathsheba in cat. no. 28.[3] A study at Bowdoin College Museum of Art, possibly of Ceres, also reflects a similar profile.[4] □

NOTES

1 Ghelfi 1997, 102 (August 23, 1640); Grimaldi 1968, pl. 185; Mahon and Turner 1989, 143.

2 Hazlitt, Gooden & Fox 1988, no. 28, fig. 28; Mahon and Turner 1989, 143, no. 430, pl. 334; Brooke 1998, 75–76, no. 32. Another drawing of a seated female nude made in the same session as the Hazlitt sheet is in the collection of Jean Bonna (Brugerolles and Strasser 2006, 38–40, no. 19, pl. 19).

3 New York, The Metropolitan Museum of Art, inv. 63.75.2; Bean 1979, 187, no. 245 (also repr. Turner and Plazzotta 1991, 26, fig. 5, as a study for the figure of Ganymede).

4 Brunswick, Maine, Bowdoin College Museum of Art, 1956.24.221 (Stone 1991, 214, 24, pl. F24).

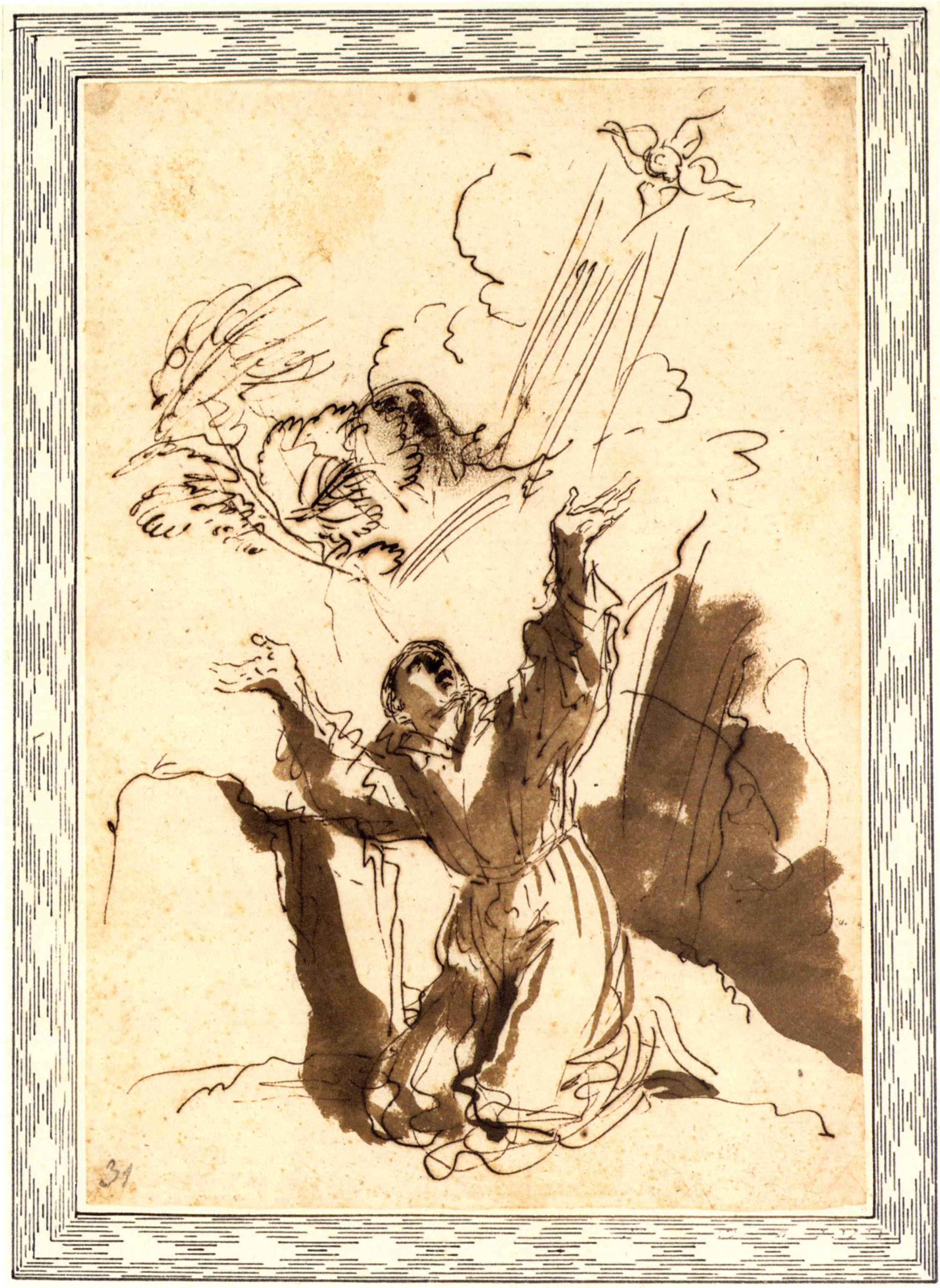
31

29.

SAINT FRANCIS RECEIVING THE STIGMATA

ca. 1642
Pen and brown ink, brush with brown wash
25.6 × 18.4 cm (10 1/8 × 7 1/4 in.)
Numbered in graphite at lower left: *31*
London, Courtauld Institute of Art Gallery, D.1952.RW.1369

PROVENANCE Casa Gennari / Bouverie family / Sir Robert Witt, L.2228B, *verso* (see p. 16).

EXHIBITIONS London 1977, no. 38; London 1991, no. 96.

BIBLIOGRAPHY Blunt 1956, 76; Hammer et al. 1977, 18; Mahon and Turner 1989, 42; Mahon 1991, 34; Turner and Plazzotta 1991, 31n92, 31n97, 32n108, 126, fig. 96; Turner et al. 1995, 98.

ACCORDING TO TRADITION, Francis of Assisi beheld a vision in 1224 while praying on Mount Alverna: he saw a seraphlike figure whose arms were outstretched to form the shape of the Cross. While contemplating the vision, Francis found that the marks of Christ's wounds appeared on his hands, feet, and body. Popular in Christian art, this subject was treated by Guercino on a number of occasions.

In this swiftly executed drawing, Saint Francis kneels with arms raised, looking up at the vision. The urgency of the calligraphic penwork is apparent in the seemingly random but well-judged lines that make up the figure of the saint and in the lower swirls of drapery. That sense of urgency is emphasized by the robust application of wash.

Guercino started to draw Saint Francis on a larger scale higher up the page—a partially obscured face is apparent at the sheet's upper center—but he must have realized that this would leave no space to draw the vision, and he repositioned the saint lower down. Guercino then drew over his initial marks, mutating the face and raised right arm into verdant foliage and clouds.

Given the number of times Guercino treated the subject of Saint Francis throughout his career and the relative similarity of his solutions, it is extremely difficult to identify the painted work that catalogue number 29 might relate to. It seems most likely to be a study for a canvas (now in the Mittelrheinisches Landesmuseum, Mainz) that Guercino made for Padre Giovan Battista d'Este; two other sheets have also been related to that painting.[1] In a drawing that is nearly the same size as catalogue number 29, a somewhat larger-scale Saint Francis strikes a very similar pose but looks to the right instead of upward. The location of his head corresponds to the initial placement on catalogue number 29, and it is tempting to think of that drawing as directly preceding the Courtauld sheet.[2] □

NOTES

1 Nicholas Turner in Turner et al. 1995, 98, when discussing a related drawing then in the collection of Jak Katalan; Sir Denis Mahon, opinion noted in the auction catalogue when that same drawing was sold, Sotheby's, London, July 10, 2002, lot 63. Both authorities also relate Louvre inv. 6881 to the composition (repr. Loire 1990, 103, no. 41).

2 Sold Christie's, New York, January 10, 1996, lot 315, 24.2 × 17.8 cm (recto and verso; only recto illustrated).

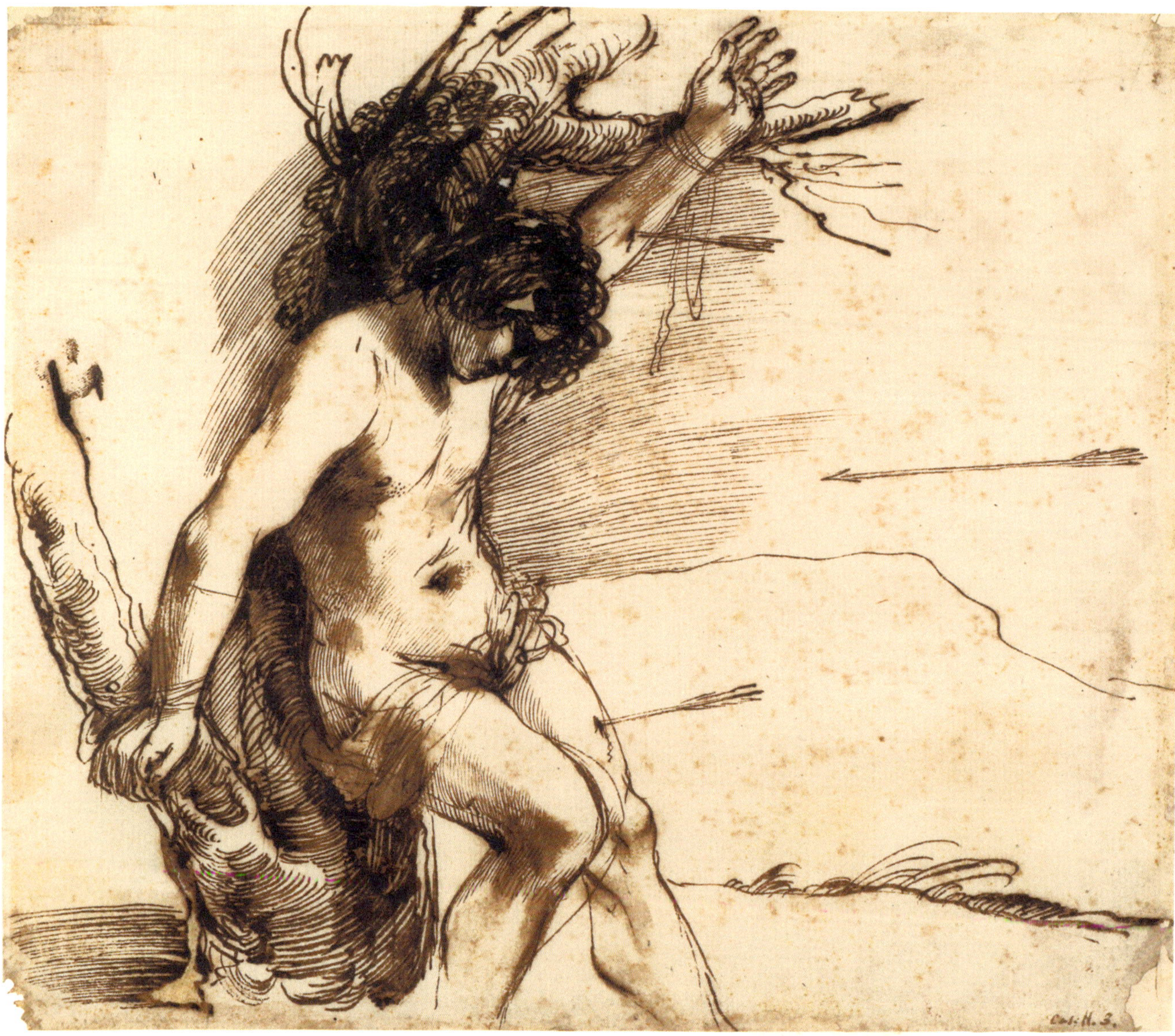

30.
SAINT SEBASTIAN

ca. 1642
Pen and brown ink, brush with brown wash
19.4 × 22.9 cm (7⅝ × 9 in.)
Inscribed in brown ink at lower right: *cas.H.3*
London, Courtauld Institute of Art Gallery, D.1952.RW.1377

PROVENANCE Casa Gennari / Bouverie family / Sir Robert Witt, L.2228B, *verso* (see p. 16).

EXHIBITIONS London 1925, no. 43; London 1953a, no. 52; London 1977, no. 37.

BIBLIOGRAPHY Arts Council 1953, 20; Blunt 1956, 76; Marangoni 1959, 13, pl. 15; Hammer et al. 1977, 18.

ACCORDING TO CHRISTIAN TRADITION, in the fourth century A.D. the Roman soldier Sebastian was sentenced to die for having converted to Christianity. His executioners shot him repeatedly with arrows and left him for dead, but he survived and was nursed back to health, only to be clubbed to death some time later.

Here, Guercino emphasizes the drama of the scene as the saint, pierced by two arrows, slumps against the tree to which he is bound. A third arrow in midair creates a sense of immediate danger. Guercino used a number of other devices to heighten the feeling of instability and tension: strong compositional diagonals; a scene cropped at the bottom, like a "close-up"; multiple planes of insistent parallel hatching; and angled tufts of grass on a nearby knoll that enclose the space. The dark, dense lines of the tree contrast with the light, meandering pen strokes used for the bindings of the left wrist and the blood trickling from the wounds. Only a single pentimento occurs, in the saint's right knee.

Guercino employed wash sparingly and in an unusually restrained manner on this sheet. The predominant use of pen hatching makes it likely that the drawing dates to later in the artist's career, even though the drama and robustness of the figure recall the bold compositions Guercino produced as a young man, during his *prima maniera*. It is not possible to link the sheet definitively to a particular commission or painted work; the artist treated the subject a number of times, often showing a half-length, inactive figure. In spirit, the drawing comes closest to Guercino's full-length *Saint Sebastian* in the Palazzo Pitti, Florence, datable to 1652, which shows the saint tied to a tree with a putto hovering above.[1] Yet the clean lines and confident draftsmanship of catalogue number 30 do not fit well with the late date of that painting. It perhaps compares best with the drawings *Primavera* (1642) and *Semiramis* (1645), at Windsor Castle.[2]

The inscription in the lower right corner seems likely to be an eighteenth-century storage note for the drawing and was added after the corner had been torn. □

NOTES

1 Salerno 1988, 359, no. 289, fig. 289.

2 Windsor Castle, Royal Library, invs. RL 2526 and RL 2575, respectively (M&T 106, 114; Mahon and Turner 1989, 61, 65, nos. 106, 114, pls. 111, 119).

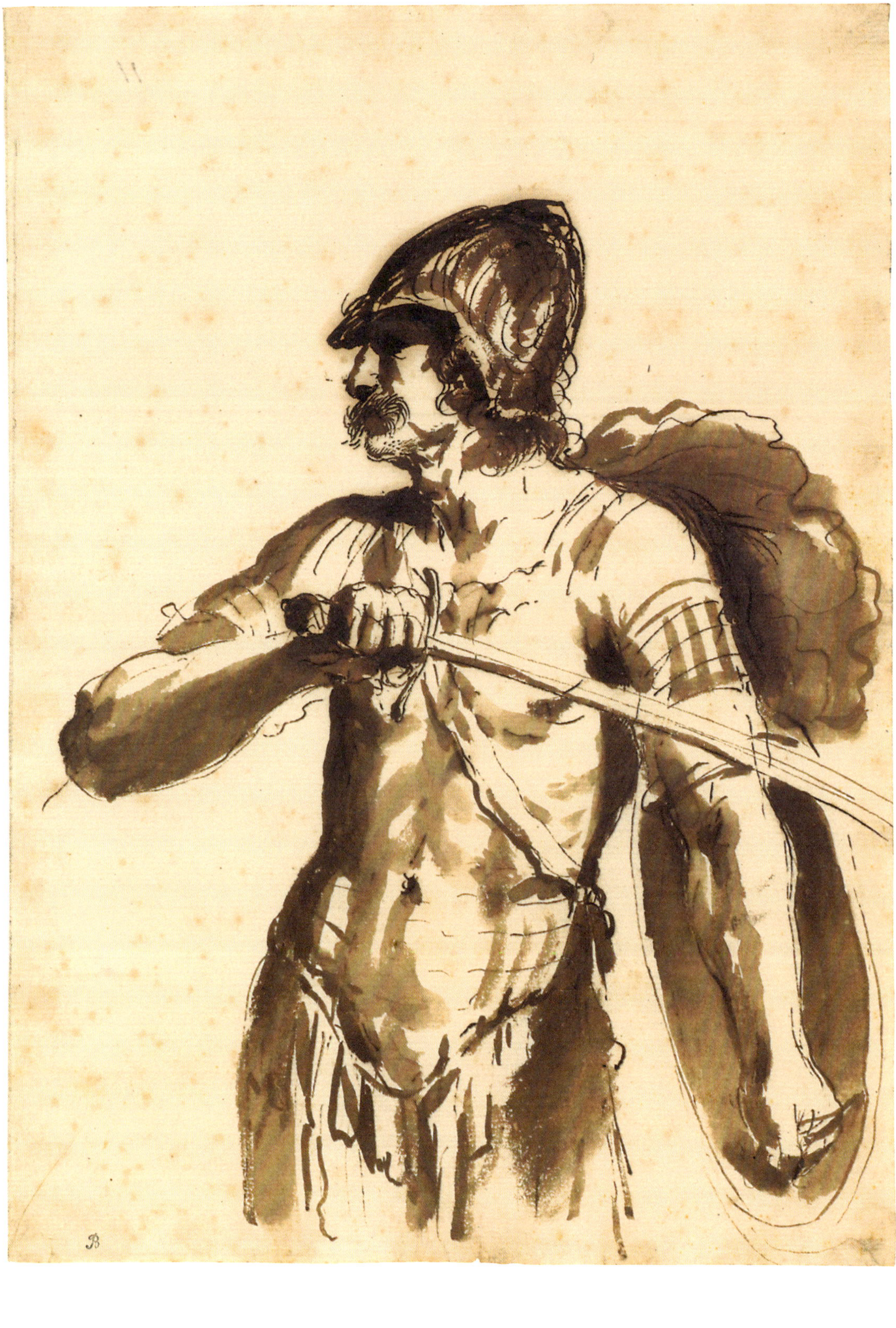

31.
A WARRIOR

1645
Pen and brown ink, brush with brown wash
26.5 × 19.4 cm (10 3/8 × 7 5/8 in.)
Numbered in brown ink at top right of verso: *11*
London, Courtauld Institute of Art Gallery, D.1952.RW.1368

PROVENANCE Casa Gennari / John Bouverie, L.325, and Bouverie family / Sir Robert Witt, L.2228B, *verso* (see p. 16).

EXHIBITIONS London 1977, no. 31; London 1991, no. 141.

LITERATURE Blunt 1956, 76; Horton 1960, 7, 9, 13, 19, fig. 6; Mahon 1967, 14n37; Hammer et al. 1977, no. 31; Brejon and Volle 1988, 247; Czére 1989, 86; Mahon and Turner 1989, 66, 77; Loire 1990, 55; Turner and Plazzotta 1991, 31n92, 31n94, 31n97, 32n108, 165, 171, 172, 262, fig. 141.

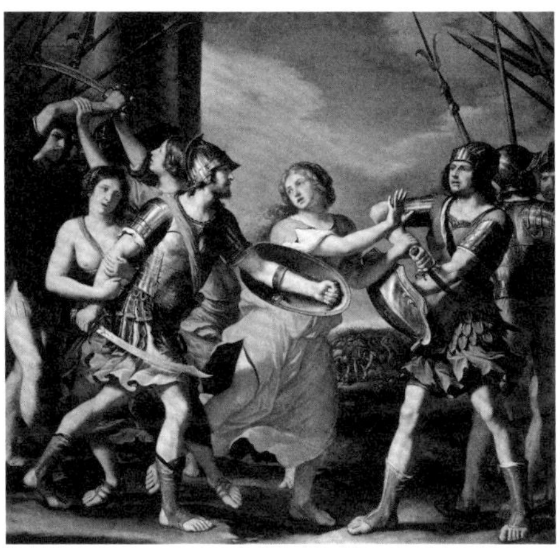

FIGURE 31.1
Guercino. *Hersilia Separating Romulus and Tatius*, 1645.
Oil on canvas, 253 × 267 cm (99 1/2 × 105 in.). Paris, Musée du Louvre, 85. Photo: Erich Lessing/Art Resource, New York

IN DRAWING THIS HELMETED SOLDIER, Guercino clearly reveled in the dramatic effects of contrasting textures. Fluid applications of a thin wash represent the hard and smooth surfaces of the armor. Ruffled brush lines evoke an extraneous piece of flying drapery at right. The artist particularly enjoyed juxtaposing that fluid softness with both the short pen strokes of the warrior's unshaven chin and the longer, twisting lines of his bristly moustache. The lower parts of the drawing consist almost entirely of wash, applied in many cases with the tip of the brush. In fact, Guercino was able to create details with brush and wash so effectively that pen lines were unnecessary. By its nature, the extensive use of wash in the drawing provides strong effects of light and shade; darker inks make deep shadows, including an almost black area on the warrior's right shoulder.

The distinctive pose held by the warrior—with his right arm bent so that he holds his sword across his body—makes it likely that the drawing is a study for the soldier on the right (Tatius) in Guercino's painting *Hersilia Separating Romulus and Tatius* (fig. 31.1).[1] The painting was made in 1645 for a French patron, Louis Phélypeaux de La Vrillière, secretary of state to King Louis XIII; it was one of three canvases Guercino sent to decorate the gallery of Phélypeaux's grand residence in Paris. In *Hersilia Separating Romulus and Tatius*, the artist has raised Tatius's shield-bearing left arm as well as his right elbow and lowered his right hand. In fact, in catalogue number 31 a few pen lines under the warrior's sword-bearing hand indicate that Guercino considered a lower placement on the drawing too. As Nicholas Turner and Carol Plazzotta point out, the artist had considerable difficulty with the foreshortening of that arm in the painting, in contrast with the adept handling of space in the drawing. □

NOTES

1 Salerno 1988, 300, no. 226. As observed by Mahon and Turner 1989, 66, no. 115, 166, no. 574; and Turner and Plazzotta 1991, 171–72. The drawing for the principal warrior, formerly in the Rudolf Collection, was sold at Sotheby's, New York, January 12, 1994, lot 23.

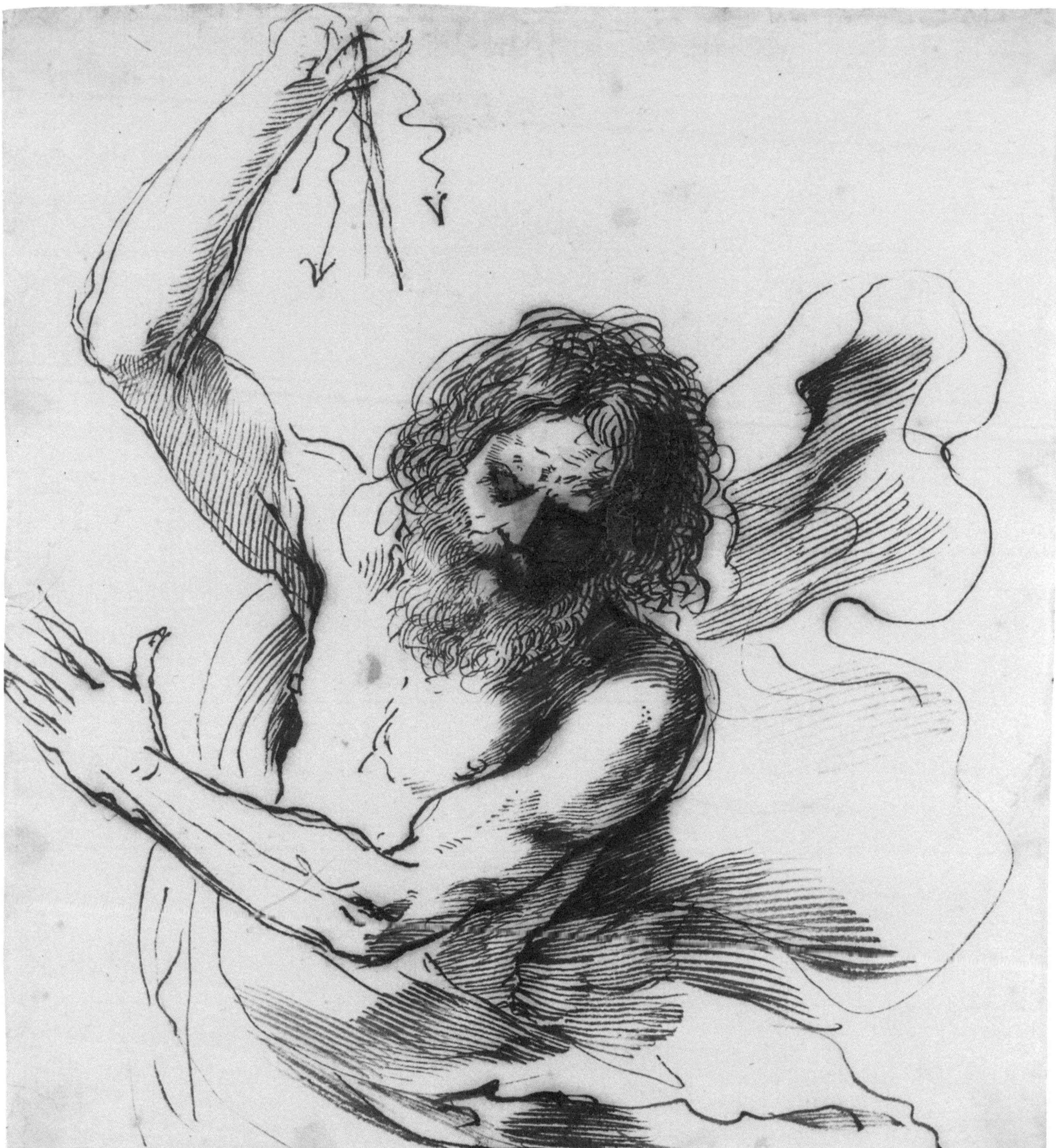

32.
JUPITER THROWING A THUNDERBOLT

ca. 1645
Pen and brown ink
20 × 18.7 cm (7⅞ x 7⅜ in.)
London, Courtauld Institute of Art Gallery, D.1952.RW.1361

PROVENANCE Casa Gennari / Bouverie family / Sir Robert Witt, L.2228B, *verso* (see p. 16).

EXHIBITIONS Not previously exhibited.

BIBLIOGRAPHY Blunt 1956, 76.

WHILE THIS DRAWING does not relate to a known painting, it is a good example of the energy inherent in Guercino's draftsmanship. The pose of the vengeful god is active: he raises his thunderbolt-wielding hand high and swings his left arm vigorously across his body. Guercino's penwork contributes to the sense of motion. In both right and left forearms, the artist drew the outlines several times, producing a blurring, kinetic effect, and in the god's wildly flying drapery, meandering calligraphic lines aptly convey the turbulence. The shadows consist mostly of varied sequences of parallel hatching, which give the impression of light moving across the figure (and, in places, echo the tidy undulating lines of an engraver's burin). These straight lines contrast with the rounded ones forming the god's wiry and unkempt hair.

In 1626, Guercino made studies of Jupiter and Semele for an engraving by the Centese printmaker G. B. Pasqualini (1595–1631),[1] but cat. no. 32 does not seem to relate to those studies: here Jupiter is clearly more wrathful than seductive. The style of the drawing fits better with a much later dating of about 1645, and the areas of dense hatching compare with the penwork in other drawings dating to that time, including one of Samson and Delilah, and studies for Atlas.[2] □

NOTES

1 Mahon and Turner 1989, 20, no. 36, pl. 37.

2 Turner and Plazzotta 1991, 172–73, no. 143; 176, no. 146.

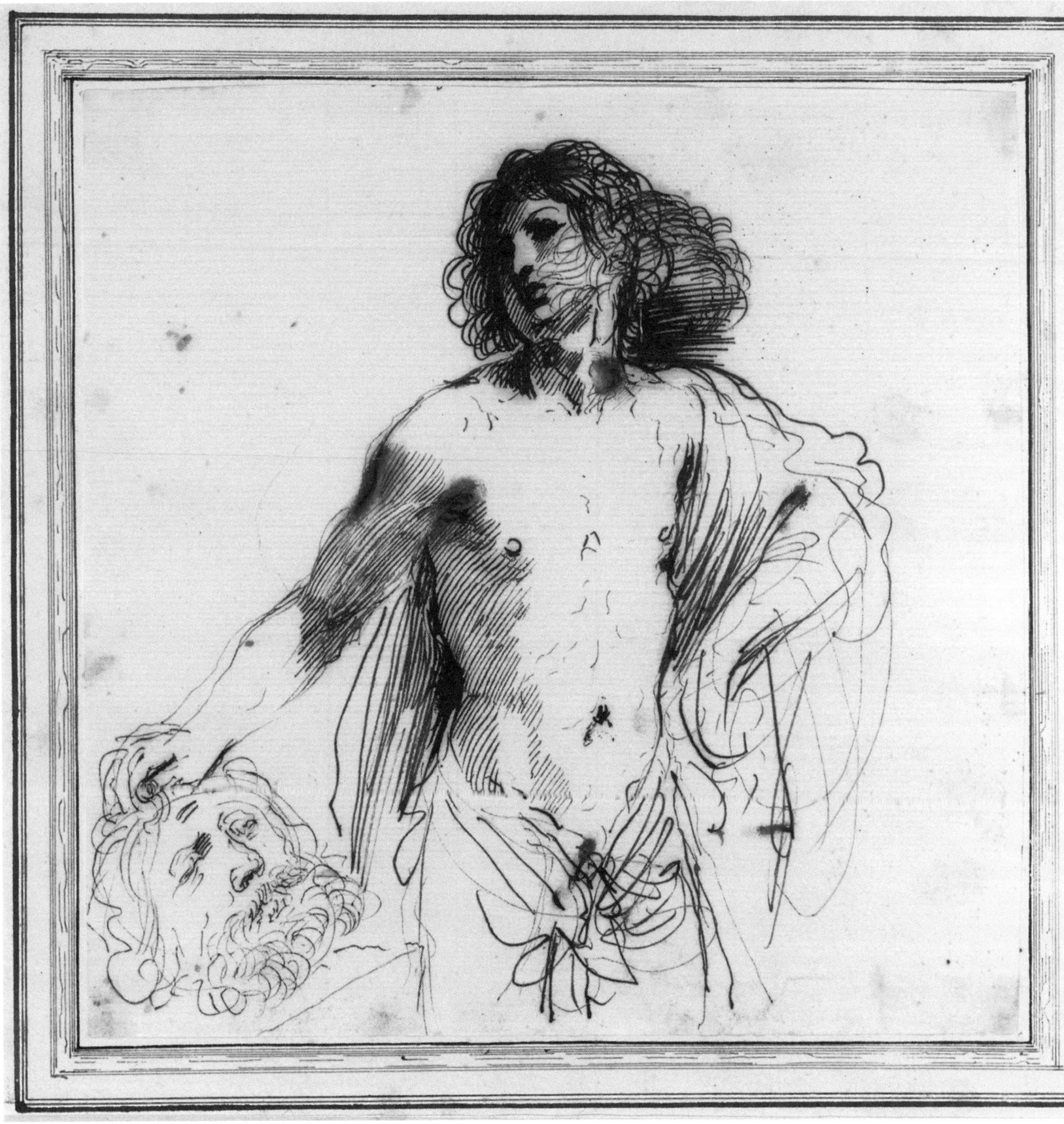

33.
DAVID WITH THE HEAD OF GOLIATH

ca. 1650
Pen and brown ink, brush with brown wash
18.8 × 18.8 cm ($7^{3}/_{8} \times 7^{3}/_{8}$ in.)
London, Courtauld Institute of Art Gallery, D.1952.RW.1363

PROVENANCE Casa Gennari / Bouverie family / Sir Robert Witt, L.2228B, *verso* (see p. 16).

EXHIBITIONS Not previously exhibited.

BIBLIOGRAPHY Blunt 1956, 76.

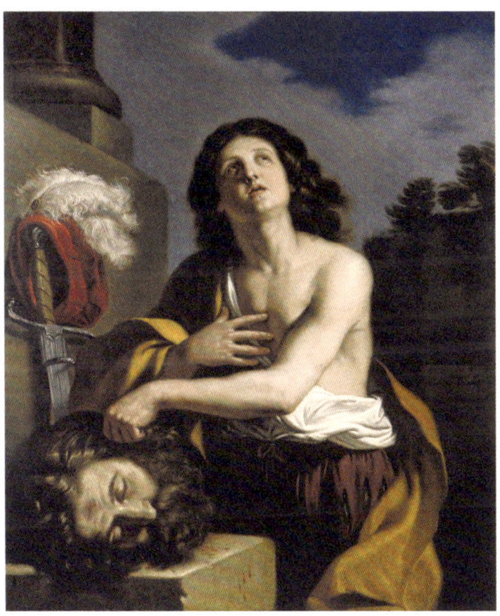

FIGURE 33.1
Guercino. *David with the Head of Goliath*, 1650. Oil on canvas, 120.5 × 102 cm ($47^{1}/_{2} \times 40^{1}/_{8}$ in.). Private collection

WHILE GUERCINO seems to have been more willing than many artists to reach for a new piece of paper when he grew dissatisfied with a composition on which he was working, he would sometimes make radical changes to a design on the same sheet. In catalogue number 33, he significantly altered the position of David's head. At first, Guercino placed it just above the figure's left shoulder, looking down and away from the head of Goliath. But then the artist scored through these features with a series of horizontal lines and drew the head in a more upright pose, with the youthful David, future king of the Israelites, looking confidently over the head of his defeated adversary, the Philistine giant Goliath. A number of wavy lines across the hero's left cheek are the remains of the hair as originally drawn.

The rest of the composition has been hurriedly mapped out. Rapid draftsmanship suggests a left arm partly covered with drapery, while two strong lines show the wrist placed against the body in a way that is readable only when viewing the drawing from a distance. A tangled junction of lines represents drapery around the waist, and a clever mix of long and short strokes conveys the bending of the right arm and shadow upon it.

Goliath's head, resting on a block of stone, is noted in a series of faint lines, the artist presumably keen to concentrate on the head and expression of the hero instead. Goliath's facial features and traditional curly beard are supplemented by two small sets of short horizontal lines on his forehead, indicating his wound.

Catalogue number 33 was probably a preparatory drawing for *David with the Head of Goliath* (fig. 33.1), for which Guercino was paid by Lodovico Fermi of Piacenza on October 12, 1650.[1] Like the drawing, the painting shows a half-length David, but the young hero looks skyward to thank God for his victory. Two drawings, one at the Fogg Art Museum and another at Windsor Castle, probably reflect earlier stages of Guercino's thoughts for the project. Both show David half length and wearing a plumed hat; the Fogg sheet has him leaning on a ledge contemplating Goliath's head, and in the Windsor sheet he stands in front of a wall holding the head, which rests on a slab in the lower right corner.[2] □

NOTES

1 Ghelfi 1997, 149, no. 430 (October 12, 1650); Salerno 1988, 342, no. 272 (location as "London, Trafalgar Galleries").

2 Cambridge, Mass., Fogg Art Museum, inv. 1965.385 (Stone 1991, 214, no. 28, pl. D28). An early copy of this drawing was sold at Jean-Marc Delvaux, Paris, March 28, 2001, lot 15; Windsor Castle, Royal Library, inv. RL 2944 (M&T 358; Mahon and Turner 1989, 126, 358 [not ill.]), called "Ascribed to," but not there related to the 1650 picture.

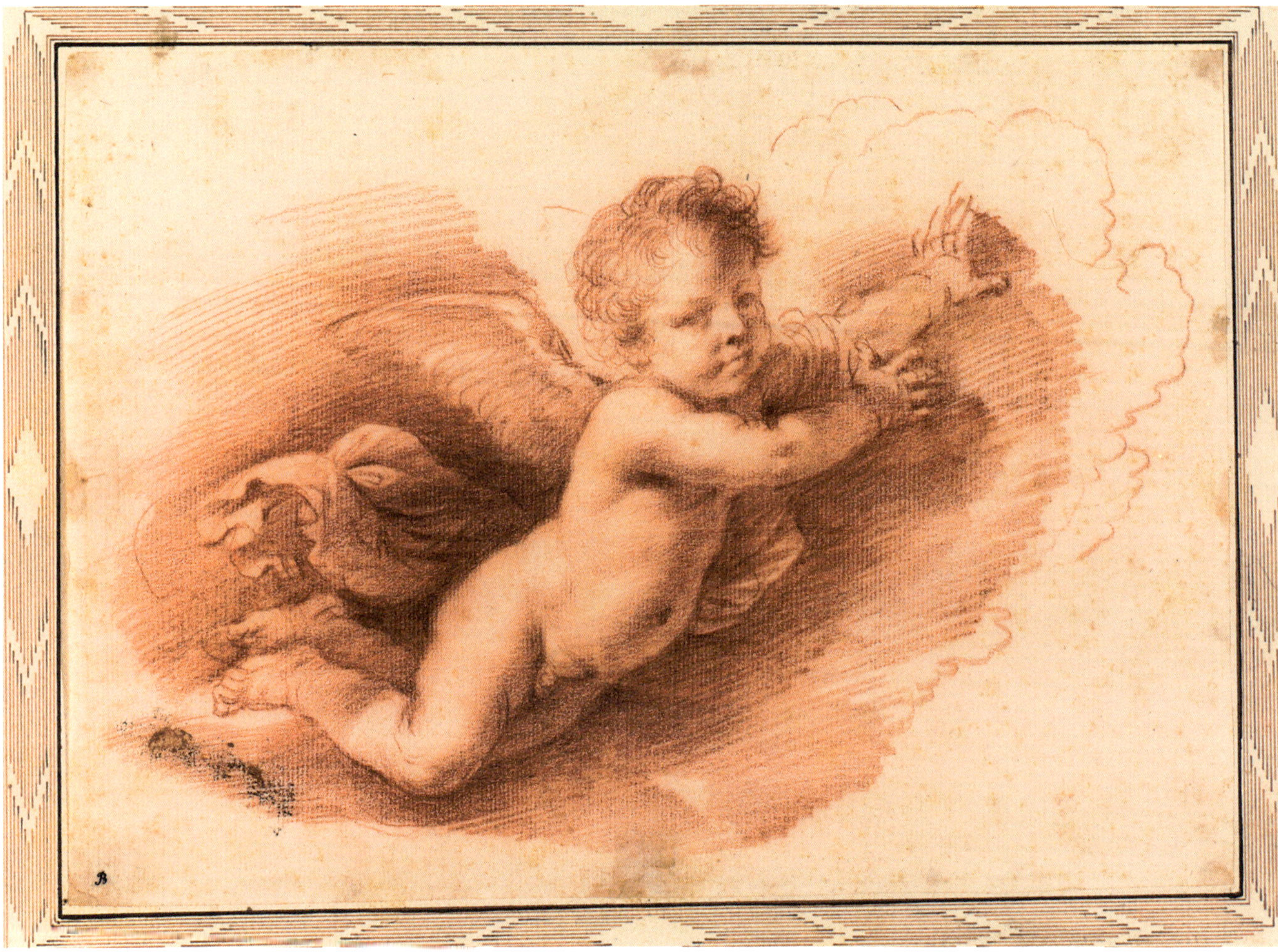

34.
STUDY OF A FLYING PUTTO

ca. 1650
Red chalk
20.5 × 28.9 cm (8 1/8 × 11 3/8 in.)
London, Courtauld Institute of Art Gallery, D.1952.RW.1861

PROVENANCE Casa Gennari / John Bouverie, L.325, and Bouverie family / "Oriolo, Florence," Sir Robert Witt, L.2228B, *verso* (see p. 16).

EXHIBITIONS London 1977, no 41; London 1991, no. 154.

BIBLIOGRAPHY Blunt 1956, 76; Hammer et al. 1977, 19; Turner and Plazzotta 1991, 31n92, 32n97, 182, fig. 154.

LATER IN HIS CAREER, Guercino increasingly used red chalk, a medium he had employed sporadically—although with great effect—throughout his life. Whereas in many of his later drawings he uses chalk in a linear, penlike fashion, in catalogue number 34 he creates a highly finished effect by carefully rounding and shaping the body. The putto is lit strongly from above left, and subtle gradations of red chalk demark shadows on the white of the paper. Vigorous, dense hatching carves out a space for the flying child, and carefully worked curling tendrils of drapery suggest motion. In only a few areas does Guercino release control, and rapid draftsmanship is evident in the drapery on the left arm and in the shadows defining the fingers of the left hand.

As Nicholas Turner and Carol Plazzotta have observed, this drawing resembles a number of putti in paintings from the 1640s and 1650s, but it does not seem to relate directly to any of them.[1] It may have served, no doubt along with other similar drawings, as a model from which putti in paintings could be derived. In fact, the noticeably smudged lines of the drawing indicate that a counterproof was taken from the sheet, which would have provided an additional—reversed—pose. □

NOTES

1 Turner and Plazzotta 1991, 182.

EXHIBITIONS AND LITERATURE CITED

EXHIBITIONS CITED

ADELAIDE 1968
Master Drawings of the 17th Century from the Witt Collection. Adelaide, South Australia, 1968.

AUCKLAND 1960
Old Master Drawings from the Witt Collection. Auckland City Art Gallery, New Zealand, September–October 1960.

BOLOGNA 1968
Il Guercino (Giovanni Francesco Barbieri, 1591–1666): Catologo critico dei Disegni. Palazzo dell'Archiginnasio, Bologna, September 1–November 18, 1968.

BOLOGNA 1991
Il Guercino 1591–1666. Dipinti e Disegni, Il Guercino e la bottega. Museo Civico Archeologico, Bologna, September 6–November 10, 1991; Pinacoteca Civica e Chiesa del Rosario, Cento; Schirn Kunsthalle, Frankfurt; National Gallery of Art, Washington, D.C.

CAMBRIDGE 1991
Guercino, Master Draftsman: Works from North American Collections. Arthur M. Sackler Museum, Cambridge, Massachusetts, February 15–March 31, 1991; National Gallery of Canada/Musée des Beaux-Arts du Canada, Ottawa, May 3–June 16, 1991; Cleveland Museum of Art, Cleveland, August 27–October 13, 1991.

GENOA 1992
Genova e Guercino: Dipinti e disegni delle Civiche Collezioni. Galleria di Palazzo Rosso, Genoa, May 21–August 23, 1992.

LEEDS 1868
National Exhibition of Works of Art. Leeds, 1868.

LONDON 1923
Winter Exhibition 1923–1924. Burlington Fine Arts Club, London, 1923.

LONDON 1925
Italian Art of the Seventeenth Century. Burlington Fine Arts Club, London, 1925.

LONDON 1937
Exhibition of Drawings of the Bolognese School. W. Gernsheim, London, May 10–June 10, 1937.

LONDON 1938
17th-Century Art in Europe. Royal Academy, London, January 3–March 12, 1938.

LONDON 1943
Drawings of the Old Masters from the Witt Collection. Victoria and Albert Museum, London, January–May 1943.

LONDON 1948
Catalogue of an Exhibition of Selected Paintings, Drawings and Sculpture from the Collection of the Late Hugh Baker. Exhibition No. 877. The Leicester Galleries, Leicester Square, London, March 1948.

LONDON 1953
Drawings by Old Masters. Royal Academy of Arts, London, 1953.

LONDON 1953A
Drawings from the Robert Witt Collection at the Courtauld Institute of Art. The Arts Council of Great Britain, London, 1953; York City Art Gallery, York, June 6–27, 1953; Peterborough Art Gallery, Peterborough, July 4–25, 1953.

LONDON 1955
Artists in 17th-Century Rome. Wildenstein & Co., London, June 1–July 16, 1955.

LONDON 1958
Drawings from the Witt Collection. Courtauld Institute of Art, London, 1958.

LONDON 1965
Newly Acquired Drawings for the Witt Collection. Courtauld Institute Galleries, London, October 1965–March 1966.

LONDON 1971
Italian Drawings of the Seventeenth and Eighteenth Centuries from the Witt Collection. Courtauld Institute Galleries, London, March–April 1971.

LONDON 1977
Drawings by Guercino and Other Baroque Masters. Courtauld Institute Galleries, London, February–March 1977.

LONDON 1988
European Drawings: Recent Acquisitions. Hazlitt, Gooden & Fox, London, November–December 1988.

LONDON 1991
Drawings by Guercino from British Collections. British Museum, London, May 17–August 18, 1991.

LONDON 1991A
Master Drawings from the Courtauld Collection. Courtauld Institute Galleries, London, 1991.

LONDON 1993
Drawings from the J. Paul Getty Museum. Royal Academy of Arts, London, October 30, 1993–January 23, 1994.

LOS ANGELES 1976
Old Master Drawings from American Collections. Los Angeles County Museum of Art, Los Angeles, April 29–June 13, 1976.

LOS ANGELES 1984
In Honor of Ebria Feinblatt, Curator of Prints and Drawings, 1947–1985. Los Angeles County Museum of Art, Los Angeles, 1984.

LOS ANGELES 1996
Figure Drawings. J. Paul Getty Museum, Los Angeles, December 17, 1996–April 6, 1997.

LOS ANGELES 1998
Two Centuries of Drawings from Bologna. J. Paul Getty Museum, Los Angeles, December 15, 1998–February 28, 1999.

LOS ANGELES 1998A
Landscape Drawings 1500–1900. J. Paul Getty Museum, Los Angeles, June 9, 1998–August 23, 1998.

LOS ANGELES 1999
The Body Beautiful: Artists Draw the Nude (1440–1880). J. Paul Getty Museum, Los Angeles, December 14, 1999–February 27, 2000.

LOS ANGELES 2002
Mise-en-Page: The Art of Composing on Paper. J. Paul Getty Museum, Los Angeles, December 17, 2002–March 9, 2003.

LOS ANGELES 2003
Casting Characters: Portraits and Studies of Heads. J. Paul Getty Museum, Los Angeles, November 4, 2003–March 9, 2004.

LOS ANGELES 2004
Visions of Grandeur: Drawing in the Baroque Age, J. Paul Getty Museum, Los Angeles, June 1–September 12, 2004.

MANCHESTER 1962
Loan Exhibition of Master Drawings from the Witt and Courtauld Collections. Whitworth Art Gallery, Manchester, November 17–December 22, 1962.

MONTE CARLO 1966
Dessins italiens du XVe et du XVIIIe s. de la collection H. de Marignane. Palais des Congrès, Monte Carlo, May 29–June 4, 1966.

NEW YORK 1993
Drawings from the J. Paul Getty Museum. Metropolitan Museum of Art, New York, May 24–August 8, 1993.

PARIS 1971
Dessins du XVIe et du XVIIe s. dans les collections privées françaises. Galerie Claude Aubry, Paris, December 1971.

PARIS 1990
Le Guerchin en France. Musée du Louvre, Paris, May 31–November 12, 1990.

PARIS 1999
Dominique-Vivant Denon: L'oeil de Napoléon. Musée du Louvre, Paris, October 20, 1999–January 17, 2000.

SASKATCHEWAN AND MONTREAL 1970
A Selection of Italian Drawings from North American Collections. Norman Mackenzie Art Gallery, Saskatchewan, January 16–February 15, 1970; Montreal Museum of Fine Arts, Montreal, March 5–April 3, 1970.

SYDNEY 1999
Michelangelo to Matisse: Drawing the Figure. Art Gallery of New South Wales, Sydney, November 20, 1999–February 27, 2000.

WELLINGTON 1973
Italian Old Master Drawings: Witt Collection, Courtauld Gallery. National Gallery, Wellington, New Zealand, 1973.

WINDSOR 1939
[Title unknown]. Eton College, Windsor, 1939.

WINDSOR 1950
[Title unknown]. Drawings Schools, Eton College, Windsor, June 1950.

LITERATURE CITED

ADAM ET AL. 2005
Nel segno del Guercino: Disegni dalle collezioni Mahon, Oxford e Cento [Guercino as Master Draughtsman: Drawings from the Mahon Collection, The Ashmolean Museum at Oxford, and Cento]. Edited by Orietta Benocci Adam. Exhibition catalogue. Rome: Roma Studios, 2005.

ARTIOLI AND MONDUCCI 1982
Artioli, Nerio, and Elio Monducci. *Dipinti "Reggiani" del bondone e del Guercino (pittura e documenti)*. Exhibition catalogue. Reggio Emilia: Ente provinciale per il turismo, 1982.

ARTS COUNCIL 1953
Drawings from the Robert Witt Collection at the Courtauld Institute of Art. Exhibition catalogue. Introduction by Anthony Blunt. London: Arts Council of Great Britain, 1953.

AUBRY 1971
Dessins du XVIe et du XVIIe s. dans les collections privées françaises. Exhibition catalogue. Paris: Galerie Claude Aubry, 1971.

BAGNI 1985
Bagni, Prisco. *Il Guercino e il suo Falsario: I Disegni di paesaggio*. Bologna: Nuova Alfa Editoriale, 1985.

BAGNI 1990
Bagni, Prisco. *Il Guercino e il suo Falsario: I Disegni di figura*. Bologna: Nuova Alfa Editoriale, 1990.

BAMBACH 2005
Bambach, Carmen. "Seated Nude Young Man in Nearly Frontal View." In *Disegno, giudizio e bella maniera: Studi sul disegno italiano in onore di Catherine Monbeig Goguel*, edited by Philippe Costamagna, Florian Härb, and Simonetta Prosperi Valenti Rodinò. Milan: Silvana Editoriale, 2005: 178–79.

BEAN 1966
Bean, Jacob. *Italian Drawings in the Art Museum, Princeton University: 106 Selected Examples*. Princeton: The Art Museum, Princeton University, 1966.

BEAN 1967
Bean, Jacob. Review of *Omaggio al Guercino: Mostra di dipinti restaurati e dei disegni della collezione Denis Mahon di Londra* by Denis Mahon. *Master Drawings* 5, no. 3 (Winter 1967).

BEAN 1979
Bean, Jacob. *17th-Century Drawings in the Metropolitan Museum of Art*. New York: Metropolitan Museum of Art, 1979.

BICART-SÉE 1999
Bicart-Sée, Lise. "Le Christ prêchant." In *Dominique-Vivant Denon: L'oeil de Napoléon*, 461. Edited by Pierre Rosenberg. Exhibition catalogue. Paris: Éditions de la Reunion des Musées Nationaux, 1999.

BISOGNI 1975
Bisogni, Fabio. "A Fragment of Guercino's Pesaro Altarpiece." *Burlington Magazine* 117, no. 867 (June 1975): 338–43.

BLUNT 1956
Blunt, Anthony. *Hand-List of the Drawings in the Witt Collection*. London: London University, 1956.

BLUNT AND TROUTMAN 1962
Blunt, Anthony, and Philip Troutman. *Loan Exhibition of Master Drawings from the Witt and Courtauld Collections*. Exhibition catalogue. Manchester: University of Manchester, 1962.

BOCCARDO 1992
Boccardo, Piero. *Genova e Guercino: Dipinti e disegni delle civiche collezioni*. Exhibition catalogue. Genoa: Nuova Alfa Editoriale, 1992.

BONFAIT 1990
Bonfait, Olivier. "Il pubblico del Guercino: Ricerche sul mercato dell'arte nel XVII secolo a Bologna." *Storia dell'arte* 68 (1990): 71–94.

BORA 1976
Bora, Giulio. *I Disegni del Codice Resta*. Bologna: Emmere Studio, 1976.

BOTTARI 1966
Bottari, Stefano, Renato Roli, and Anna Ottani Cavina. *Guercino, Disegni*. Milan, 1966.

BRADFORD AND BRAHAM 1991
Bradford, William, and Helen Braham. *Master Drawings from the Courtauld Collection*. Exhibition catalogue. London: Courtauld Institute Galleries, 1991.

BREJON AND VOLLE 1988
Brejon de Lavergnée, Arnauld, and Nathalie Volle. *Seicento, le siècle de Caravage dans les collections françaises*. Exhibition catalogue. Paris: Éditions de la Réunion des musées nationaux, 1988.

BROOKE 1998
Brooke, Xanthe. *Mantegna to Rubens: The Weld-Blundell Drawings Collection*. Exhibition catalogue. London: Merrell Holberton, 1998.

BROOKS 2003
Brooks, Julian. *Graceful and True: Drawing in Florence c. 1600*. Exhibition catalogue. Oxford: Ashmolean Museum, 2003.

BRUGEROLLES AND STRASSER 2006
Brugerolles, Emmanuelle, and Nathalia Strasser. *Carnets d'études 4: Dessins italiens de la collection Jean Bonna*. Exhibition catalogue. Paris: École nationale supérieure des beaux-arts, 2006.

BRYDGES 1829
Brydges, Sir Egerton. *Memoirs and Characters of the Peerage*, vol. 2. London, 1829; manuscript expansion of *A Biographical Peerage of the Empire of Great Britain*, 1808, with extensive comments on the life and character of his contemporaries, and occasional annotations on names, death dates, arms, and incidental matters.

BURLINGTON FINE ARTS CLUB 1925
Catalogue of an Exhibition of Italian Art of the Seventeenth Century. Exhibition catalogue. London: Burlington Fine Arts Club, 1925.

BYAM SHAW 1989
Byam Shaw, James. Review of *Italian Drawings in the J. F. Willumsen Collection*, by Chris Fischer. *Burlington Magazine* 131, no. 1036 (July 1989): 493.

CALABI 1928
Calabi, A. *Francesco Bartolozzi, catalogue des estampes*. Bologna: Guido Modiano, 1928.

CAVIGGIOLI 1966
Caviggioli, G. A. *Catalogue de l'exposition de dessins italiens du XVe et du XVIIIe s. de la collection H. de Marignane*. Exhibition catalogue. Monte Carlo, 1966.

COURTAULD 1958
Drawings from the Witt Collection. Exhibition catalogue. London: Courtauld Institute of Art, 1958.

COURTAULD 1966
Newly Acquired Drawings for the Witt Collection. Exhibition catalogue. London: Courtauld Institute of Art, 1966.

COURTAULD 1971
Italian Drawings of the Seventeenth and Eighteenth Centuries from the Witt Collection. Exhibition catalogue. London: Courtauld Institute Galleries, 1971.

CRICCO AND PAOLO DI TEODORO 2004
Cricco, Giorgio, and Francesco Paolo di Teodoro. "Giovanni Francesco Barbieri: Il Guercino (1591–1666), Gran disegnatore e felicissimo coloritore." In *Itinerario nell'arte: Da Giotto all'eta barocca* 2. Bologna: Zanichelli, 2004: 992–95.

CZÉRE 1989
Czére, Andrea. *Disegni di artisti bolognesi nel museo delle belle arti di Budapest*. Bologna: Nuova Alfa Editoriale, 1989.

DAVIS 1984
Davis, Bruce. *In Honor of Ebria Feinblatt, Curator of Prints and Drawings, 1947-1985*. Los Angeles County Museum of Art, Los Angeles, 1984.

DAVIS 1997
Davis, Bruce. *Master Drawings in the Los Angeles County Museum of Art*. Los Angeles: Los Angeles County Museum of Art, 1997.

DUVAL 1829
Duval, Amaury. *Monuments des arts du dessin* 3. Paris: M. Brunet Denon, 1829.

EBERT-SCHIFFERER 1991
Ebert-Schifferer, Sybille. *Giovanni Francesco Barbieri: Il Guercino, 1591–1666*. Exhibition catalogue. Frankfurt: Schirn Kunsthalle Frankfurt, 1991.

EMILIANI 1959
Emiliani, Andrea. *Mostra di disegni del seicento emiliano nella Pinacoteca di Brera*. Exhibition catalogue. Milan: Brera, 1959.

ETON 1950
"The Drawings Schools: Pictures from Sir Robert Witt's Collection." *Eton College Chronicle* (June 4, 1950): unpaginated.

FAIETTI 1993
Faietti, Marzia. "Two New Guercino Drawings in Bologna." *Master Drawings* 31, no. 1 (Spring 1993): 47–54.

FEINBLATT 1976
Feinblatt, Ebria. *Old Master Drawings from American Collections*. Exhibition catalogue. Los Angeles: Los Angeles County Museum of Art, 1976.

FISCHER 2002
Fischer, Chris. "Guercino Drawings in Denmark." *Bulletin de l'Association des Historiens de l'Art Italien* 8 (2002): 4–17.

GETTY 1985
"Acquisitions 1984," in *The J. Paul Getty Museum Journal* 13 (1985): 195.

GETTY 1986
"Acquisitions 1985," in *The J. Paul Getty Museum Journal* 14 (1986): 236.

GETTY 1990
"Acquisitions 1989," in *The J. Paul Getty Museum Journal* 18 (1990): 190.

GHELFI 1997
Ghelfi, Barbara, ed., with the consultation of Denis Mahon. *Il Libro dei conti del Guercino*. Venice: Nuova Alfa Editore, 1997.

GIBBONS 1977
Gibbons, Felton. *Catalogue of Italian Drawings in the Art Museum, Princeton University*. Vol. 1. Princeton: Princeton University Press, 1977.

GOLDMAN 1988
Goldman, Paul. *Looking at Prints, Drawings and Watercolours: A Guide to Technical Terms*. London: British Museum Publications, 1988.

GOLDNER 1993
Goldner, George R. *Checklist of Drawings from the J. Paul Getty Museum*. Exhibition catalogue. New York: Metropolitan Museum of Art, 1993.

GOLDNER, HENDRIX, AND PASK 1992
Goldner, George, Lee Hendrix, and Kelly Pask. *European Drawings 2: Catalogue of the Collections*. Malibu: J. Paul Getty Museum, 1992.

GOLDNER, HENDRIX, AND WILLIAMS 1988
Goldner, George, Lee Hendrix, and Gloria Williams. *European Drawings 1: Catalogue of the Collections*. Malibu: J. Paul Getty Museum, 1988.

GRIMALDI 1968
Grimaldi, Nefta Barbanti. *Il Guercino: Gian Francesco Barbieri, 1591–1666*. Bologna: Edizioni Bologna, 1968.

GRISWOLD 1991
Griswold, William. Review of *Guercino, Master Draftsman: Works from North American Collections*, by David Stone. *Burlington Magazine* 133, no. 1062 (September 1991): 643–45.

HAMMER ET AL. 1977
Hammer, Martin, Terence O'Hair, and Gerard Neil. *Drawings by Guercino and Other Baroque Masters*. Exhibition catalogue. London: University of London, 1977.

HAZLITT, GOODEN & FOX 1988
European Drawings: Recent Acquisitions. Exhibition catalogue. London: Hazlitt, Gooden & Fox, 1988.

HELD COLLECTION 1970
Selections from the Drawings Collection of Mr. and Mrs. Julius S. Held. Exhibition catalogue. Binghamton: University Art Gallery at the State University of New York, Binghamton, 1970.

HORTON 1960
Horton, Anne K. "A Drawing by Guercino." *Allen Memorial Art Museum Bulletin* (Oberlin College, Ohio) 18 (1960): 5–19.

KLEPAC 1968
Klepac, Lou. *Master Drawings of the 17th Century from the Witt Collection*. Exhibition catalogue. Adelaide, South Australia: Hyde Park Press, 1968.

LEICESTER 1948
Catalogue of an Exhibition of Selected Paintings, Drawings and Sculpture from the Collection of the Late Hugh Baker (Leicester Galleries). Exhibition catalogue. London: Ernest, Brown & Phillips Ltd., 1948.

LIEURE 1989
Lieure, Jules. *Jacques Callot: Catalogue raisonné de l'oeuvre gravé*. 2 vols. San Francisco: Alan Wofsy Fine Arts, 1989. (Orig. pub. Paris, 1924–27.)

LOIRE 1990
Loire, Stéphane. *Le Guerchin en France*. Exhibition catalogue. Paris: Éditions de la Réunion des musées nationaux, 1990.

MACANDREW 1983
Macandrew, Hugh. *Italian Drawings in the Museum of Fine Arts, Boston*. Boston: The Museum, 1983.

MAHON 1955
Mahon, Denis. *Artists in 17th-Century Rome, to save Gosfield Hall for the Nation as a residential nursing home with hospital wards for the elderly sick and infirm of limited means*. Exhibition catalogue. London: Wildenstein & Co., 1955.

MAHON 1967
Mahon, Denis. *I Disegni del Guercino della collezione Mahon*. Exhibition catalogue. Bologna: Edizioni Alfa, 1967. (Corrected reprint of part of: *Omaggio al Guercino*. Exhibition catalogue. Cento, June–October 1967. Bologna: Edizioni Alfa, 1967.)

MAHON 1967A
Mahon, Denis. *Omaggio al Guercino: Mostra di dipinti restaurati e dei disegni della collezione Denis Mahon di Londra*. In *Master Drawings*, vol. 3, no. 5. Bologna: Edizioni Alfa, 1967.

MAHON 1991
Mahon, Denis. *Il Guercino. Dipinti e Disegni, Il Guercino e la bottega*. Exhibition catalogue. Bologna: Nuova Alfa Editoriale, 1991.

MAHON *DIPINTI* 1968
Mahon, Denis. *Il Guercino (Giovanni Francesco Barbieri, 1591–1666): Catalogo critico dei Dipinti*. Exhibition catalogue. Bologna: Edizioni Alfa, 1968.

MAHON *DISEGNI* 1969
Mahon, Denis. *Il Guercino (Giovanni Francesco Barbieri, 1591–1666): Catalogo critico dei Disegni*. Exhibition catalogue. Bologna: Edizioni Alfa, 1969.

MAHON AND EKSERDJIAN 1986
Mahon, Denis, and David Ekserdjian. *Guercino: Drawings from the Collections of Denis Mahon and the Ashmolean Museum*. Exhibition catalogue. Oxford: Burlington Magazine Publications Ltd. and the Ashmolean Museum, 1986.

MAHON AND TURNER 1989
Mahon, Denis, and Nicholas Turner. *The Drawings of Guercino in the Collection of Her Majesty the Queen at Windsor Castle*. Cambridge: Cambridge University Press, 1989.

MAHON, PULINI, AND SGARBI 2003
Mahon, Denis, Massimo Pulini, and Vittorio Sgarbi. *Guercino: Poesia e sentimento nella pittura del '600*. Exhibition catalogue. Milan: DeAgostini, 2003.

MALOON AND RAISSIS 1999
Maloon, Terence, and Peter Raissis. *Michelangelo to Matisse: Drawing the Figure*. Exhibition catalogue. Sydney: Art Gallery of New South Wales, 1999.

MALVASIA ED. 1841
Malvasia, Carlo Cesare. *Felsina pittrice: Vite de' pittori bolognesi*. 2 vols. Rev. edition edited by Giampietro Zanotti. Bologna, 1841.

MARANGONI 1959
Marangoni, Matteo. *Guercino: I Grandi Maestri del Disegno*. Milan: Aldo Martello Editore, 1959.

MILKOVICH 1970
Milkovich, Michael. *Selections from the Drawing Collection of Mr. and Mrs. Julius S. Held*. Exhibition catalogue. Binghamton: University Art Gallery, 1970.

NEGRO, PIRONDINI, AND ROIO 2004
Negro, Emilio, Massimo Pirondini, and Nicosetta Roio. *La Scuola del Guercino*. Exhibition catalogue. Modena: Artioli Editore, 2004.

PASINI 2002
Pasini, Pier Giorgio. *Guercino ritrovato collezioni e committenze riminesi, 1642–1660*. Exhibition catalogue. Milan: Rizzoli, 2002.

POPHAM 1938
Popham, A. E. Review of *Seventeenth-Century Art in Europe at Burlington House: The Drawings*, by A. E. Popham. *Burlington Magazine* 72, no. 418 (January 1938): 19.

POPHAM 1938A
Popham, A. E. *Catalogue of the Exhibition of 17th-Century Art in Europe*. Exhibition catalogue. 2nd ed. London: Royal Academy of Arts, 1938.

PULINI 2001
Pulini, Massimo. *Guercino, racconti di paese: Il Paesaggio e la scena popolare nei luoghi e nell'epoca di Giovanni Francesco Barbieri*. Exhibition catalogue. Milan: Motta, 2001.

PULINI 2003
Pulini, Massimo. *Le Collezioni ritrovate di Guercino*. Exhibition catalogue. Milan: Rizzoli, 2003.

RA 1938
17th-Century Art in Europe, an illustrated souvenir of the exhibition of 17th-Century art in Europe at the Royal Academy of Arts, London, 1938. Exhibition catalogue. London: William Clowes and Sons, 1938.

RA 1953
Drawings by Old Masters. Exhibition catalogue. London: William Clowes and Sons, 1953.

RA 1993
Drawings from the J. Paul Getty Museum. Exhibition catalogue. London: Royal Academy of Arts, 1993.

RAGGHIANTI 1938
Ragghianti, Carlo Ludovico. "Notizie e Letture." *La Critica d'Arte* 3 (1938): xvii–xxx.

REVELEY 1820
Reveley, Henry. *Notices Illustrative of the Drawings and Sketches of Some of the Most Distinguished Masters in All the Principal Schools*. London: Longman, Hunt, Rees, Orme and Brown, 1820.

RICCÒMINI 1969
Riccòmini, Eugenio. *Il Seicento ferrarese*. Milan: Silvana Editoriale d'Arte, 1960.

ROLI 1972
Roli, Renato. *G. F. Barbieri: Guercino*. Milan: Aldo Martello Editore, 1972.

RUSSELL 1923
Russell, Archibald G. B. *Drawings by Guercino*. London: Edward Arnold & Co., 1923.

SALERNO 1988
Salerno, Luigi. *I Dipinti del Guercino*. Rome: Ugo Bozzi Editore, 1988.

SAVILLE GALLERY 1929
Drawings by Old Masters. Exhibition catalogue. London: Saville Gallery, 1929.

SPEAR 1994
Spear, Richard E. "Guercino's 'prix-fixe': Observations on Studio Practices and Art Marketing in Emilia." *Burlington Magazine* 136, no. 1098 (September 1994): 592–602.

STONE 1991
Stone, David M. *Guercino, Master Draftsman: Works from North American Collections*. Exhibition catalogue. Cambridge, MA: Harvard University Art Museums, 1991.

STONE 1991A
Stone, David M. Review of *Drawings by Guercino from British Collections*, by Nicholas Turner and Carol Plazzotta. *Burlington Magazine* 133, no. 1062 (September 1991): 632–35.

TERNOIS 1962
Ternois, Daniel. *Jacques Callot: Catalogue complet de son oeuvres dessiné*. Paris: Nobele, 1962.

TROUTMAN 1960
Troutman, Philip. *Old Master Drawings from the Witt Collection*. Exhibition catalogue. Auckland, New Zealand: Auckland City Art Gallery, 1960.

TROUTMAN 1973
Troutman, Philip. *Italian Old Master Drawings: Witt Collection, Courtauld Gallery*. Exhibition catalogue. Wellington, New Zealand: National Art Gallery, 1973.

TURNER 1991
Turner, Nicholas. *Guercino: Drawings from Windsor Castle*. Exhibition catalogue. Washington, D.C.: National Gallery of Art, 1991.

TURNER 1991A
Turner, Nicholas. "Guercino als zeichner." In *Giovanni Francesco Barbieri: Il Guercino, 1591–1666*, edited by Sybille Ebert-Schifferer. Exhibition catalogue. Frankfurt: Schirn Kunsthalle Frankfurt, 1991: 345–54.

TURNER 1994
Turner, Nicholas. "John Bouverie as a Collector of Drawings." *Burlington Magazine* 136, no. 1091 (February 1994): 90–99.

TURNER 2001
Turner, Nicholas. *European Drawings 4: Catalogue of the Collections*. Los Angeles: J. Paul Getty Museum, 2001.

TURNER 2005
Turner, Nicholas. "An Unpublished Drawing by Guercino for *Elijah in the Desert Fed by Ravens*." *Master Drawings* 43, no. 4 (Winter 2005): 508–11.

TURNER AND HENDRIX 1997
Turner, Nicholas, and Lee Hendrix. *Masterpieces of the J. Paul Getty Museum: Drawings*. Los Angeles: J. Paul Getty Museum, 1997.

TURNER AND PLAZZOTTA 1991
Turner, Nicholas, and Carol Plazzotta. *Drawings by Guercino from British Collections*. Exhibition catalogue. London: British Museum Press, 1991.

TURNER ET AL. 1995
Turner, Nicholas, et al. "St. Francis Kneeling in a Landscape Contemplating a Crucifix." In *The Katalan Collection of Italian Drawings*, 98–99. Exhibition catalogue. Poughkeepsie, NY: Trustees of Vassar College, 1995.

V. AND A. 1943
Drawings of the Old Masters from the Witt Collection. Exhibition catalogue. London: Victoria and Albert Museum, 1943.

VAN TUYLL 1991
Van Tuyll van Serooskerken, Carel. *Guercino (1591–1666): Drawings from Dutch Collections*. Exhibition catalogue. Haarlem: Teylers Museum, 1991.

VARRIANO 1973
Varriano, John. "Guercino, Bonfanti, and *Christ among the Doctors*." *Record of the Art Museum* (Mount Holyoke College, Massachusetts) 32, no. 1 (1973): 11–15.

VARRIANO 1974
Varriano, John. *Drawings by Guercino and His Followers*. Exhibition catalogue. South Hadley, MA: Mount Holyoke College, 1974.

VARRIANO 1984
Varriano, John. "Christ among the Doctors." In *Handbook of the Collection: Mount Holyoke College Art Museum*, edited by Jean C. Harris. South Hadley, MA: The Museum, 1984: 24.

VITZTHUM 1970
Vitzthum, Walter. *A Selection of Italian Drawings from North American Collections*. Exhibition catalogue. Saskatchewan: Norman Mackenzie Art Gallery and Montreal Museum of Fine Arts, 1970.

WARING 1868
Waring, J. B. *National Exhibition of Works of Art at Leeds, 1868*. Exhibition catalogue. Leeds: The Executive Committee, 1868.

INDEX

Page numbers in *italics* refer to illustrations. Page numbers in **bold** refer to individual catalogue entries.

ABOUT THE AUTHOR

JULIAN BROOKS, Assistant Curator of Drawings at the J. Paul Getty Museum, is a specialist of Italian sixteenth- and seventeenth-century drawings. From 2000 to 2003 he was Print Room Supervisor at the Ashmolean Museum, Oxford, where he co-curated, with Catherine Whistler, and wrote the catalogue for, the exhibition *Graceful and True: Drawing in Florence c. 1600* (Oxford, 2003). He received his doctorate from the University of Oxford in 1999; his thesis studied *The Drawings of Andrea Boscoli (c. 1560–1608).*